MW00906717

Corporate Performance Management Best Practices

"Bob Paladino's writing blends his skill as a business leader, consultant, and teacher to deliver guidance that can harness the power of integrated effort toward the same goal. As you read it, you can visualize the difference it makes when individuals and departments are working with a compelling and clear end in mind all while chartering their improvement and progress toward the goal.

Whether Bob is 'hands on' helping businesses achieve the performance they desire or putting his principles into a guidebook for business leaders, he always leaves you and your organization with a different mindset and a set of tools to raise the bar and achieve far more than what existed before.

For any business leader wanting to accelerate performance and get his or her organization moving in a new direction, Bob's *Corporate Performance Management Best Practices* supplies the roadmap, toolkit, and guidance you need. With just a few talented people who believe in your vision and the principles in Bob's book, you can achieve your mission and achieve results that your team probably didn't imagine possible."

—Brad Wheeler
President, Genworth Financial Trust Company

Bob illuminates a clear path to developing and executing corporate performance management. This proven, easily-understood and executed method to connect strategy, metrics and performance management is one from which companies of any size can benefit."

—Mike Premo
President and CEO, ARC Corp

"Many companies struggle to successfully implement best practices and drive strategy through their organization. Bob Paladino transforms theoretical approaches and applies them to real life case studies by sharing the ways companies have adopted and adapted the use of the balanced scorecard and performance management within their companies. Bob continues to demonstrate that success is possible no matter the industry, the size of the company or the operating culture."

—Joseph Martucci
Performance Lead, PSE&G

"Bob Paladino's straight-forward, easy-to-use methods break down the obstacles keeping organizations from world-class performance. This book extends Bob's approach with tools to make even the best organizations better."

—Mark C. Lack
Manager, Strategy Analytics & Business Intelligence,
Mueller, Inc.

"Much has been written about the theory of creating strategic alignment and creating a sustainable improvement system. Theory is sometimes hard to implement. Bob leverages his practical experiences in showing how his concepts have been implemented and proven successful. His are the best "how-to" books on the subject."

—Mark Voigt
Senior Director, Diebold, Inc.

"Bob Paladino's career experience as a chief performance officer comes to light in this book that provides a roadmap for any company to accelerate its business improvement program. The book is grounded in actual case studies, so no there is no theory, but rather a practical template to improve your financial, customer, process, and people results; public, nonprofit and government organizations take note."

—Ted B. Miller, Jr.
President, 4M Investments, LLC
Chairman, Intercomp Global Services
former Chairman, Crown Castle International
former Chairman, M7 Aerospace

"Bob Paladino's wisdom and experience are evident in this book. The true value is from the logical, real world case studies focused on improving performance, whether a novice or experienced organization."

—Robin Ellingson
Learning & Development Director
Midwest Fortune 500 Insurance Company

Corporate Performance Management Best Practices

Founded in 1807, John Wiley & Sons is the oldest independent publishing company in the United States. With offices in North America, Europe, Asia, and Australia, Wiley is globally committed to developing and marketing print and electronic products and services for our customers' professional and personal knowledge and understanding.

The Wiley Corporate F&A series provides information, tools, and insights to corporate professionals responsible for issues affecting the profitability of their company, from accounting and finance to internal controls and performance management.

Corporate Performance Management Best Practices

A Case Study Approach to Accelerating CPM Results

BOB PALADINO

WILEY

John Wiley & Sons, Inc.

Published by John Wiley & Sons, Inc., Hoboken, New Jersey.
Published simultaneously in Canada.

For general information on our other products and services or for technical support, please contact our Customer Care Department within the United States at (800) 762-2974, outside the United States at (317) 572-3993 or fax (317) 572-4002.

Wiley also publishes its books in a variety of electronic formats. Some content that appears in print may not be available in electronic books. For more information about Wiley products, visit our website at www.wiley.com.

Library of Congress Cataloging-in-Publication Data

Paladino, Bob, 1959-
  Corporate performance management best practices : a case study approach to accelerating CPM results/Bob Paladino.
      p. cm. — (Wiley corporate F&A series)
  Includes bibliographical references and index.
  ISBN 978-1-118-47858-5 (cloth); ISBN 978-1-118-50746-9 (ebk);
  ISBN 978-1-118-50769-8 (ebk); ISBN 978-1-118-50745-2 (ebk)
  1. Organizational effectiveness—Case studies.   2. Performance—Management—Case studies.   3. Management—Case studies.   4. Health care reform—Case studies.   I. Title.
  HD58.9.P348 2013
  658.4′013–dc23   2012030209

Printed in the United States of America.

10 9 8 7 6 5 4 3 2 1

To My Family

Thank you to my parents, Albert and Dorothy, for their continued support. Special admiration to my wife, Ellen, and to my children, Joseph and Natalie, for keeping me inspired.

To Our Freedom

I am grateful to have freedom of speech and faith and have immense respect for those who have preserved it. Consistent with prior books, I continue to donate royalties to fund injured soldiers and to the United Flight 93 Tower of Voices Memorial near my home. It contains 40 wind chimes; sounds of the wind are a living memory of the 40 persons honored, many whose last contact was through their voices. To express your appreciation, please go to www.honorflight93 .org and www.saluteheroes.org, both IRS Section 501(c) (3) nonprofit organizations.

And unto whomsoever much is given, of him much shall be required.
—Mark 12:48

To Principled Living

I tithe earnings to numerous nonprofit organizations to assist others to become self-reliant, self-assured, and prosperous.

Be great in act, as you have been in thought.
—William Shakespeare

Contents

Preface

WHAT DO AWARD-WINNING COMMERCIAL, NONPROFIT, and government organizations know about corporate performance management (CPM) that eludes other executives? How do you organize your leadership and management teams, establish structure and governance, bring out the best in your employees, find hidden talent, take on sacred cows, and unlock innovation to accelerate and realize breakthrough results? The CPM *Improve Performance* best practices, maturity model, and 10-Step problem-solving approach described in this book will enable you to chart your progress to excellence. Ten-step teams averaged over $450,000 per team in annual earnings improvements derived from their 12-week problem-solving cycle. Learn from dozens of high-performing teams and professionals at MidMichigan Health who delivered outstanding results: tens of millions in earnings improvements balanced with customer, process, and people results.

From the author of *Five Key Principles of Corporate Performance Management*—the number one best-selling CPM book for five years running—and *Innovative Corporate Performance Management*—the number two best-selling CPM book for three years running—this dynamic book expands Principle 4: Improve performance for your organization to fast-track results. The author partnered with the MidMichigan Health system executive and management teams and chronicles their journey and results. This book provides:

- **Five Key Principles of CPM**—a self-scoring diagnostic with 30+ best practices
- **Five Key Principles of CPM**—the program roadmap
- **Principle 4: Improve performance**—a program maturity model to chart your course
- **Principle 4: Improve performance**—35 new best practices to accelerate results

- **Principle 4: 10-step problem solving**—case studies to improve business units, shared services functions, and core and support processes
- **Practical insights** from 10-step team leaders on how they achieved outstanding results

Teams leveraged corporate performance management, 10-step problem solving, best practices, problem statements, goal statements, customer requirements, team charters, team roles, customer surveys, process map choke points, fishbone diagrams, creative design exercises, To-Be six-way design matrices, benchmarking, change management, and communications plans. Consider this book a field guide that you can apply to your organization. It provides practical executive and management examples and is brimming with insights and tools to help you achieve results. *Corporate Performance Management Best Practices* will help improve performance in your organization.

As for the roadmap, Chapter 1 provides an introduction to the Five Key Principles of Corporate Performance Management and Innovative Corporate Performance Management, shares an executive summary of the first seven rounds of team results that amassed millions in savings, and provides the views of MidMichigan Health executives on the 10-step team program.

Chapter 2 shares Five Key Principles of Corporate Performance Management's 34 best practices and introduces the Carnegie Mellon University (CMU) five-stage Capability Maturity Model, which served as a useful framework for charting the maturation of MidMichigan Health's CPM 10-step program.

Chapter 3 provides the strategic context and key market and industry forces impacting MidMichigan Health, the company's CPM program and journey, and a summary case study to introduce the 10-step Improve Performance approach deployed by dozens of teams.

Chapter 4 chronicles MidMichigan Health's journey to excellence and the maturing of its 10-step program through five rounds of teams. It optimizes the program in round 6 for an entire hospital and formal launch of five system-wide teams in round 7. For each of the seven rounds of teams, six elements are reviewed:

1. CMU maturity model level definition
2. Leadership rationale
3. Team areas of focus
4. Team results
5. Positive outcomes
6. Opportunities for improvement

Chapter 5 shares 35 new best practices that were instrumental to the success of the seven-plus rounds of teams. Examples range from steering committee governance to team member selection, from the use of behavioral modeling to benchmarking, and from team roles to time boxing team life cycles. The best practices are arranged to mirror a team's life cycle.

Chapter 6 describes finance, human resources, and supply chain management shared services teams from a practitioner's perspective by walking through the 10-step teams' working papers in narrative form. Cases include:

- **Finance.** Accounts Payable and Disbursements, *Smart Spending*
- **Finance.** Financial and Management Reporting, *Streamline Information*
- **Human Resources.** New Employee Requisitions, *Simplify Hiring*
- **Supply Chain Management.** New Product Requisitions, *Manage Innovation*

Chapter 7 shares the journey of two teams focused on MidMichigan Health system laboratory services and pharmacy services. Traditionally, these services have operated within each of the four medical centers (hospitals) supporting core hospital operations, patients, and general and specialty medical practice areas. They were structured vertically inside their respective hospitals. The two 10-step teams changed this paradigm forever by reorienting and repositioning these service lines as "horizontal" strategic business units with clear and singular executive leadership to be optimized and to serve all four medical centers.

Chapter 8 focuses on core and specialty services within the MidMichigan Health care system. Core or central to the medical centers, the Emergency Department (ED) often is the first point of contact for patients. Should ED diagnoses warrant further services, patients will experience the care coordination process through discharge. MidMichigan Health provides numerous specialty services. The orthopedics services team focused largely on hip and joint replacements and women's health services team focused on preventive mammographic screening. Cases include:

- **Emergency Department.** Improve throughput, customer scores, and revenue.
- **Care Coordination.** Improve medical outcomes.
- **Orthopedic Services.** Standardize and save.
- **Women's Health Services.** Grow the business.

Chapter 9 outlines a systematic approach for completing a self-scoring diagnostic to baseline your CPM Improvement program and to chart your course toward providing best-in-class and world-class customer, financial, process, and people results. Sections provide three blueprints, including the five-level CMU maturity model; CPM Five Key Principles 34 Core Best Practices; and CPM 10-Step Improve Performance 35 Best Practices Blueprint to enable your journey to excellence.

Acknowledgments

THIS BOOK WOULD NOT HAVE been possible without special contributions from dozens of professionals. More important than their contributions to this book is the recognition they deserve for efforts to advance the field of corporate performance management, the results they achieved for their organizations and their unselfish team centered approach to performance.

Individual commitment to a group effort—that is what makes a team work, a company work, a society work, a civilization work.

—Vince Lombardi

The CPM Steering Committee consisted of executives and leaders:

- Greg Rogers, President, MidMichigan Medical Center—Midland, Executive Vice President, MidMichigan Health
- Francine Padgett, Chief Financial Officer, Senior Vice President, and Treasurer, MidMichigan Health
- Scott Currie, Vice President and Chief Financial Officer, MidMichigan Medical Center—Midland
- Mike Erickson, Vice President of Facility Services, MidMichigan Medical Center—Midland
- Mike Larson, Vice President and Chief Information Officer, MidMichigan Health
- Lorie Mault, Director Labor Relations, MidMichigan Health
- Deb Mills, Director of Corporate Performance Management, MidMichigan Health
- Diane Nold, Vice President, MidMichigan Medical Center—Midland
- Jeff Wagner, Vice President of Supply Chain, MidMichigan Health
- Dr. Lydia Watson, Vice President of Medical Affairs, MidMichigan Medical Center—Midland
- Shelli Wood, Vice President and Chief Nursing Officer, MidMichigan Medical Center—Midland

The next professionals participated on and contributed to high-performing CPM 10-step business improvement teams (in alphabetical first-name order).

Team Members	Title	Affiliate	Credentials
Alicia Kozak	Accountant	MidMichigan Health (Health)	MBA
Amanda Taylor	Admitting Manager	Midland	CHAM
Amy Behmlander	Pharmacy Operations Manager	Midland	PharmD
Amy Livsey-Sommer	Rehabilitation Services Manager	Midland	OTRL
Andrea Millard	RN	Midland	RN, BSN
Andrea Muladore	Former Manager	Midland	
Ann Archuleta	Supply Contracts Administrator	Midland	MBA, CMRP
Ann Dull	Director of Orthopedics and Rehabilitation Services	Midland	PT, MBA, DPT
Ann Niinisto	Office Assistant	Michigan Physicians Group (MPG)	
Anna Goka	Lead Radiation Therapist—Radiation Oncology	Midland	RT
Ashlee Ritchie	Accountant	Health	
Ashley Bugbee	RN	Home Care	RN
Barb Bailey	Medical Assistant	MPG	MLT(ASCP)
Barbara Schaffer	Scheduler	Midland	
Beau Hultquist	Former Senior Analyst	Health	
Ben Faulk	Financial Analyst	Health	CPA, M.Acc.
BettyAnn Eash	Infection Prevention Coordinator	Midland	RN, BSC, CIC
Bev Wackerle	Director of Physician Services and Primary Care Strategic Business Unit	Midland	CPMSM

Team Members	Title	Affiliate	Credentials
Bill Geyer	Physician Liaison Imaging Services	Midland	RT(R)
Bob Berg	Manager	Health	
Bob D. Cowger	RN	Midland	
Bob Francisco	Facilities Operations Manager	Gratiot	CHFM
Bob Green	Manager Radiology Services	Gratiot	
Bonnie Cline	Insurance Account Representative	Gratiot	
Brad VanFulpen	Former Financial Analyst	Health	CPA
Brian McCarthy	Director of Neurosciences, Surgery Services	Midland	
Bridget Banfield	Patient Service Specialist	MPG	
Bryan Cross	Director of Pharmacy	Midland	PharmD, MBA
Carmen Terwillegar	Registered Nurse	Midland	RN
Carol Carbeno	Office Coordinator— Rehabilitation Services	Clare	
Carole Calvert-Baxter	Director, Center for Women's Health	Midland	MA, LLPC
Carolyn Leadholm-Wittke	Nurse Practitioner	Midland	
Carolyn VanWert	Case Manager and Quality Analyst	Gladwin	RN
Cecilia Jerome	Physician Recruitment Coordinator	Midland	BA, MBA
Chandra Morse	Vice President and Corporate Compliance Officer	Health	MBA, CPHRM
Cheryl Bennett	Accountant	Health	MBA
Cheryl Kotenko	Manager of Financial Reporting	Health	CPA, MBA
Cheryl Volkmann	Physician Assistant	Midland	

(continued)

Team Members	Title	Affiliate	Credentials
Cheryl Yesney	Vice President	MPG	
Chris Sheets	Data Coordinator—Operating Room	Midland	Bachelor in Business
Christie Mann	Case Manager	Midland	RN
Christy Weber	Materials Management Supply Contract Analyst	Midland	
Cindy Fillmore	Administrative Director, Laboratory Services	Health	MT(ASCP), MBA
Cindy Hough	Surgical Services Purchasing Coordinator	Clare	RN
Cindy Orvosh	Data Security Analyst	Midland	
Cinthia Brooks	Manager of Financial Planning and Analysis	Health	BBA, MBA
Colleen Such	Inventory Management Specialist	Midland	BBA
Cory Wheeler	CT Scanning Lead Technologist	Midland	RT(R)(CT)
Courtney Szelski	Manager, Radiation Oncology	Midland	BS, RT(R)(T)
Danielle Alward	Practice Manager	MPG	
Dave Koutz	Director of Facilities	Gratiot	BSBA
Dean Cornell	LIS Administrator	Midland	BS in Medical Technology
Deana Cramer	Former Social Worker	Midland	
Deb Hitt	Director, Patient Support Services	MPG	
Deb Mills	Director of Corporate Performance Management	Health	B. Math
Deb Sharpe	Director of Patient Financial Services	Midland	
Deb Smith	Manager Cardiopulmonary, Cardiac/Pulmonary Rehab and Sleep Labs	Gratiot	RRT, RPSGT
Denise Przepiora	Administrative Assistant	MPG	

Team Members	Title	Affiliate	Credentials
Dennis Bauer	Manager	Midland	
Dennis Ouillette	Gamma Knife Manager	Midland	RN, BS
Diane Nold	Vice President of Professional Services	Midland	RRT
Diane Strahota	Manager	MPG	
Don Lynch	Finance Manager	Health	
Doug Nye	Manager II	Midland	
Dr. Michael Stack	Physician	MPG	
Erik Robinette	Director of Business Development—Isabella County	Health	BS, RPSGT
Faith Morley	Lead Clerk	Midland	
Francine Padgett	Senior Vice President	Health	MBA, CPA, HFMA Fellow
Fred Kagarise	Manager of Corporate Reimbursement	Health	
Gail Pelkey	Breast Health Nurse	Midland and MPG	RN, CBPN-IC
Georgette Walters	Emergency Department Nurse Manager	Gladwin	RN, BSN
Glenn King	Vice President and Chief Nursing Officer	Clare	RN, MSN, MBA
Greg Ghilardi	Director of Total Compensation	Health	BBA, MS, SPHR
Greg Rogers	Executive Vice President of MidMichigan Health and President and CEO of MidMichigan Medical Center–Midland	Midland	CPA, FHFMA
Heather Wager	Accounting Supervisor	Health	CPA
Jan Overly	Manager	Midland	
Jan Penney	Director of Cardiovascular, Emergency, andCritical Care Services	Midland	RN, BSN

(continued)

Team Members	Title	Affiliate	Credentials
Janet Foor	Vice President of Nursing	Gladwin	RN, MSN
Jason Hunt	Accounting Supervisor	Health	CPA
Jason Williams	Manager of System Integration	Midland	EMBA, BS RT(R)
Jeanne Genovese	Nurse Manager	Midland	RB, BS
Jeff Wagner	Vice President	Health	
Jen Hickerson	Management Analyst	Health	
Jennifer Miller	Accounting Supervisor	Health	
Jeramie Soderberg	Accountant	Health	CPA
Jerri Liphard	Director of Nursing, Medical/Surgical/Observation Units	Midland	MBA, RN-BC
Jill Roby-Snyder	Vice President of Operations	Home Care	RN, BBA
Joan Herbert	Director, Oncology Strategic Business Unit	Midland	Pharm D
Joanne Cergnul	Property Management Specialist	Health	
Jodi Herman	Manager, Health Information Management	Midland	RHIA
John Shaffer	Manager of Emergency Medical Services	Midland	AD in Fire Science, BSC in Organization Administration
John Urban	Supervisor Imaging Services	Midland	RT(N), CNMT, MSA
Jolene Reyes	Scheduling Supervisor	Midland	
Jon Athey	Materials Management Specialist	Midland	
Josh Clark	Desktop Specialist	Midland	
Josh Gustavison	Senior IT Specialist	Midland	AD in Applied Science

Team Members	Title	Affiliate	Credentials
Josh Wiggins	Vice President and Controller	Health	
Josie Brigham	Scheduler/Secretary	Midland	
Joyce Carrick	Neurology Specialty Coordinator	Midland	Certified Surgical First Assistant
Judi Graves	Corporate Accounting Manager	Health	
Julie Foster	Risk Manager	Midland	RN, BSN
Julie Sanders	Quality Analyst and Education	Home Care	AD in Nursing
Julie Simon	Specialty Surgery and Observation Manager	Midland	RN-BC
June Galbraith	Obstetrics and Surgical Care Unit Manager	Gratiot	RN
Karen Koutz	Program Director, Wound Treatment Center	Midland	BSC
Kari McDowell	Accountant	Health	BS in Accounting
Karma Beutel (McGaw)	RN	Midland	RN, ED
Katherine Warren	RN	Midland	RN
Kathi Wilford	Former Planning Analyst	Health	MBA
Kathleen Ludwig	Office Assistant—Breast Health Program	Midland	
Kathy Akin	Manager	MPG	
Katie Sias	Pharmacy Clinical Coordinator	Midland	PharmD
Kay Wagner	Director of Quality	Health	MSN, RN
Kellie Warner	Clinical Documentation Specialist	Clare	BAA, RN
Ken Spencer	Pharmacy Supervisor	Gladwin	RPh, MBA
Kendra Huckins	Human Resources Strategic Partner	Health	MBA

(continued)

Team Members	Title	Affiliate	Credentials
Kevin Isbister	Equipment and Supply Manager	Home Care	
Kevin Russell	Director of Ancillary Services	Gladwin	MT(ASCP)
Kevin Wing	Pay Management Manager	Health	BBA in Accounting and Management
Kim Gerhardt	Pharmacist	Midland	RPh
Kim Hartnagle	Financial Counselor	Midland	
Kim Lisee	Clerk	Midland	
Krista Klein	Value Analysis Coordinator	Midland	
Kristina Moore	Financial Analyst	Health	
Kristy Brown	Internal Auditor	Health	
Lauree Hoag	Invasive Imaging Inventory Coordinator	Midland	BBA
Laurie Krebs	Pay Management Specialist	Midland	
Liezel Radey	Manager of Physical Rehabilitation	Gratiot	PT
Linda Clark	RN	Midland	
Lisa Grabmeyer	Patient Financial Services Cashier	Midland	
Lisa Minns	Nurse Manager— Rehabilitation Center andDirector—Office of Recipient Rights	Gratiot	RN, CRRN
Lisa Weston	Employee Service Representative	Health	
Liz Minbiole	Director of Finance and Controller	MPG	MBA, CPA
Lorie Mault	Director of MyHR Service and Talent Acquisition Centers, Employee and Labor Relations and Strategic Partners	Health	MSA, PHR, CLRS

Team Members	Title	Affiliate	Credentials
Lydia Watson	Staff Gynecologist and Vice President of Medical Affairs	MPG/Midland	BA, MD
Lyn Boyce	Manager, Case Management and Discharge Planning	Gratiot	RN, BSN
Lyn Hintz	Supervisor Diagnostic Radiology/Transcription Services	Midland	RT(R)
Lynn Bruchhof	Vice President of People Resources	Health	BA, MA in Organization Development and Human Resources
Lynne Carlson	Financial Analyst	Health	
Magan Graf	Patient Transporter	Midland	
Marion Lapeer-Cook	Patient Transporter	Midland	
Mark Bush	Former CEO	Gratiot	
Mark Kozak	Compensation Analyst	Health	MBA
Mary Bell	Medical Surgical and Operating Room Manager	Gladwin	RN, BSN
Mary Chamberlin	Patient Account Specialist	Midland	
Mary Jane Hoshaw	Manager, Diabetes Center and Clinical Nutrition Services	Midland	MS, RD
Mary Jo Jahn	Ultrasound Technician	Midland	
Mary Jo Letts	Scheduler	Midland	
Mary Petersen	RN Case Manager	Midland	RN, BSN
Matt Nobis	Director of Internal Audit	Health	BA, MBA, CPA
Matt Streitmatter	Marketing Manager	Health	
Megan Mallory	RN	Midland	RN
Melanie Mickle	HRIS Human Resource Information System Manager	Health	

(continued)

Team Members	Title	Affiliate	Credentials
Melisa McLeod	Invasive Imaging Supervisor	Midland	RN, BSN
Melissa Dunkle	Lead Tech Diagnostic Imaging	Clare	RT(R)(CT)
Melissa Simmons	Patient Service Specialist	MPG	
Melodie Dodman	Accountant	Health	BS in Business Administration
Michael Bruzewski	Labor and Employee Relations Specialist	Health	MSA, PHR
Michael Rogers	Former Specialist, HR	Health	
Michael Thom	Operating Room Purchasing Coordinator	Midland	MS, RN, CNOR
Michelle Brady	Director of Emergency and Inpatient Services	Clare	RN, BSN
Mike Bersani	Manager, Clinical Nutrition, Food Services, Environmental Services, Laundry	Clare	CDM, CFPP
Mike Erickson	Vice President Facilities and Construction	Midland	CBET, MS, MBA
Mike Graham	Financial Analyst	Health	CPA
Molly Sheltraw	Human Resources Manager	Health	MSA, PHR
Nicole Krantz	Clinical Support Tech	Home Care	
Pam Wieske	Manager, Quality Management Department	Midland	BSN, RN
Paula Buning	Nurse Manager, Emergency Department, Cardiac Catheter and Interventional Radiology	Gratiot	RN, BSN
Paula Chermside	Vice President	MPG	MHA, MBA
Penny Martin	Regional Director	MPG	MA
Polly McKimmy	Practice Manager	MPG	MMCC
Rachel Aultman	Operations Director	Home Care	RN, BSN, OCN
Rachel Peltier	Nursing Administration	Gratiot	RN, BSN

Team Members	Title	Affiliate	Credentials
Rachelle Druelle (Wenglikowski)	Former Pay Management Specialist	Midland	
Randy Crites	Network Analyst	Gratiot	BS in Computer Science
Randy Wyse	Director of Laboratory Services	Midland	
Rebecca Messing	Former Human Resources Generalist	Health	
Renae Foco	Admitting Supervisor	Midland	CHAM
Rich Weiler	Manager of Respiratory Care	Midland	MSA, RRT
Richard Reynolds	President and CEO	Health	CPA, FHFMA
Roberta Ryan-Dankert	Database Administrator	Midland	
Robin Nelson	Patient Relations Manager, Privacy Officer, and Recipient Rights Advisor	Midland	MSA
Robin Whitmore	Vice President, Nursing and Clinical Services	Gratiot	RN, MSN, MBA
Rod Zapolski	Director of Imaging	Midland	MSA, RT(R)
Ronette Parks	Vice President	MPG	
Ruth Kitzmiller	Director of Surgical Services	Midland	RN, BSN, MSA
Sally DeSloover	Senior Programmer/Analyst	Midland	BS in Computer Information Systems
Sandra Blank	Director of Customer Service	Midland	BA
Sandy Postal	Pay Specialist	Midland	
Sara Silvestro	Group Leader	Clare	MT(ASCP)
Sarah Hills	Talent Management Specialist	Health	BS
Scott Currie	Vice President and Chief Financial Officer	Health	
Shannon Brantley	Data Integrity Manager	Home Care	

(continued)

Team Members	Title	Affiliate	Credentials
Shelli Wood	Vice President and Chief Nursing Officer	Midland	RN, BSN, MBA
Sherry Taunt	Former Vice President	Health	
Stephanie Petras	Emergency Department Manager	Midland	RN, BSN, MA, MSA, CEN
Sue Heber	Manager, Health Information Management	Clare	RHIA
Tammy Beyer	Patient Account Representative	MPG	
Tammy Pero	Referral Specialist	MPG	
Tammy Terrell	Director of Nursing	Gratiot	RN, BSN
Tara Schmitt	Human Resources Strategic Partner	Health	BBA, PHR
Tara Tigner	Supervisor Supply Distribution	Midland	
Teresa Bailey	Nurse Manager, Peri-Operative Services and Ambulatory Surgery	Gratiot	RN, BSN
Terry Thrush	RN Shift Administrator	Midland	RN, BSN
Tiffany Lavack	Billing Account Representative	MPG	
Tim Sassin	Department of Pharmacy Clinical Coordinator	Midland	PharmD, BCPS
Tim Watkins	Manager, Acute Care EMR	Midland	
Tina Church	Patient Financial Services Manager	Midland	BA
Tom Elsen	Facilities Manager	Midland	BBA (pending)
Toni Phillips	Patient Service Specialist	MPG	
Tonia VanWieren	Nursing Director, Maternity Unit/Pediatrics	Midland	RN, BSN
Tori Meyer	Cost Budget Analyst	Health	
Tracie Hopkins	Manager of Critical Care and Value Analysis Chair	Midland	RN, BSN, CCRN

Team Members	Title	Affiliate	Credentials
Tracy Klapish	Physician Liaison	Midland	BS, MBA
Tricia Mangapora	Laboratory Quality Process Manager	Midland	MT(ASCP)
Tricia Sommer	Director of Business Planning and Development	Midland	MBA, FHFMA
Vic Morgan	Vice President and Chief Financial Officer	Health	BBA in Accounting
Vickie Colbry	Manager of Critical Care Unit, Cardiac Catheterization Lab, Progressive Unit, and Pediatrics	Gratiot	RN
Victor Hosfeld	Medical Physicist	Midland	MS
Warren Johnson	Marketing Director	Health	APR
Wendy Wackerle	Physical Therapy Assistant	Home Care	
Wieslaw Herdzik	Financial Analyst	Health	MBA
Zack Luick	Former Manager	Midland	

CHAPTER ONE

Introduction

I'm a great believer in luck, and I find the harder I
work the more I have of it.

—*Thomas Jefferson*

MANY COMPANIES, GOVERNMENTS, AND NONPROFITS
are experiencing turbulence and challenges. Several factors have
converged to create unprecedented pressures and they are finding it
essential to accelerate their corporate performance management (CPM) journeys for results. My first two books on CPM studied dozens of award-winning
companies and provided a roadmap of their core and innovative best practices for others to emulate. I am grateful to you as a reader for helping them
to become best sellers. This book takes a more focused view on one company
that has earned numerous awards and chronicles its business improvement
program while on its journey to excellence.

In my first book, *Five Key Principles of Corporate Performance Management*, published in 2007 by John Wiley & Sons, I researched over 100 award-winning companies and shared over 30 common core best practices grouped by the Five Key Principles.

Principle 1: Establish and deploy a CPM office and officer.
Principle 2: Refresh and communicate strategy.
Principle 3: Cascade and manage strategy.
Principle 4: Improve performance.
Principle 5: Manage and leverage performance.

Executives from 14 commercial, government, and nonprofit organizations generously shared their case stories in that book. They had earned an impressive roster of awards and honors, including:

- U.S. President's Malcolm Baldrige National Quality Award (MBNQA)
- Kaplan & Norton Global Balanced Scorecard Hall of Fame Award
- Deming Quality Award
- American Productivity & Quality Award (APQC) Best Practice Partner award
- State quality awards
- *Fortune* magazine's "100 Best Companies to Work For"
- Several other honors and awards in each case

In the first book, I shared my personal journey of leading Crown Castle International's Global CPM efforts while reporting to the chief executive officer (CEO). Crown earned several notable awards and honors:

- The *Wall Street Journal* ranked Crown in the top 20 most improved in shareholder value (out of over 4,000).
- The company's share price appreciated from $1 to over $30 during my tenure.
- The company earned the globally recognized Balanced Scorecard Hall of Fame Award from Drs. Kaplan and Norton.
- The company won the APQC Best Practice Partner award.

This was the beginning of the Five Key Principles model (shown in Exhibit 1.1) that has since been used by dozens of organizations to emulate these early winners.

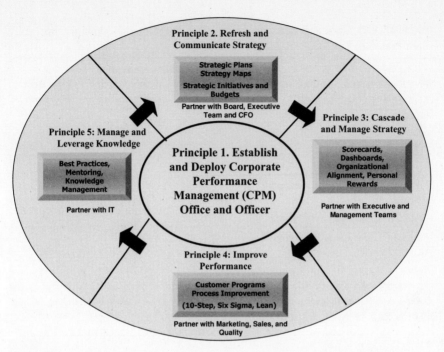

EXHIBIT 1.1 Five Key Principles of Corporate Performance Management

Source: Bob Paladino, *Five Key Principles of Corporate Performance Management* (Hoboken, NJ: John Wiley & Sons, 2007), p. 4. © Copyright 2010 Bob Paladino and Associates, LLC.

With regard to excellence, it is not enough to know, but we must try to have and use it.

—Aristotle

In my second book, *Innovative Corporate Performance Management* (John Wiley & Sons, 2011), I researched dozens of companies that were thriving during the worst recession in American history. In short, the 11 commercial, government, and nonprofit organizations that shared their cases had amassed over 175 notable national awards, including all of those noted earlier. I was astonished to discover that these organizations have devised 132 innovative best practices beyond the core best practices; the core and innovative best practices are stratified in Exhibit 1.2.

EXHIBIT 1.2   Core and Innovative Corporate Performance Management
Best Practices

Five Key Principles of Corporate Performance Management	Core Common Best CM Practices	New Innovative, Company-Specific Best Practices	Total Best Practices
Principle 1: Establish and deploy a CPM office and Officer	8	8	16
Principle 2: Refresh and communicate strategy	6	39	45
Principle 3: Cascade and manage strategy	9	31	40
Principle 4: Improve performance	5	30	35
Principle 5: Manage and leverage knowledge	6	24	30
Totals	34	132	166

Source: Bob Paladino, *Innovative Corporate Performance Management* (Hoboken, NJ: John Wiley & Sons, 2011), p. xii. © Copyright 2011 Bob Paladino and Associates, LLC.

This research also provided a CPM Core Process Blueprint, which provides a roadmap for organizations to migrate from the current state to emulate award-winning organizations. The blueprint of core CPM processes is shown in Exhibit 1.3.

The blueprint of key processes also formalized key roles and responsibilities for each core process; the roles included process sponsors, process owners, process facilitator, and process participants.

> All truths are easy to understand once they are discovered; the point is to discover them.
>
> —**Galileo Galilei**

CORPORATE PERFORMANCE MANAGEMENT BEST PRACTICES

Corporate Performance Management Best Practices builds on prior research and expands on Principle 4: Improve performance. I was grateful to partner with

EXHIBIT 1.3 CPM Principles 1 to 5 Blueprint and Key Supporting Processes

CPM PRINCIPLES 1–5 ROADMAP	Year 1				Year 2				Year 3	
Key Supporting Processes	Q1	Q2	Q3	Q4	Q1	Q2	Q3	Q4	Q1	Q2
Principle 1: Establish and Deploy CPM Office										
• Executive Sponsorship and Trusted Advisor process										
• Recruit, Train and Manage Enterprise CPM Expert process										
• CPM Principles 2–5 Management process										
• Manage CPM Centers of Excellence process										
Principle 2: Refresh and Communicate Strategy										
• Strategic Planning process										
• Enterprise Risk Management process										
• Budgeting and Strategic Initiative process										
• Strategic Communications and Change Management processes										
Principle 3: Cascade and Manage Strategy										
• Corporate Balanced Scorecard process										
• Business and Support Unit Balanced Scorecard processes										
• Team and Personal Scorecard and Goal processes										
• BSC Automation and Meeting Management processes										
Principle 4: Improve Performance										
• Customer and Competitor Survey and Innovation processes										
• Quality Improvement and Innovation processes										
• Benchmarking process										
Principle 5: Manage and Leverage Knowledge										
• Best Practice and Innovation Sharing process										
• Mentor and Development process										

Source: Bob Paladino, *Innovative Corporate Performance Management* (John Wiley & Sons, 2011, Hoboken, NJ), p. 36.

the MidMichigan Health system executive and management teams and chronicle their journey and results. This book provides:

- *Five Key Principles of CPM* self-scoring diagnostic with 30+ best practices
- *Five Key Principles of CPM* Program Roadmap
- *Principle 4: Improve performance program maturity model* to chart your course
- *Principle 4: Improve performance* 35 new best practices to accelerate results
- *Principle 4: 10-step problem-solving* case studies to improve business units, shared services functions, and core and support processes
- *Practical insights* from 10-Step team leaders on how they achieved outstanding results

Teams leveraged real-time voice-of-the-customer surveys, net promoter scoring, internal and external benchmarking, creative exercises, prioritization techniques, and more. Consider this book a field guide that you can readily apply to your organization.

I will share the journey of applying CPM best practices and understanding the obstacles and lessons learned necessary to help accelerate your results. How does an organization apply best practices? What does an organization experience, and what adjustments does it make to realize value? What are the five levels of maturity? What resources does it take? How long does it take to go from the starting point to full maturity? This book addresses these and many more questions. It chronicles the journey the vast majority of organizations are on, striving to attain awards that a select few earn.

I have been honored to participate on the journey toward excellence with a special company and a dynamic team at MidMichigan Health system. I invite you to join me in tracing their journey of deploying CPM methods to accelerate results and explore their progress from level 1 (initial), to level 3 (defined), to level 5 (optimized), often referred to as best in class, and understand program best practices that enabled their metamorphic transformation.

In short, how has a Michigan hospital system applied the Five Key Principles of Corporate Performance Management to emulate award-winning organizations? How has the diverse employee base dealt with headwinds, including the collapse of the auto industry on its doorstep, unprecedented government intrusion, declining reimbursement (revenue) rates, reductions in customer/patient population, and new national competitors to improve performance across dozens of key measures? This book chronicles MidMichigan's CPM journey with a distinct focus on Principle 4: Improve performance, and offers best practices and key insights on how it tackled the sacred cows, proactively myth-busted to refute long-held beliefs, and applied disciplined problem-solving methods to get it right to benefit patients, communities, doctors, and employees. Consider this book a field guide or implementers' guide that you can readily apply to your organization.

How have MidMichigan stayed focused, avoided the pitfalls, and achieved breakthrough results in the financial, customer/ patient, operational, and people perspectives of the business? How has it translated the cases and best practices into actions that employees can understand and support? The lessons learned and best practices apply to all organizations on the journey to excellence.

Trust one who has gone through it.

—**Virgil**

Corporate Performance Management Best Practices not only provides universal, innovative best practices but also brings you a proven implementation model that has accelerated breakthrough results. Learn practical techniques that have been adopted at all levels in the organization, from a facilities manager to the chief nursing officer, from a human resources supervisor to the chief financial officer, and from an hourly patient transportation worker to the chief executive officer.

Corporate Performance Management Best Practices moves well beyond traditional how-to books and offers a fresh approach for rapidly deploying solutions to accelerate and improve performance.

EXECUTIVE VIEWS ON CPM

The 10-step program offers a simpler, less complicated approach [than Six Sigma or lean] to solving real-world problems in a team environment. It has been a very effective and successful tool for our organization.

—Adelberto J. "Al" Adan, MBA, FACHE, Executive Vice
President and COO, MidMichigan Physicians Group, and Vice
President, MidMichigan Medical Center–Midland

Provides a structured approach to process improvement that is easy to learn and is data driven. Requires you to move quickly and encourages you to think outside the box.

—Scott Currie, Vice President and Chief Financial
Officer, MidMichigan Medical Center–Midland

Bob Paladino's 10-step program brought a logical, repeatable process to MidMichigan Health. Following the disciplined step-by-step process, you peel back the onion to expose the true cause of the issue that you are working on. We drove home results that would not have been achievable without the program.

—Mike Erickson, Vice President of Facility Services, MidMichigan Medical Center–Midland

I believe the CPM training provided our staff with the tools and clarity to really focus on results/outcomes that aligned with our system strategic goals and objectives. Once the team was selected and team roles were identified, the team followed the code of conduct and quickly gathered a tremendous amount of information which were then used to make decisions on our new process. The 12-week deadline at first seemed impossible but the team bonded quickly and came to a solution that we knew would create efficiencies and cost/time savings for our facility.

—Lorie Mault, MSA, PHR, Director of Labor Relations, MidMichigan Health

The 10-step process has provided MidMichigan Health with a consistent systematic methodology to approach problem solving. Within this structured framework which has defined beginning, middle and end dates, our multidisciplinary teams have been extremely successful in identifying solutions that result in measurable changes to improve quality, efficiency, patient satisfaction, and financial results aligning with our strategic initiatives.

—Deb Mills, Director of Corporate Performance Management, MidMichigan Health

It WORKS! A process that has a defined beginning, middle and end has been very effective for our organization. This process has been valuable in assisting us with problem solving, changing processes, and implementing these changes in a very disciplined and timely manner. While a great deal of work is accomplished by our teams, the members of the teams have fun and feel a great sense of accomplishment.

—Diane Nold, Vice President, MidMichigan Medical Center–Midland

From my perspective the value of the 10-step program for MidMichigan Health has been its ability to "focus" the organization. The 10-step program focuses on:

Facts;
Operations and solving "real" problems;
Cross-functional collaboration;
Utilizing innovation and best practices for its solutions; and
Success and accountability.

By setting the bar that each team must have some type of "hard" dollar impact (revenue or expense reduction).

—Francine Padgett, Chief Financial Officer, Senior Vice
President and Treasurer, MidMichigan Health

I have been particularly impressed with how the 10-Step Program helps each team (many of whom have never worked together before) solve problems in unique, enlightening ways, ultimately affording us financial wins and improvements in our abilities to take care of our patients.

—Dr. Lydia Watson, Vice President of Medical Affairs,
MidMichigan Medical Center–Midland

The value is the ability of the process to direct focus to the root cause of an issue and to accomplish an action plan in a defined period of time.

—Shelli Wood, Vice President and Chief Nursing Officer,
MidMichigan Medical Center–Midland

However beautiful the strategy, you should occasionally look at the results.

—Winston Churchill

 ## MIDMICHIGAN AWARDS, HONORS, AND RESULTS

According to the MidMichigan Health 2011 Community Report, MidMichigan Health has earned several honors and awards and realized several safety improvements, which are described next.

Awards and Honors

- For the third consecutive year, MidMichigan Health was selected as one of the best health systems in the country by Thomson Reuters, scoring in the top 20 percent of 285 organizations nationwide. Top-quintile performers are proven to have much better patient outcomes, higher-quality care, and better patient satisfaction scores.
- MidMichigan Medical Center–Gratiot received the HealthGrades 2011 Outstanding Patient Experience Award™. This distinction ranks the Medical Center among the top 5 percent of hospitals nationwide, based on an analysis of patient satisfaction data for 3,797 U.S. hospitals.
- MidMichigan Medical Center–Gladwin was recognized for quality improvement in clinical performance by the Michigan Center for Rural Health.
- MidMichigan Medical Center–Gladwin was named one of the nation's top-performing hospitals on key quality measures by the Joint Commission, the leading accreditor of health care organizations in America. It is one of only 405 U.S. hospitals to earn the distinction.
- MidMichigan Medical Center–Clare met rigorous national standards to earn the Joint Commission's Gold Seal of Approval™ for health care quality and safety. The Joint Commission's unannounced on-site review serves as an independent audit of quality and patient safety.
- The RehabCentre at MidMichigan Medical Center–Gratiot received three-year accreditation from the Commission on Accreditation of Rehabilitation Facilities, the fifth consecutive accreditation for the inpatient rehabilitation and the second for the stroke specialty program.
- MidMichigan Medical Center–Gratiot and Bariatric Surgeon Ernest Cudjoe, M.D., earned the American Society for Metabolic and Bariatric Surgery Bariatric Surgery Center of Excellence designation for the second consecutive year.
- The inpatient medical/pediatric care unit at MidMichigan Medical Center–Gratiot received the 2010 Professional Research Consultants 5-Star Excellence Award for Quality of Care. Recipients scored in the top 10 percent of PRC's national database in confidential interviews for units rated "excellent."
- The Michigan Peer Review Organization awarded MidMichigan Gladwin Pines special recognition for efforts to reduce the use of physical restraints on facility residents. The focus was based on a 2008 to 2011 patient safety quality improvement initiative.

Safety Improvements

According to MidMichigan Health's quality reports, several affiliates of Mid-Michigan Health ranked in the top 10 percent nationwide for listed achievements (national core measure abbreviations in parentheses):

- Aspirin at arrival (AMI-1). AMI patients who received aspirin within 24 hours before or after hospital arrival
- Aspirin prescribed at discharge (AMI-2). AMI patients who are prescribed aspirin at hospital discharge
- Beta blocker prescribed at discharge (AMI-5). AMI patients who are prescribed a beta blocker at hospital discharge
- Evaluation of LVS function (HF-2). Heart failure patients with documentation in the hospital record that the LVS function was evaluated before arrival, during hospitalization, or is planned for after discharge
- Adult smoking cessation advice/counseling (HF-4). Heart failure patients who have a history of cigarette smoking within 12 months who are given advice/counseling
- Blood cultures collected in the ED before first antibiotic received (PN-3b). Pneumonia patients whose initial emergency room blood culture specimen was collected prior to first dose of antibiotics
- Antibiotic selection non-ICU Patients (PN-6b). Immuno-competent non-ICU patients with CAP who receive an initial antibiotic regimen during the first 24 hours that is consistent with current guidelines
- Resident falls with injury. Number of falls with serious injury

Results

MidMichigan Health has embraced the Five Key Principles of Corporate Performance Management by focusing first on three principles concurrently:

Principle 1: Establish and deploy a CPM office and officer.
Principle 3: Cascade and manage strategy.
Principle 4: Improve performance.

Given the market pressures noted, the focus of this book is on Principle 4 so I highlight some of the results identified by the 10-step improvement teams and reported in the CPM 10-Step Team Status Report of CPM MidMichigan Health dated March 15, 2012. Case studies, including detailed results, working papers, key tips, and techniques, are shared in later chapters.

Financial Improvements
- Improved earnings by over $16,000,000 annually from rounds 1 to 7 teams
- Improved earnings by over $89,000,000 in the next five years
- Beyond these earnings, identified one-time cash award of $26,400,000
- Increased revenue for neurology procedures by $128,000 per annum
- Increased procurement card savings by $400,000 per annum
- Increased revenue by $300,000 per annum through reduced leave before treatments
- Reduced mileage reimbursement by $200,000 per annum
- Reduced account receivable write-offs by $85,000 per year
- Reduced sales tax expenditures by $75,000 per annum
- Reduced procurement costs for orthopedic replacements by $397,000 per annum
- Improved revenue by $647,000 per annum through more accurate diagnoses and billings
- Reduced medical insurance rejections by $200,00 per annum
- Reduced software expenses by $300,000 per annum

Customer/Patient Improvements
- Improved emergency department patient satisfaction to "Excellent (highest) Rating" from 40 percent to 52 percent
- Achieved top HCAPS (Hospital Consumer Assessment of Healthcare Providers and Systems) patient scores across all hospitals in state of Michigan
- Decreased inpatient length of stay for degenerative nervous system disorders by 2.9 days, resulting in a total savings of $400,000 per annum (net of adjusted reimbursement)

Process Improvements
- Reduced cycle time to review new, innovative medical products from 161 days to 31 days
- Reduced financial budget complexity across the system by 52 percent from 21,000 to 9,000 lines of detail in one year
- Reduced page counts across the system in management/financial reports by 35 percent in one year
- Increased customer volume, additional 600 mammographic screenings per annum
- Reduced emergency room cycle time by 30 minutes
- Reduced month-end financial statement close from 10 days to 5 days

People and Technology Improvements
- Reduced nursing turnover on medical surgical floors by 43 percent in first year
- Reduce employee requisition cycle time from 45 days to 38 days
- Reallocated four finance department full-time equivalents from traditional finance activities to CPM champion responsibilities
- Trained 56 nurses on neurology procedures to establish neurology step-down unit

 MY PROMISE

Corporate Performance Management Best Practices provides practical executive and practitioner best practice examples on how to embrace and deploy a CPM *Improve Performance* program using integrated CPM processes. I am fortunate to have been part of the journey with this special company and others and am glad to share practical truths to help you with yours.

Honesty is the first chapter in the book of wisdom.

—Thomas Jefferson

2

Corporate Performance Management Core Best Practices

> It is possible to fail in many ways . . . while to succeed is possible only in one way.
>
> —*Aristotle*

THIS CHAPTER DESCRIBES THE FIVE KEY PRINCIPLES of corporate performance management (CPM) and core best practices model. This model, developed in prior research, provides the foundation and strategic context for the material in the rest of the book. I have supplemented these core best practices with selected examples of innovative best practices based on research from my second book, *Innovative Corporate Performance Management*, published in 2011 by John Wiley & Sons. The discovery and application of best practices is a continuous learning experience. This book builds on the prior two with an expanded set of best practices focused on Principle 4: Improve performance.

> The beginning is the most important part of the work.
>
> —**Plato**

PRINCIPLE 1: ESTABLISH AND DEPLOY A CPM OFFICE AND OFFICER

The optimal first step to becoming a high-performing CPM enterprise is deploying *Principle 1: Establish and deploy a CPM office and officer* for your enterprise. The CPM office and officer are at the center of the five CPM principles and facilitate deployment of the remaining four principles. Although not all winners have started with this step, they have all, at some point, come to the realization that a CPM office and officer are necessary. Principle 1 consists of several best practice elements, shown next.

Core Best Practices (recognized and used by all case companies)

- **Executive sponsorship.** The chief executive officer (CEO) actively sponsors the CPM office and CPM projects for a sustained period and with the right visibility to enable maturity.
- **Organizational level and reporting relationship.** The CPM office executive reports to the CEO or CEO direct report.
- **CPM office staff.** Office staff consists of a small senior team experienced in change programs.
- **Leadership, influence factors.** Able to organize cross-organizational, virtual teams to drive results in all CPM methods.
- **Ownership of CPM processes and methods.** The office owns or substantially influences the portfolio and methods of CPM processes enterprise wide.
- **CPM, industry, and company knowledge.** The CPM team possesses deep expertise in strategic planning, initiative management, balanced scorecard (BSC), and knowledge management. One or more team members have deep industry and company-specific knowledge to help guide resolution of project issues.
- **Collaborative maturity.** Experienced in working horizontally and vertically through the organization.
- **Ability to learn.** Open to new ideas, methods, and approaches; able to streamline, integrate, and adapt methods; able to think concurrently.

New Innovative Best Practices: Selected Examples

- Cargill Corn Milling (CCM)'s CPM Office works effectively across a complex, multiple entity enterprise including Cargill Corporate, Cargill's segment operations, and multiple geographies in a complex matrix organization.
- Public Service Electric & Gas (PSE&G) has demonstrated its CPM industry leadership with top decile results in several utility benchmarks and hosted numerous visits from other companies to showcase the CPM office organization and its processes.
- Lockheed Martin Information Systems & Global Services (IS&GS) optimizes the return on investment of its CPM office by minimizing the number of full-time personnel.
- Sharp Healthcare has an expanded, formalized performance improvement infrastructure consisting of champions, change agents, an executive steering committee, and a CEO council.

> I have never let my schooling interfere with my education.
>
> **—Mark Twain**

PRINCIPLE 2: REFRESH AND COMMUNICATE STRATEGY

Many enterprises are challenged to effectively translate their strategies to operations and communicate their strategies to employees. *Principle 2: Refresh and communicate strategy*, consists of several best practice elements, shown next.

Core Best Practices (recognized and used by all case companies)

- **Strategic planning.** Leverage the strategic planning process as either owner or partner to understand changing market conditions including competitor, supplier, rival, and potential entrants and substitutes in the marketplace.
- **Core and adjacent products and services.** Define and determine core and adjacent products and products and services to focus on highest probabilities for success.

(continued)

- **Strategic plan.** Produce a comprehensive strategic plan.
- **Strategy mapping.** Develop corporate- and department-level strategy maps containing objectives along four perspectives, including financial, customer/constituent, process, and people. Observe strategy map design parameters of 20 to 25 objectives.
- **Link strategic planning and budgeting processes.** Link strategic planning to the budgeting process, partner with finance to provide for a seamless continuum.
- **Communications plan.** Communicate strategy throughout the organization using a comprehensive communications plan.

New Innovative Best Practices: Selected Examples

- CCM strategic planning process sources innovative ideas from employees, referred to as Ideas to Innovation (i2i), customers, expert panels, suppliers, and other stakeholders. Innovative product ideas, service ideas, operation ideas, or business model ideas must survive each step of strategic review analysis.
- The City of Coral Springs strategic planning process involves customers enabling key requirements, secured from over 15 customer input sources, to be included in strategic goals, Key Intended Outcomes, and cascaded down through the organization. This strategic planning process has been recognized as a best practice by numerous third-party organizations, such as the National Performance Review, American Productivity and Quality Center, Government Finance Officers Association publications, the Florida Institute of Government programs, and Fitch.
- Delta Dental Kansas has developed and managed the strategic S-curve described as the profile in sales and unit sales for the rollout of innovative new, ancillary products.
- PSE&G, in a strategic business innovation, pioneered innovation strategy with placement of solar panels on over 200,000 utility poles, an industry first on this scale.
- PSE&G, in a second strategic business innovation, pioneered the strategy of deep-water wind farm consisting of 96 turbines located 20 miles offshore to reduce visual signature.
- M7 Aerospace uses several separate but integrated analytics (core and adjacency, five forces, and Strengths, Weaknesses, Opportunities, and Threats [SWOT]) to innovate and formulate strategy; this is far more comprehensive and inventive than most companies.

We are what we repeatedly do. Excellence then, is not an act, but a habit.

—**Aristotle**

PRINCIPLE 3: CASCADE AND MANAGE STRATEGY

Principle 3: Cascade and manage strategy focuses on translating the outputs from Principle 2 into strategic objectives and measures that are actionable by employees. A key influence on development of these best practices and credit goes to Kaplan and Norton, co-inventors of the balanced scorecard methodology and experiences from leading one of their largest consulting divisions. Principle 3 consists of several best practices, shown next.

Core Best Practices (recognized and used by all case companies)

- **Partner with business owners.** Partner with line and staff leadership team members to gain support and influence as partners to help them achieve results.
- **Develop level 1 BSC.** Translate strategy into level 1 BSC measures and measure targets at the highest organizational level.
- **Leverage proven BSC or comparable method.** Observe BSC or comparable design parameters, assigning one to two measures to each strategy map objective.
- **Cascade BSC to lower levels.** Cascade and align level 1 BSC to levels 2, 3, 4, and so on, depending on organizational and accountability structures.
- **Align support services.** Identify and define measures for all support services that align with levels 1 and below.
- **Align teams and individual employees.** Define personal BSCs for teams and/or individuals that align with higher-level and support services BSCs.
- **Link compensation.** Align rewards, recognition, and compensation programs to the BSC.
- **Manage using measures.** Manage BSC meetings to address the appropriate mix of strategic and operational issues; link these issues with Principle 4: Business improvement.

(continued)

- **Automate measurement.** Implement CPM software to manage BSC program with links to other principles.

New Innovative Best Practices: Selected Examples

- CCM Senior Leadership Team (SLT) introduced the Performance Measure Alignment Matrix to identify measures that must appear on business plans produced during the annual business planning process. For example, to promote the *Be innovative* value, the SLT decided that every business plan must include the metric of implemented idea savings.

- The City of Coral Springs has incentive programs to encourage initiative and innovation; these include the Instant Employee Recognition Program, the Project and Performance Bonus Program, and the Gain Sharing Program.

- The City of Coral Springs established process owners and process measure metrics (cycle time, cost, customer satisfaction) to identify variation and to initiate innovation. In process measures, for instance, emergency medical services response times are tracked daily to determine if there is unacceptable variation and corrective action or innovation is taken.

- Delta Dental Kansas (DDKS) draws from numerous external and inventive data sources to secure benchmark and competitive information to inform its BSC results.

- Lockheed Martin IS&GS has embedded innovation into its BSC objectives and measures. P9 is champion solutions for citizen-to-government interaction, which is measured by the number of customer solution awards.

- M7 Aerospace utilizes an innovative shared or virtual BSC to link and align multiple business units and supporting departments to deliver on customer requirements.

The only good is knowledge and the only evil is ignorance.

—**Socrates**

PRINCIPLE 4: IMPROVE PERFORMANCE

Principle 4: Improve performance, focuses on improving customer and competitor intelligence, and business improvement processes. Key influences on this section were my training and facilitation of GE Six Sigma Black Belt teams; collaboration with Motorola University, the pioneers of six sigma; and exposure and use of quality methods, such as the 10-step approach, priority action matrices, and Plan, Do, Check, and Act (PDCA). In concert with Principle 3, if your BSC indicates underperformance, it is incumbent on you to launch an initiative to improve performance. Principle 4 consists of several best practices, shown next.

Core Best Practices (recognized and used by all case companies)

- **Prioritize improvement projects.** Identify and prioritize strategic and operational initiatives projects to improve the organization's performance along financial, customer or constituent, process, and people dimensions.
- **Leverage customer-facing processes.** Develop and exercise customer- and constituent-facing processes to understand and recalibrate processes around changing customer needs. Gather customer and competitor intelligence using regular customer surveys, focus groups, call centers, and related methods and approaches.
- **Leverage process improvement methods.** Design and maintain an ongoing process improvement methods and problem solving to identify and eliminate root causes of issues.
- **Realize value from benchmarking.** Leverage benchmarking and comparative methods to identify and regularly improve core and support processes.
- **Create a performance culture.** Create a virtual community of practitioners to coordinate initiative completion.

New Innovative Best Practices: Selected Examples

- Be Innovative is a CCM value. CCM utilizes a formal approach, i2i, to systematically capture and track innovative ideas relating to new discoveries, cost efficiencies, process improvements, and creative ways to meet business goals and objectives. In addition, CCM supports a culture of innovation through quarterly and annual recognition, monthly BSC communications, an innovation Web site, sponsoring location innovation champions, and a business unit innovation team.

(continued)

- CCM has formalized innovation in its key work process, Manage Idea & Concept Generation, where the company utilized an external resource to help create the innovation process and to provide it with a database for tracking innovative ideas before bringing this capability in-house. The i2i process supports CCM's values of Be Innovative and Promote Collaboration.

- The City of Coral Springs goes beyond traditional training on performance improvement methods to encourage innovation. Its work system design is based on four principles that support city values and encourage innovation. They are customer focus, empowerment, continuous improvement, and team-based operations.

- Poudre Valley Health System starts building relationships with patients and other customers long before they come to the organization seeking services and continues throughout their care and after their discharge.

- PSE&G has innovated performance management in the utility and gas industries and is the benchmarking and best practices clearinghouse for multiple participating companies.

An investment in knowledge always pays the best interest.

—**Benjamin Franklin**

PRINCIPLE 5: MANAGE AND LEVERAGE KNOWLEDGE

Principle 5: Manage and leverage knowledge, focuses on capturing and reusing enterprise-wide intellectual property to leverage the organization's best minds, best practices, and innovations. As enterprises increasingly rely on knowledge workers, it is essential to have core knowledge management (KM) processes embedded in the organization to capture and propagate best-in-class and world-class results. In concert with Principle 3, if your BSC informs you of a location that performs in the top quartile or top decile, it is advantageous to understand, document, and share this location's winning formula with all locations. Principle 5 best practices are shown next.

Core Best Practices (recognized and used by all case companies)

- **Develop KM processes.** Establish and leverage best practice identification, gathering, and sharing processes and technology solutions.
- **Leverage technology.** Partner with the information technology (IT) function to launch and maintain KMS.
- **Develop expert locator systems.** Design and use expert locator systems to capture a systems employee skills inventory within the enterprise to accelerate problem solving in Principle 4 and to optimize human capital.
- **Link KM with Principle 4: Improve process performance.** Link best practice or KM processes with Principle 4 processes to capture solutions and innovations.
- **Share best practices.** Share best practices with strategic planning processes to better understand core competencies and possible strategic advantages.
- **Maintain a virtual KM network.** Establish and maintain virtual network of KM experts throughout the enterprise to optimize results.

New Innovative Best Practices: Selected Examples

- Using a more sophisticated, expanded model than most award-winning companies, CCM transfers relevant knowledge and best practices from and to not only customers but also suppliers and partners. Can we keep the same sentence design and start with CCM?
- CCM leverages numerous forum and approaches to best practice sharing including centers of expertise (COEs), process development groups (PDGs), and cross-functional improvement teams *for innovation*. For instance, the Mill-Feed PDG team works with Cargill Sweeteners Europe to collect, transfer, and share best practices for mill and feed operations for 31 worldwide mills. Examples of COEs include Cargill IT, IT, energy risk management, maintenance and reliability, and corporate procurement.
- City of Coral Springs Process Improvement teams not only drive organizational innovation but also share nationally (and win awards). The emergency medical response process improvement team was the state's team showcase winner and placed fourth overall in the nation in 1998. The Citation System Improvement Team was the state's team showcase winner in 2005 and competed in the nationals in May 2006.

(continued)

- DDKS's employee I.D.E.A. program fosters innovation by providing an avenue for employees to share ideas, suggestions, and feedback regarding the organization, tied to the company's strategy map.
- Poudre Valley Health System links its knowledge, innovation best practice sharing to its competency, leadership, and development models.
- PSE&G pioneered best practice sharing among over 20 gas and 20 electric companies.

Don't be afraid to see what you see.

—**Ronald Reagan**

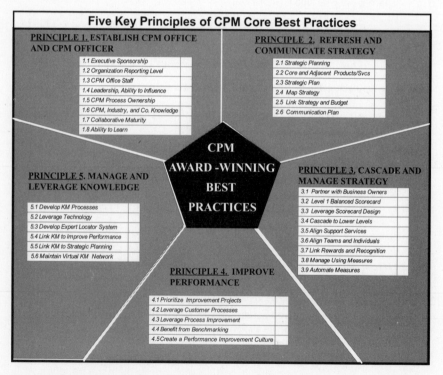

EXHIBIT 2.1   Best Practices Diagnostic Scored on One-to-Five Maturity Scale

CPM MATURITY MODEL AND BEST PRACTICE PENTAGON SCORING DIAGNOSTIC

Organizations adopting the CPM best practice model follow a predictable pattern of maturing their capabilities. This pattern mirrors the model developed by Carnegie Mellon University's (CMU) Capability Maturity Model (CMM).[1] CMU CMM provides a continuum along which maturity can be developed incrementally from one level to the next. I refer to this framework to chronicle MidMichigan Health's evolution in Chapter 4. The levels are:

- **Level 1 initial.** Typically processes at this level are undocumented and in a state of dynamic change, tending to be driven in an ad hoc, uncontrolled, and reactive manner by users or events. The environment for the processes is chaotic or unstable.
- **Level 2 repeatable.** At this level, some processes are repeatable, possibly with consistent results. Process discipline is unlikely to be rigorous, but where it exists, it may help to ensure that existing processes are maintained during times of stress.
- **Level 3 defined.** At this level, sets of defined and documented standard processes are established and subject to some degree of improvement over time. These standard processes are in place (i.e., they are the As-Is or current state processes) and used to establish consistency of process performance across the organization.
- **Level 4 managed.** At this level, using process metrics, management can effectively control the As-Is process. In particular, management can identify ways to adjust and adapt the process without measurable losses of quality or deviations from specifications. Process capability is established from this level.
- **Level 5 optimized**. At this level, the focus is on continually improving process performance through both incremental and innovative technological changes/improvements.

Combining the CPM Best Practices model and the CMU CMM provides a useful diagnostic and project management tool to manage and accelerate their combined adoption in your organization Exhibit 2.1 provides an example of how an organization has used the best practices as a diagnostic to manage and navigate during its journey.

NOTE

1. Mark C. Paulk, Charles V. Weber, Bill Curtis, and Mary Beth Chrissis, "Capability Maturity Model for Software, Version 1.1," Carnegie Mellon University, February 1993.

3

Corporate Performance Management at MidMichigan Health

Hide not your talents. They for use were made.
What's a sundial in the shade?

—*Benjamin Franklin*

 ## STRATEGIC CONTEXT AND CPM APPROACH

MidMichigan Health is a nonprofit health system, headquartered in Midland, Michigan, dedicated to providing quality, comprehensive health care throughout the middle of Michigan and beyond.

It covers a 12-county region with four medical centers in Midland, Alma, Clare, and Gladwin, as well as urgent care centers, home care, nursing homes, physicians, medical offices, and other specialty health services.

Mission, Vision, Values

MidMichigan Health conducts a thoughtful and comprehensive strategic review and incorporates input from its leaders to formulate its mission, vision, and values. The mission, vision, and values are described next.

Our Patients are the focus of everything that we do.

Our Mission is to provide excellent health services to improve the quality of life for people in our communities.

Our Vision is to be an integrated health system providing seamless care to each person we serve.

Our Values . . .

- **Excellence**. We offer nothing less than the best. We adhere to the highest standards possible in clinical care and customer service. We continuously measure ourselves and constantly strive to improve.
- **Integrity.** We do the right thing, each time, every time. We treat each individual with compassion and respect, demonstrating the pinnacle of professionalism and dignity. We communicate openly and honestly. We recognize the unique individuality of each person. In all that we do, we exemplify the highest ethical standards.
- **Teamwork.** We provide individual commitment to a group effort. Collaboration benefits everyone, most importantly our patients. It promotes efficiency, fosters professional and organizational growth, encourages learning, and stimulates innovation.
- **Accountability.** We accept responsibility for all we do. We are accountable for the outcomes of our efforts. We are responsible to the communities we serve, to our patients, and to one another. We recognize that as health care providers we occupy a position of trust.

MidMichigan Health has more than 6,000 employees, physicians, and volunteers and provided $76.7 million in community benefits in fiscal year 2011.

MidMichigan Health is a partnership of health providers, services and facilities in the heart of Michigan. It is a non-profit, tax-exempt organization, led by a board of directors and a 145-person corporate membership. All excess revenues go back into providing care, upgrading services technology and facilities, fairly compensating employees, and creating a supportive work environment.

MidMichigan Health acts as a parent organization to 14 subsidiaries and has various joint ventures and management contracts.

During fiscal year 2011, MidMichigan Health provided $75.5 million in charity care, community benefit, and community-building services to the more than 500,000 people in the 12-county region.

MidMichigan Health also contributes significantly to the health of our local economies. As the second-largest employer in Midland County and the largest employer in Clare, Gratiot, and Gladwin Counties, MidMichigan Health employs more than 4,800 people who, combined, earn more than $100 million in annual wages and benefits. In addition, we purchase more than $15 million in goods and services from local businesses.

System-wide, MidMichigan Health has:

- More than 4,800 employees
- 450 physicians and advanced practice providers
- More than 1,250 volunteers
- Annual gross revenues approximately $1.1 billion
- Assets valued at more than $590 million
- 461 hospital beds at four medical centers
- 185 licensed nursing home beds
- 20 licensed assisted living beds

A hallmark of MidMichigan Health is the quality of its medical facilities and campuses, which have been enhanced by the generosity of local foundations and donors.[1]

Key Market and Industry Trends

A full discussion about trends in health care could consume volumes. This section focuses on a few highlights to provide meaningful context for MidMichigan Health's operating environment and its corporate performance management (CPM) program. These highlights include:

- Declining government and private/commercial insurance provider reimbursement rates, most notably the federal Medicare and Medicaid rates.
- Prolonged and deep nationwide recession and persistent unemployment above 8.0 percent. Adding those who are underemployed or dropped out of the market (another 8 to 9 percent), total unemployment reaches over 16 percent. Michigan has been impacted due largely to the traditionally dominant, now-challenged automotive sector. Further, many upstream sector suppliers have closed or drastically reduced production and employee levels, which translates into patients in a medical system context.

- Outmigration of U.S. population from the North and Midwest to the South and in particular away from Michigan.
- Emergence of regional and national providers or competitors.
- Expansion of nontraditional players into health care services, such as Walgreens and Wal-Mart.
- Trending shortage of general and specialty practice physicians commanding increasing salaries.
- Movement toward more hospital-employed versus private practice doctors.
- National health care debate and myriad of legal challenges injected uncertainty in and disrupted traditional planning and practices.

Design is not just what it looks like and feels like. Design is how it works.

—Steve Jobs

 ## MIDMICHIGAN HEALTH CPM PROGRAM OVERVIEW AND JOURNEY

In December 2009, I was invited by Francine Padgett, chief financial officer (CFO) of MidMichigan Health, to visit with her and Greg Rogers, executive vice president of MidMichigan Health and president, MidMichigan Medical Center–Midland, MidMichigan Health's flagship hospital. We discussed how to establish a CPM program and emulate best practices from award-winning health care companies, essentially CPM programs as outlined in my first book, *Five Key Principles of Corporate Performance Management.*[2] We launched efforts in three of the five key principles:

- **Principle 1: Establish and deploy a CPM office and CPM officer.** This effort included the formation of the CPM office sponsored by the chief executive officer (CEO) of Midland and the CFO of MidMichigan Health. Later it was led on a day-to-day basis by a new director of CPM.
- **Principle 3: Cascade and manage strategy.** We developed and deployed balanced scorecards for the flagship medical center, Midland, and key strategic business units (SBUs).
- **Principle 4: Improve performance.** This effort took place through a pilot round 1 set of several 10-step business improvement teams focused on

the system's five corporate goals: quality, growth, operational excellence, collaboration, and people. Round 1 teams exceeded expectations and the CPM program gained traction.

Action is eloquence.

—William Shakespeare

To address industry and market pressures, MidMichigan Health decided to focus significant resources on Principle 4: Improve performance, the primary emphasis of this book.

 ## PRINCIPLE 4: IMPROVE PERFORMANCE, 10-STEP BUSINESS IMPROVEMENT APPROACH

The 10-step business improvement (BI) methodology (developed by my firm) incorporates best-of-breed quality tools, change management techniques, and team dynamics disciplines into an integrated, proven approach for delivering results from each team inside 12 weeks. Topics for the 10-step team were selected by the steering committee and aligned with corporate strategic goals. Teams participate in the next steps and timeline during their 12-week life cycle.

- **Step 0 Pre-reading.** Reading material is distributed one to two weeks prior to the first two days of training.
- **Steps 1–5 Training.** Week 1 training involves teams developing "As-Is or current state" working papers and content during the first two-day training including breakout sessions.
- **Steps 1–5 Fieldwork.** During weeks 2 through 5, teams validate key findings primarily from voice-of-customer surveys and data review and analytics.
- **Steps 6–10 Training.** Week 6 training consists of teams drafting "To-Be, or desired future state" pilot, and full implementation working papers and content during the second two-day training including breakout sessions.
- **Steps 6–10 Fieldwork.** During weeks 7 through 11, teams validate To-Be, pilot and full implementation plans.
- **Week 12.** Teams assemble for celebration and reception and to transfer the new process to the process owner. Teams then disband.

A steering committee with regular biweekly meetings for team leader status updates provides the governance for each team cycle and ensures that recommendations are deployed and results are realized.

Round 1, consisting of four 10-step teams, identified significant earnings improvements and foreshadowed future rounds. Under the careful direction of Rogers and Padgett, the CPM program blossomed enterprise wide. The five-level maturation of this approach is described more fully in Chapter 4. Teams have evolved from being focused on simple, single-location and single-process-centered objectives to being focused on sophisticated, system-wide, multilocation, multidisciplined, and multifaceted objectives. Commensurate with this maturity has been significant financial and nonfinancial value delivered by teams.

Exhibit 3.1 summarizes the portfolio of rounds 1 through 7 and the $16,590,840 value of team earnings improvements (middle column) plus a one-time value cash infusion of $26,400,000. MidMichigan Health matured its CPM 10-step program from level 1 (basic) through level 5 (optimized) during the first five rounds. Stated differently, each team created on average $460,857

EXHIBIT 3.1 Summary of 10-Step Team Results, Rounds 1 to 7

		Team	Net Income Year One	Annual Net Impact Future Years	Earnings Five Year Total
Round 1	1.	Central Scheduling	$ 55,000	$ 55,000	$ 275,000
	2.	Oncology (Midland)	84,000	84,000	420,000
	3.	Print (Midland)	32,000	32,000	160,000
	4	Disbursement (System)	750,000	750,000	3,750,000
Round 2	5.	Center for Women's Health	75,000	75,000	375,000
	6.	Patient Placement	110,000	110,000	550,000
	7.	Emergency Department (Midland)	158,000	158,000	790,000
	8.	Budget (System)	75,000	75,000	375,000
	9.	Orthopedics (System)	397,000	397,000	1,985,000
Round 3	10.	Financial Reporting (System)	300,000	300,000	1,500,000
	11.	Care Coordination I and II (System)	647,240	647,240	3,236,200
	12.	Neuro In/Out Migration (Midland)	128,000	128,000	640,000
	13.	Patient Referral (MPG)	209,000	209,000	1,045,000
	14.	New Products (Invasive Imaging and OR VATs—System)	84,600	84,600	423,000

		Team	Net Income Year One	Annual Net Impact Future Years	Earnings Five Year Total
Round 4	15.	Human Resources Requisition (System)	109,000	109,000	545,000
	16.	Financial Statement Close (System)	75,000	$ 75,000	375,000
	17.	PTO/COB (System)	1,650,000	1,650,000	8,250,000
	18.	Value Analysis Team— General Only (System)	41,000	41,000	205,000
Round 5	19.	Cash Processing (System)	55,000	55,000	275,000
	20.	Home Health Patient Scheduling (Home Care)	214,000	214,000	1,070,000
	21.	Inventory (Midland)	166,000	166,000	830,000
	22.	Patient Safety (Midland)	150,000	150,000	750,000
	23.	Patient Transportation (Midland)	48,000	48,000	240,000
Round 6	24.	Nursing	254,000	298,000	1,444,000
	25.	Physicians	35,000	437,000	1,783,000
	26.	Emergency Department/ Inpatient	190,000	918,000	3,862,000
	27.	Outpatient / Ancillary Services	420,000	2,036,000	8,563,000
	28.	Facilities	(46,000)	631,000	2,740,000
	29.	Revenue Cycle Management	591,000	1,459,000	6,429,000
	30.	Purchased Goods and Services	588,000	849,000	3,983,000
	31.	Benchmarking	375,000	2,032,000	21,400,000
Round 7	32.	HIPAA and Security Processes (System)	186,000	186,000	930,000
	33.	Laboratory Integration (System)	1,700,000	1,700,000	8,500,000
	34.	Patient Scheduling (System)	80,000	80,000	400,000
	35.	Pharmacy (System)	292,000	292,000	1,460,000
	36.	Quality and Core Measures (System)	60,000	60,000	300,000

(continued)

EXHIBIT 3.1   (*Continued*)

Team	Net Income Year One	Annual Net Impact Future Years	Earnings Five Year Total
Total Earnings for Rounds 1–7	10,337,840	16,590,840	89,858,200
Average Earnings Improvement per Team	287,162	460,857	2,496,061
One-Time Cash Infusion		26,400,000	

in annual earnings improvements. Year 1 varies due to timing of investments and expenses required to attain the annual run rate of earnings improvements noted.

For instance, Round 6 consisted of seven 10-step teams. These teams built on the first five rounds of experience and leveraged 10-step trained leaders so the round "Optimized for a Business Unit, a business unit is higher order than a single process" and identified $8,660,000 in annual earnings improvements for one hospital in the MidMichigan Health system. This translates into $50,204,000 over five years.

Round 7 consisted of a set of five 10-step teams that "Optimized for the Health Care System" and identified a one-time cash infusion of $26,400,000 and annual earnings improvements of $2,318,000; annual earnings improvements amounted to $11,590,000 over five years.

Round 8, consisting of a set of five 10-step teams, was launched and was engaged in its fieldwork during the preparation of this book.

Rounds 9 to 10, consisting of five teams each, has been scheduled for deployment over the next six months.

In addition to improving earnings, teams made significant improvements in dozens of nonfinancial measures, including increased preventive medical screenings and inpatient patient satisfaction scores, reduced emergency department patient wait times, reduced cycle times to hire nurses, and improved patient medical outcomes. Further, improvements included reduced medical and surgical floor nurse turnover, reduced cost per hip replacement, simplified walk-in patient payment processing, and reduced patient scheduling and registration cycle times.

So what is the 10-step approach used by the teams? At this point, it would be useful to walk through a subset of one team's working papers to build foundational understanding of the 10-step approach.

PRINCIPLE 4: IMPROVE PERFORMANCE, 10-STEP BUSINESS IMPROVEMENT CASE STUDY

This section provides highlights from the planning and budgeting 10-step team working papers but is not all-inclusive; rather, it offers strategic context and foundational understanding to aid in understanding subsequent chapters. Detailed case studies in Chapters 6 through 8 provide more in-depth understanding of the approach. Exhibit 3.2 displays the 10-step BI approach.

Step 1: Have We Identified the Right Areas of Focus?

The first step ensures that the team has identified the right customer segments, both external and internal, and their key service requirements. Experience has shown that customer groups and their requirements may not be obvious. These requirements are continuously evolving and are often refined as the team gains further insights throughout the first five steps.

Exhibits 3.3 and 3.4 show two customer segments requirements depicted in "5 Ups" format. Customer requirements would be attributes of service valued by customers such as timeliness, pricing, and quality. The 5 Ups format is very simply projected to capture them in declining pain-point format. The aim is for team to reduce cycle time, reduce costs, and reduce defects or error rates. In Exhibit 3.3, the team shows internal customer department manag-

AS-IS Current State	1. Have we identified the right areas of focus?
	2. What is the initial goal statement? Team charter?
	3. What are three to five customer requirements/complaints?
	4. What is the current process (map) and issues?
	5. What are the prioritized choke points, issues, and root causes?
TO-BE Future State	6. What are future state or desired frocess attributes?
	7. What improvement level is expected – final goal statement?
	8. What should the future process be (new map)?
GAP	9. What are the barriers to improvement? Countermeasures?
Implementation	10. What do we pilot? Results? What is the full implementation plan?

EXHIBIT 3.2   10-Step Business Improvement Approach

Customer Group: Department Managers

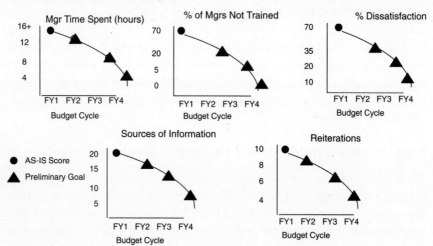

EXHIBIT 3.3 Department Manager Customer 5 Ups Requirements

ers. For example, "Manager Time Spent" is estimated at 16 hours per budget cycle (the solid circle indicating current state), and the team expects to reduce it to 12 hours in year 1, 8 hours in year 2, and 4 hours in year 3. In turn, each measure in the exhibit captures team estimated improvements over the next three years.

In Exhibit 3.4, the team depicted the finance department budget leaders titled "Administration," those finance personnel who administer the budget process. One might call them process owners; their requirements are charted with the current state and future targets for the team to attain.

Brainstorming

The team now sets its sights on brainstorming the causes of current performance. It identified numerous reasons by customer group:

Overall Issues and Concerns
- Communication (consistent)
- Training
- Standardization (forms/affiliates)
- Terminology
- Cycle time too long
- Technology

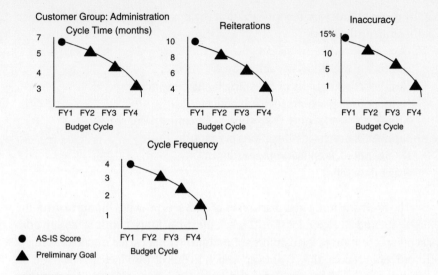

EXHIBIT 3.4 Administration Customer 5 Ups Requirements

- Amount of detail (too much detail)
- Manual inputs
- Set expectations sooner
- Accounting jargon

Department Manager's Budgeting Concerns
- Support from finance
- Ease of forms and data
- Access to information
- Standardization of the process
- Tools (technology available)
- Fewer touch points

Finance Department's Budgeting Concerns
- Time spent from start to finish (kickoff/packet submission) to expected

Data Sets

The team identified key data sets to better understand the As-Is situation. Data sets provide insights and facts to better analyze and validate and refine the goal statement. Data sets also provide the basis for refining or adjusting the scope of the project. The team determined that the next data sets would be useful to gather during fieldwork:

- Number of line items in each budget
- Number of potentially overlapping budget line items
- Number of cost centers for each budget
- Number of overlapping costs centers for similar departments
- Number of overhead allocations per month
- Number of reclassifications per month
- Other data sets

The brainstorming and discussion of data sets provides inputs to draft the team goal and direction for the 12-week life cycle. Since teams by design consist of representatives from different functions with a varied understanding of the current process, the 10-step approach in Step 1 also focuses the team on establishing a baseline or common understanding of the current situation. The next two templates call for defining the preliminary problem statement and preliminary goal statement.

Issue/Problem   Lack of adequate training, communication, and technology in the budgeting process leads to numerous iterations, lower customer satisfaction, and extensive cycle time.

Goal Statement   Reduce cycle time in the budget process by 50% for fiscal year 2012, which will provide more efficiency by reducing iterations to result in a 60% increase in customer satisfaction.

Step 2: What Is the Initial Goal Statement? What Is the Team Charter?

This step identifies team roles and code of conduct, both key inputs into formulation of the team charter. These topics are described next.

Team Roles

For the team to perform at a consistently high level and be self-correcting, it adopts a proven set of roles. The training includes a self-assessment for each team member to understand his or her behavioral profile. The self-identified and team-validated profile enables team members to self-select into the role they are best suited for and to enhance the team's productivity. The roles described at a high level for the planning and budgeting team volunteers included those shown in Exhibit 3.5.

Code of Conduct

The team established a code of conduct to be observed during team meetings and phone calls in order to remain highly productive to meet its ambitious goals. The code of conduct incorporates the cultural dimensions the teams believed to be important to maintain good morale and working relationships. The code of conduct includes the next elements (for emphasis or importance, the team highlighted key words in italics):

No cell phones/PDAs, iPads, etc.
Set meeting *agenda*, allocate time
Subject Matter Experts are not team members
Ensure *timeliness* (calendar integrity, start/stop on time)
Involve *everyone* (round robin)
One idea at a time (*no flops*)
No *judgment* of other's ideas (brainstorm)
Obtain *consensus*

Role	Team Member
Sponsor: Mentors the team leader	Jeff W
Team Leader: Provides inspirational and project management expertise	Cinthia B
Time Keeper: provides clarity during meetings and overall project timeline	Alicia K
Recorder: Visually displays concepts and data during meetings	Kristina M
Scribe: Maintains project records and working papers	Erik R
Monitor: Ensures team is following the 10-step methodology	Jason H
Process Observer: Ensures all team members are participating	Deb M
Spokesperson: Functions as ambassador of goodwill and interfaces with other teams	Josh W
Subject Matter Experts: Interviewed for expertise	Courtney S and Georgette W

EXHIBIT 3.5 10-Step Team Roles and Roster

Prepare *before* meeting
Clearly define *goals*—get agreement
Define *roles*
Define tool to meet objective
Be courteous . . . show *respect*
Commit to staying in meeting
No side discussions
Take turns talking
Foster *honesty, openness, trust* (no ridicule for throwing out idea)
Two-knock rule (any team member can knock on the table to temporarily suspend meeting conversations and reset discussion)
Have *fun*

Team Charter

The team charter provides clarity of direction and to communicate a common understanding among team members; it consists of the following elements:

- Issue/Problem
  Lack of adequate training, communication, and technology in the budgeting process leads to numerous iterations, lower customer satisfaction, and extensive cycle time.
- Goal Statement
  Reduce cycle time in the budget process by 50% for the next fiscal year, which will provide more efficiency by reducing iterations to result in a 60%.
- Constraints
  - Customers have limited time
  - Seriousness of project
  - Competing projects
  - Current technologies/strategies
  - Inconsistent expectations across affiliates
- Assumptions
  - New technology enhancements will make for less constraints.
  - Administrative support for change.
- Team Guidelines
  Included in code of conduct.
- Resources
  Included in roles but also consider adding subject matter experts not contemplated during the project planning phase (before the two-day training that resulted in the scope of this charter).

- Preliminary Project Plan
    (10-step milestone level)
    - Steps 1–5 Training: Week 1
    - Steps 1–5 Fieldwork: Weeks 2–5
    - Steps 6–10 Training: Week 6
    - Steps 6–10 Fieldwork: Weeks 7–11
    - Celebration and Team Turnoff: Week 12

Step 3: What Are Three to Five Customer Requirements/Complaints?

The team conducted a survey or focus group of customers in each targeted segment to ensure there is clear understanding of the current issues and to identify areas that offer opportunities for refinement. Exhibit 3.6 provides just one of over a dozen survey results that helped guide the team to sharpen its focus. The voice of the customer consisted of multiple questions and topics.

Department managers identified the highest-priority challenges as training, need more information, and assumptions with the planning and budgeting process. The full survey provided additional insights into the issues and root causes.

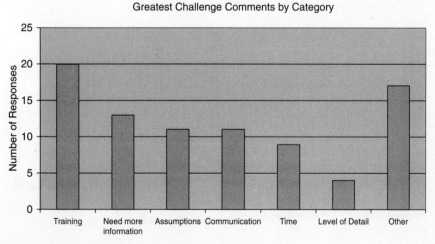

EXHIBIT 3.6 Customer Survey Results

Step 4: What Are the Current Process (Map) and Issues?

Due to the space constraints, I have omitted the planning and budgeting process map and its dozens of choke points, or challenges. This approach illuminates the current state and provides team members, leader, and sponsor with a snapshot of the complexity of the current state and the dominant and subordinate issues to contend with. The team identified over 24 choke points or opportunities to improve the As-Is process.

Step 5: What Are the Prioritized Choke Points, Issues, and Root Causes?

Based on the additional information provided by steps 1 through 4, the team is well positioned to develop a root cause or fishbone diagram to group causes for the issues (see Exhibit 3.7). In the interest of brevity, the fishbone quality tool and alternative uses are discussed in depth in Chapter 6. The team voted on the primary root causes depicted by the lightning bolts as in cycle time with subroot causes including inconsistency, excessive approvals, and lack of lack of documentation, to name a few.

During the first five weeks, the team conducts fieldwork and iterates through steps 1 through 5 to realize a deeper understanding of the current state and to enable ample fact gathering to validate and/or myth-bust

Fishbone: "Major" Causes and "Minor" Causes

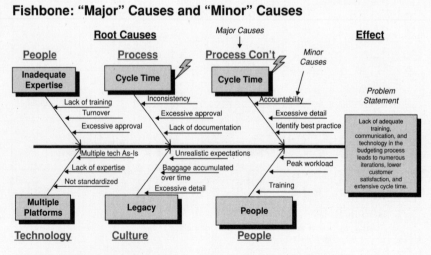

EXHIBIT 3.7 Root Cause Diagram Major and Minor Causes

the As-Is process. The case studies in Chapters 6 through 8 provide more in-depth examples, data sets, customer survey results, and analytics for review. This team and others reconvene for a two-day offsite training and breakout sessions to walk through steps 6 through 10 to design the future state, implementation, and change management plans. These steps are described next.

Step 6: What Is Future State or the Desired Process Attributes?

Through a series of creative and logical benchmarking steps, the team designed future state attributes and groups them as shown in Exhibit 3.8. These are critical exercises. The detailed cases in Chapters 6 through 8 provide more insights into their use and outputs.

Step 7: What Improvement Level Is Expected—Final Goal Statement?

The team is encouraged to dream big and agrees to reduce cycle time for the budget process by 57% over the next two fiscal years by leveraging technology, reducing the level of granularity, implementing a shared service model,

Process	Technology	People/Skills
• Reduce line detail • Eliminate allocations • Materiality limits • Consolidate cost centers • Variable-based budgeting • Clear communication plans • Identify key performance measures	➢ Integrate assumptions/targets ➢ Interface historical data ➢ Automated calculations and spreads ➢ Electronic budget review and revision ➢ Automated approvals ➢ Electronic notifications ➢ Variance analysis	➢ Training for managers ➢ Shift focus, forward thinking ➢ Clear communication plans
	Policy ➢ Hold managers accountable for x high-level line items ➢ Materiality limits ➢ Linkage to strategic plan through scorecards	**Partners** ➢ Managers ➢ Finance ➢ Administration and board

EXHIBIT 3.8 Future State Design Elements

and eliminating allocations, resulting in cost avoidance of approximately $375,000 over a five-year period. This will be accomplished by making the listed changes.

Year 1
- Reduce cycle time 38 percent by utilizing the data warehouse (the new decision support system).
- Reduce the number of line items by over 57 percent from 21,000 to 9,000 lines by condensing the current 767 cost centers and 487 expense accounts into 581 cost centers and 56 expense accounts,
- Implement a shared service staffing model.
- Place a $100,000 threshold on allocations, reducing the total number of allocations by 26.

The foregoing process changes will result in a 33 percent reduction in the level of effort spent on budget while allowing the focus of effort to shift from 90 percent clerical and 10 percent analytical to a 50 percent effort in both clerical and analytical while increasing the relevancy of the budget significantly.

Year 2
- Reduce cycle time by an additional 19 percent resulting in a total cumulative reduction of 57 percent in cycle time to date.
- Move toward rolling forecasts.
- Continue the reduction of cost centers as allowed by a transition to managing by benchmarking and scorecards.
- Implement a shared service model throughout the system where appropriate.
- Eliminate allocations.

The results of the foregoing process changes would include an additional 22 percent reduction in the level of effort spent on budget with 75 percent of effort being dedicated to analysis and solutions while providing an even greater increase in the relevancy of the budget and continuing to transform the budget to align more with MidMichigan Health's strategic plan and balanced scorecard metrics.

Step 8: What Should the Future Process Be (New Map)?

Due to space limitations, the process map and step descriptions are not shown here. As one could expect, the process was greatly simplified to align with the changes based on best practices noted in steps 6 and 7.

Topic:	
Driving Forces ++	Restraining Forces – –
Administration	Administration
Strategic plan	Training and expertise
Health care reform	Technology
Time management	Historical expectations
Standardization	Time, EMR rollout
Value-added analysis	Resources, training facilities
	Lack of understanding

EXHIBIT 3.9   Change Management Force Field Analysis

Step 9: What Are the Barriers to Improvement? Countermeasures?

Since the new process will impact all department managers and employees in the coming planning and budgeting cycle, the team carefully considers developing a force field analysis and a stakeholder change management plan with key action items (see Exhibit 3.9). The force field identifies major supporting trends that the team will leverage to deploy the new process and the major restraining forces that will have to be addressed. It is interesting to note that administration appears as both a driving force and restraining force due to divergent views about the current budget process.

Consequently, the team develops a more granular view of stakeholders through the molecule map (see Exhibit 3.10) where CFOs and CEOs are broken out separately from department managers.

The team recognized that these two stakeholders require different tactics and messengers prior to the deployment of the future state process. The communications plan shown in Exhibit 3.11 captures the audiences/stakeholders, actions, owner of the action item, timing, and status.

Step 10: What Do We Pilot? Results? What Is the Full Implementation Plan?

The team disaggregated the planning and budgeting process into key elements for implementation over three business cycles, or annual plans. The results

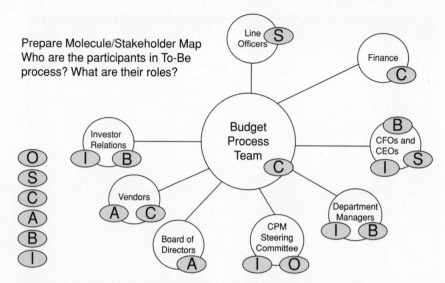

Prepare Molecule/Stakeholder Map
Who are the participants in To-Be
process? What are their roles?

Legend: O=Originator, S=Sponsor, C=Change Agents (Implementers), A=Advocate, B=Blocker, I=Informers

EXHIBIT 3.10   Change Management Molecule Map

Stakeholder Communication Action Plan

Stakeholder To whom	Action/ Message	Owner	How	When	Status
Investor Relations Purchasing/ HR/Finance	Modify data feeds Investor Relation	Josh and Cinthia	Face to face	Weekly	Ongoing
Vendor	Provide training and support on new system	Josh and Cinthia	Varies	Daily	Ongoing
CFOs	Validate recommendations	Cinthia	Face to face	Biweekly	Completed
CFOs and CEOs	Present recommendations	Cinthia	Face to face	One Month	Completed
Department Managers and Line Officers	Communicate and train	Finance	Varies	Two Months	Pending

EXHIBIT 3.11   Stakeholder Communication Action Plan

Element	Current State Root Cause/Blockers	Action Proposed FY2012 Budget Cycle	Action Proposed FY2013 Budget Cycle
Time Frame	Start January – July	16 Weeks	11 Weeks
Level of Detail—Line Items	21,000 lines of detail (487 accts to 56 accts)	9,000	Continue reduction in cost centers tied to scorecards
Level of Effort Hours Spent	272 people involved Approx 9,000 hours	6,000 hours	4,000 hours
Cost Centers	767 departments	572	TBD < 572
Focus of Effort	90% clerical 10% analytical	50% clerical 50% analytical	25% clerical 75% analytical
Technology	Out of date, lack of upgraded technology such as web based	Upgrade process and technology	Effective new technology (move toward rolling forecasts)
Strategic Value	Low	Medium/high	WOW!
Relevancy	Not relevant, out of date before it was published	Measurable improvement	Timely publication / ties to scorecards
Scope and Time Horizon	Historical—Financial only	Variable based budgeting	Variable based budgeting
Allocations	Numerous, limited value allocations 56 allocations $46 million	$100k threshold = 31 allocations $45 million HR and finance shared service model	Options: Zero allocations Shared service model with one allocation

EXHIBIT 3.12 Team Results

have been astounding. The sheer complexity or level of detail went from 21,000 monthly line items of detail to 9,000 monthly line items. Numerous other results are shown in Exhibit 3.12.

CASE STUDY SUMMARY

This case provides a walkthrough of the basic steps involved and insights into the thinking and challenges facing one team to enable you to gain appreciation for the entire program. The case summary does not attempt to capture team dynamics, level of data gathering, interactions with internal customers, and many other facets contributing to the outcomes. These are described in more depth in the case studies in Chapters 6 through 8.

In summary, this chapter provided strategic context, key market and industry trends, and the rationale for MidMichigan Health leadership to focus on CPM Principles 1, 3, and 4 and, in light of the challenges it faced, concentrate primarily on Principle 4: Improve performance. During the ensuing quarters the 10-step approach matured and the number of teams expanded. The journey and maturity model are described more fully in Chapter 4.

I am a firm believer in the people. If given the truth, they can be depended upon to meet any national crises. The great point is to bring them the real facts.

—Abraham Lincoln

 NOTES

1. MidMichigan Health website, www.midmichigan.org/about/.
2. Bob Paladino, *Five Key Principles of Corporate Performance Management* (Hoboken, NJ: John Wiley & Sons, 2007).

CHAPTER FOUR

4

Principle 4: Improve Performance—The MidMichigan Health System Journey

It is a mistake to try to look too far ahead. The chain of destiny can only be grasped one link at a time.

—*Winston Churchill*

THIS CHAPTER FOCUSES ON THE JOURNEY AND MATURATION of the 10-step business improvement (BI) program to address strategic and operational challenges. It incorporates the Capability Maturity Model (CCM)[1] of Carnegie Mellon University (CMU) as a point of reference to frame and chronicle the evolution of MidMichigan Health's use of the 10-step BI methodology. Organizations adopting the corporate performance management (CPM) best practice model follow a predictable pattern of maturation from level 1 (basic)

49

through level 5 (optimized), as introduced in Chapter 3. For each level of maturity, we describe six elements:

1. CMU definition
2. Leadership rationale
3. Team areas of focus
4. Team results
5. Positive outcomes
6. Opportunities for improvement

This chapter shares how MidMichigan Health realized over $450,000 in earnings improvement per team, over eight times the targeted value, resulting in millions in earnings improvements while concurrently improving customer satisfaction scores, modernizing dozens of processes, and attaining better employee or people results.

MidMichigan Health leveraged the first five rounds of CPM teams to advance and mature its capabilities through CMU's level 1 (basic) through level 5 (optimized) model. This maturation then enabled MidMichigan Health to apply its level 5 optimized capabilities to an entire hospital in round 6 and true system-wide teams in rounds 7 and beyond.

My hope is that by reading about the maturation of the program, regardless of where you are on your journey, you will gain insights to help accelerate your program and realize broad-based results.

 ## CPM MATURITY LEVELS FOR PRINCIPLE 4: IMPROVE PERFORMANCE

CMU CMM provides a continuum along which maturity can be developed incrementally from one level to the next. Expanded program levels and elements are described one at a time in the next sections.

Education is the best provision for the journey to old age.

—Aristotle

Level 1: Initial

This section explores the six elements of MidMichigan Health's CPM level 1 maturity.

CMU Definition

Processes at this level typically are undocumented and in a state of dynamic change, tending to be driven in an ad hoc, uncontrolled, and reactive manner by users or events. This environment is chaotic or unstable.

Leadership Rationale

At the onset, well-intended leaders across the enterprise had launched projects using different tools and approaches; there was unevenness in definitions of what constituted a project, initiative, imperative, goal, committee, and program. The leadership team wanted to adopt a disciplined problem-solving approach to address ongoing challenges and to continuously improve financial, customer, process, and people results. In an effort to address the current state, the leadership team agreed to run a pilot of four 10-step teams, one each to address four topics. The CPM steering committee consisted of these executives and leaders:

- Greg Rogers, President, MidMichigan Medical Center-Midland/Executive Vice President, MidMichigan Health
- Francine Padgett, Chief Financial Officer, Senior Vice President and Treasurer, MidMichigan Health
- Scott Currie, Vice President and Chief Financial Officer, MidMichigan Medical Center–Midland
- Mike Erickson, Vice President of Facility Services, MidMichigan Medical Center–Midland
- Lorie Mault, Director of Employment and Labor Relations, MidMichigan Health
- Deb Mills, Director of Corporate Performance Management (CPM), MidMichigan Health
- Diane Nold, Vice President, MidMichigan Medical Center–Midland
- Dr. Lydia Watson, Vice President of Medical Affairs, MidMichigan Medical Center–Midland
- Shelli Wood, Vice President and Chief Nursing Officer, MidMichigan Medical Center–Midland
- Mike Larson, Vice President and Chief Information Officer, MidMichigan Health (joined the leadership team during round 8)

Due to space limitations, in Chapters 6 through 8, I share ten in-depth case studies from the over 30 teams. The selection of the four projects aligned to the company's strategic goals. MidMichigan Health has five strategic goals consisting of over 20 supporting strategies for the entire health care system. The five strategic goals include:

1. **Quality.** Become a national leader in quality, safety, and service.
2. **Growth.** Pursue clinical growth.
3. **Collaboration.** Partner with physicians, universities, and health care organizations.
4. **People.** Value our human potential.
5. **Operational excellence.** Enhance system integration.

Team Areas of Focus

The first four teams consisted on average of 10 participants, each with representation from multiple disciplines.

1. The central intake team focused on standardizing and consolidating over 100 potential points of patient registration; this team aligned with Strategic Goal E: Operational excellence
2. The oncology team focused on growing the number of patients with a joint goal of improving women's health; this team aligned primarily with Strategic Goal B: Growth.
3. The print team focused on reducing printing costs due to the proliferation of printing devices throughout the system; this team aligned with Strategic Goal E: Operational excellence.
4. The disbursement team focused initially on efficiencies of processing time and expense reports and disbursements to vendors but discovered significant spending reductions; this team aligned with Strategic Goal E: Operational excellence.

This team case study and its working papers are described more fully in Chapter 6.

Team Results

Based on my experience advising other companies, to justify personnel time and to add incremental value the organization, the minimum savings for a team should be $50,000 per annum earnings improvement. The four teams identified combined savings of $920,000 per annum, exceeding the four-team target of $200,000 per annum.

1. Central intake team: $55,000 per annum earnings improvement.
2. Oncology team: $84,000 per annum earnings improvement.

3. Print team: $32,000 per annum earnings improvement.
4. Disbursement team: $750,000 per annum earnings improvement.

During the 12-week cycle, the leadership team gained several insights into how the approach was received by the organization and on the performance of each team. Observations on positive outcomes and opportunities for improvement are in the next section.

Positive Outcomes

The next observations were considered benefits of this round and set the stage for advancing the CPM 10-step program to the next level of maturity.

- Team outcomes or results were very high and significantly exceeded the estimated dollar savings per team. Team working papers and deliverables were regarded as very high quality.
- Several teams engaged in what is now referred to as myth busting. Their data and internal customer surveys invalidated long-held beliefs on either an issue or its root cause. For example, the disbursement team was formed due to a longstanding belief that the time and expense reporting process was too cumbersome and employees were not receiving their reimbursement checks in a timely manner. The internal voice of the customer surveys dispelled this belief.
- Since the disbursement team busted a longtime myth regarding traveler satisfaction with the time and expense reporting process, it redirected its attention to savings. (This case is discussed in depth in Chapter 6.)
- Teams were enthusiastic and glad to work with their colleagues across the organization. They did not mind traveling to make their weekly team meetings or working extra hours on the team.
- The mixed levels of team member titles and authorities ranged from director of a strategic business unit to a supervisor of finance, but this did not impede the teams. All members had an equal voice and vote for team governance.
- The survey of 10-step trainees showed that 87% agreed or strongly agreed the training program was excellent; this finding validated that the pilot was not only compatible with the company culture but also was a highly desired approach to problem solving.

Opportunities for Improvement

The next observations led to adjustments in the 10-step program design that would be incorporated into subsequent rounds to enhance the program.

- One team leader attempted to play three of the nine defined roles (scribe, team leader, and reporter), which resulted in low productivity during team meetings. The baseball analogy would be for one person to attempt to play three positions at once, an impossibility to say the least. Once the team roles were separated, team productivity and creativity were greatly enhanced. Going forward, adherence to playing team roles was a clear area of focus.
- The sponsor of one team changed the scope of his team twice, which created confusion and delayed the team's ability to address the central issue. Adherence to the team governance model (voting) would be carefully monitored.
- Attendance on one team was less than 100%, which resulted in lower initial team morale and financial results. Attendance would be more closely reviewed in subsequent rounds.

You cannot escape the responsibility of tomorrow by evading it today.

—Abraham Lincoln

Level 2: Repeatable

This section explores the six elements of MidMichigan Health's CPM level 2 maturity.

CMU Definition

It is characteristic of processes at level 2 that some processes are repeatable, possibly with consistent results. Process discipline is unlikely to be rigorous, but where it exists, it may help to ensure that existing processes are maintained during times of stress.

Leadership Rationale

Recognizing the value from the round 1 pilot teams, the leadership team elected to launch round 2 and to align these teams with the five strategic goals. The importance of project alignment to strategy prompted a review all ongoing projects. The leadership team canvassed the organization for all active projects and was surprised to learn that over 180 existed. Since the second round of five 10-step teams competed for the many of the same resources as the 180 projects, Midland Medical Center chief executive officer (CEO) Greg Rogers directed the organization to cease activities on 85 projects to free up organizational capacity. The leadership team selected five teams for round 2.

Team Areas of Focus

Round 2 consisted of five teams of about ten participants each with representation from multiple disciplines.

1. The Center for Women's Health (CWH) Services team focused on growth in the number of prescreenings or mammographic procedures for prevention and early detection of breast cancer and to provide expanded outreach into the service territory. This team aligned with Strategic Goal B: Growth. This team and its working papers are described more fully in Chapter 8.
2. The patient placement team focused on ensuring that patients were properly registered and placed and that appropriate care was provided. This team aligned with Strategic Goal A: Safety.
3. The emergency department (ED) team focused on reducing cycle time in the ED, improving customer/patient satisfaction scores, and reducing the number of patients who leave before treatment. This team aligned with Strategic Goal E: Operational excellence. This team and its working papers are described more fully in Chapter 8.
4. The budget team focused on streamlining and simplifying the planning and budgeting process system-wide. This team aligned with Strategic Goal E: Operational excellence. This case was described in Chapter 3.
5. The orthopedics team focused on reducing the cost per procedure or operation, primarily for hip and knee replacements. This team aligns with Strategic Goal E: Operational excellence. This team and its working papers are described more fully in Chapter 8.

Team Results

In addition to the customer, process, and people results described in the detailed case studies, the teams identified significant annual earnings improvements. The five teams identified a total of $815,000 in per annum earnings improvements that exceeded the five-team target of $250,000 in earnings improvements.

1. The CWH team identified $75,000 per annum in earnings improvements from increase patient flows or growth.
2. The patient placement team identified $110,000 per annum earnings improvement from properly classifying patients and their revenue from reimbursement.
3. The ED team identified $158,000 in earnings improvements per annum, primarily from retaining patients due to shorter wait times.
4. The budget team identified $75,000 in annual time savings; these were soft-dollar savings for personnel who were reassigned to focus on CPM 10-step team activities.
5. The orthopedics team identified $397,000 in annual earnings improvements.

Positive Outcomes

The next observations were considered benefits of this round and set the stage for advancing the CPM 10-step program to the next level of maturity.

- Team results validated that the 10-step approach was repeatable. A broader group of employees were now trained, so there was a base of CPM champions.
- The steering committee provided a 24-hour approval of an investment (first time) in hiring personnel for the ED team to pilot a proposed solution. The results were very impressive, and financial rewards and patient satisfaction scores far exceed the investment.
- MidMichigan Health appointed a new CPM director, Deb Mills, during this round of teams, signaling its commitment to the organization. She was the former controller for MidMichigan Health's second largest hospital and widely respected. This appointment added significant creditability and capability to the CPM function.

Opportunities for Improvement

The next observations led to adjustments in the 10-step program design that would be incorporated into subsequent rounds to enhance the program.

- The orthopedics team focused on system-wide results. It involved engagement with doctors from multiple locations who were not part of the team.

The solution of more focused procurement with three of the four existing vendors therefore took more leadership team involvement than anticipated to onboard key employees.

- The patient placement team recognized that its scope was too broad, so the scope was narrowed (and renamed phase 1). The steering committee determined that a second team in the round would address phase 2.
- Several of the nearly 50 participants commented on their desire to be better prepared for the first two-day 10-step team training sessions. The leadership team requested a pre-reading package be designed for and distributed to the next round of teams.
- Upon completion of the structured two-day training (week 1), several teams were challenged during their first solo team meeting focused on fieldwork in week 2. This resulted in some storming or internal debate and delay in getting fully launched. Given that the fieldwork period is short—just four to five weeks—time is of the essence. The leadership team decided to institute a 30-minute CPM sponsor and team leader touch-base meeting prior to the full 10-step team meeting week 2.

Slow and steady wins the race.

—Aesop

Level 3: Defined

This section explores the six elements of MidMichigan Health's CPM level 3 maturity.

CMU Definition

At this level, defined and documented standard processes are established and subject to some degree of improvement over time. These standard processes are in place (i.e., they are the As-Is processes) and are used to establish consistency of process performance across the organization.

Leadership Rationale

Fresh off the success of the first two rounds of teams, by now the leadership team had established a more routinized and streamlined approach to identifying issues, selecting teams, and scheduling direct reports for training, and also deprioritizing competing activities and projects. The mix of teams aligned to corporate strategic goals and discussions started to focus on more enterprise-wide teams or system teams.

Team Areas of Focus

The third round contained five teams of about ten participants each with representation from multiple disciplines and affiliate locations.

1. The financial and management reporting team focused on streamlining the number of reports and the page count per reports as well as improving the operational content of the information for better decision making. This team aligned with Strategic Goal E: Operational excellence. This team and its working papers are described more fully in Chapter 6.
2. The care coordination team was a carryover of the round 2 patient placement team. It recognized that the life cycle of a patient started in the ED and extended through the length of stay and discharge. The team had representation from all four hospitals. The team was renamed from the patient placement team to the care coordination team to more accurately reflect its dual goal of improving the classification of patients to inpatient or outpatient status and for improving patient care; this team aligned with Strategic Goal E: Operational excellence, though it also had impact on Goal A: Quality and Goal B: Growth. This team and its working papers are described more fully in Chapter 8.
3. The neurology in-/out-migration team focused on operating the neurology specialist practice on a system basis and had representation accordingly. This team aligned with Strategic Goal B: Growth.
4. The patient referral team focused on streamlining the system-wide process of referring a patient from the general practitioner to a specialist physician, specifically reducing missing data elements that would delay appointments and visits. This team aligned with Strategic Goal E: Operational efficiency.
5. The new products team (scope on two categories of products invasive imaging and operating room) focused on reducing the system-wide cycle time starting from when a physician requested a new product to the time it was approved by the value analysis team and procured for field use. This team aligned with Strategic Goal E: Operational excellence. This team and its working papers are described more fully in Chapter 6.

Team Results

In addition to the customer, process, and people results described in the detailed case studies later in this book, the teams identified significant annual earnings improvements. The five teams identified combined savings of $1,368,000 per annum, which greatly exceeded the five-team target of $250,000 per annum earnings improvement.

1. The financial and management reporting team identified $300,000 per annum earnings improvement from the elimination of software programs in the next fiscal year.
2. The care coordination team identified $647,240 in earnings improvements per annum, one of the highest earnings improvements to date.
3. The neurology in-/out-migration team identified $128,000 in earnings improvements per annum.
4. The patient referral team identified $209,000 in earnings improvements per annum.
5. The new products (invasive imaging and operating room) team identified $84,600 in earnings improvements per annum.

Positive Outcomes

The next observations were considered benefits of this round and set the stage for advancing the CPM 10-step program to the next level of maturity.

- Level 3 proved to be the very successful in bringing together employees from across the system to optimize system, not local, results.
- Deb Mills, the new CPM director, played an active role in scheduling and facilitating team meetings throughout this 12-week cycle; the teams were grateful for and appreciative of this mentoring resource.
- Teams remained open-minded about rescoping and setting more ambitious team goals during the 12-week cycle resulted in breakthrough solutions and, accessing experts both inside and outside. The care coordination team, for instance, partnered with an expert outside organization to more accurately classify patients, resulting in significant earnings improvements.
- The incorporation of more senior clinical personnel on the teams, including physicians, resulted in more medical expertise that presaged broader physician adoption.

Opportunities for Improvement

The next observations led to adjustments in the 10-step program design that would be incorporated into subsequent rounds of teams to enhance the program.

- MidMichigan Health did not fully plan for the teams' technology needs; a few teams relied on individuals' personal laptops to develop electronic working papers. However, occasionally those employees would miss a meeting. MidMichigan Health invested in dedicated CPM laptops and projectors and provisioned a separate shared drive for file sharing and working paper storage and retrieval.
- The CPM core team was learning how to better optimize training facilities. One outside facility contained large ballrooms that enabled open and dynamic team interactions; while another third-party provider had teams tightly configured in guest hotel rooms hastily converted to team rooms, which were not conducive to high performance. In subsequent rounds, proper offsite and onsite facilities were secured, and positive team dynamics flourished.
- The cumulative portfolio of teams from prior rounds of teams greatly expanded the need to have regular follow-up with process owners, essentially recipients of team outputs. The CPM office established a regular CPM team status report to validate the rate of benefits realization and to provide assistance for any implementation issues.

A person who never made a mistake never tried anything new.

—**Albert Einstein**

Level 4: Managed

This section explores the six elements of MidMichigan Health's CPM level 4 maturity.

CMU Definition

It is characteristic of processes at this level that, using process metrics, management can effectively control the As-Is process. In particular, management can identify ways to adjust and adapt the process to without measurable losses of quality or deviations from specifications. Process capability is established from this level.

Leadership Rationale

The leadership team built on experience from prior three rounds of teams and leveraged the results of its balanced scorecard and initiative prioritization matrix to select four CPM 10-step teams for this round. All four teams were systemwide in scope. The leadership team moved beyond a mix of system and affiliate-focused teams for the first time. The process for scheduling sponsors, team personnel, facilities, pre-reading, and forecasting results was now becoming part of the organization's DNA.

Team Areas of Focus

The fourth round contained four teams of about 10 participants each with representation from multiple disciplines and affiliate locations.

1. The human resource (HR) requisition team focused on reducing the cycle time for department managers from the requisition a new employee to when a qualified candidate could be interviewed. This team aligned with Strategic Goal E: Operational excellence. This case is discussed in detail in Chapter 6.
2. The financial statement close team focused on shortening the cycle time to produce both its financial statements and management reports to bring about more rapid decision making. This team aligned with Strategic Goal E: Operational excellence.
3. The HR benefits team adopted the name PTO/COB, the acronyms associated with two primary benefits programs in its scope: PTO (paid time off bank) and COB (cash out of time off bank). This team was aligned with Strategic Goal D: People and Strategic Goal E: Operational excellence to reduce variation in these two plans across multiple medical centers and affiliates.
4. The value analysis team (VAT) focused on streamlining nine standing committees consisting of about 100 personnel dedicated to the identification and approval of new products and services for procurement. This team built on the round 3 new products team, essentially extending the scope enterprise wide to all VAT groups.

Team Results

In addition to the customer, process, and people results described in selected case studies in later chapters, the teams identified significant annual earnings improvements. The four teams identified $1,875,000 per annum earnings improvement, which greatly exceeded the four-team target of $200,000 per annum earnings improvement.

1. The HR requisition team identified $109,000 in soft-dollar savings per annum, essentially HR and hiring manager time that could saved from removing unnecessary steps in the process that could be spent on their core roles.
2. The financial statement close team identified $75,000 in soft-dollar savings per annum enabling personnel to shift from these activities to CPM direct value-creating activities on 10-step teams.
3. The PTO/COB team identified $1,650,000 per annum earnings improvement. Employees did not lose any time off or the ability to cash out existing time in the time bank.
4. The VAT team identified $41,000 per annum earnings improvement from a single product; the team opted not to extend this result to additional products in the pipeline to be conservative.

Positive Outcomes

The next observations were considered benefits of this round and set the stage for advancing the CPM 10-step program to the next level of maturity.

- MidMichigan Health demonstrated its willingness to address sacred cows. The PTO/COB team had braced itself for significant organizational push-back and possible employee frustration from changing deferred benefits, which never came to pass. The team designed a future state, or To-Be, process and criteria that were broadly accepted as fair and equitable.
- MidMichigan Health employees continued to rate the CPM 10-step training program very highly, with scores of 93.7% agree or strongly agree on 10 questions. One such question stated: "The overall quality of training I received was high." All scores exceeded those from employees in round 1 noted earlier.

Opportunities for Improvement

The next observations led to adjustments in the 10-step program design that would be incorporated into subsequent rounds of teams to enhance the program.

- The HR requisition team conducted lunch and learn training sessions throughout the system to launch its new e-requisition solution.

It encountered a few pockets of slow adoption requiring additional outreach that resulted in system-wide adoption.

- The new system-focused teams covered organizations not represented by the initial steering committee. Representatives from this steering committee and project sponsors successfully presented system recommendations to the executive corporate level for approval and adoption.
- The system-wide VAT teams were slow to adopt the team recommendations, resulting in a delay in results.

It's not enough that we do our best; sometimes we have to do what's required.

—Winston Churchill

Level 5: Optimized

This section explores the six elements of MidMichigan Health's CPM level 5 maturity.

CMU Definition

It is characteristic of processes at this level that the focus is on continually improving process performance through both incremental and innovative technological changes/improvements.

Leadership Rationale

The leadership team had been adjusting and iterating the approach, as noted in earlier phases. However, now the leadership team was fielding requests for 10-step teams from throughout the system. Leaders of strategic business units (SBUs) and support units wanted to improve their operations and financial results from the proven track record of the prior 18 teams.

Team Areas of Focus

The fourth round contained four teams of about 10 participants each with representation from multiple disciplines and affiliate locations.

- The cash processing team focused on streamlining the collection of customer (patient) funds at point of sale and registration and to reduce the fees to third-party processors. This team aligned with Strategic Goal E: Operational excellence.

- Home health care scheduling focused on optimizing the scheduling and routing of home health care personnel driving cars to patients' homes to provide care. This team aligned with Strategic Goal E: Operational excellence.
- The inventory team focused on reducing obsolete inventory and establishing reorder quantities throughout the system. This team aligned with Strategic Goal E: Operational excellence.
- The patient safety team was focused on reducing the conditions that could lead to a serious adverse event (SAE), such as a patient fall or the administration of an incorrect medication. This aligned with Strategic Goal A: Patient safety.
- The patient transportation team focused on optimizing the scheduling and usage of personnel to transport patents to reduce costs and improve the patient experience. This team aligned with Strategic Goal E: Operational excellence.

Team Results

In addition to the customer, process, and people results described in selected case studies, the teams identified significant annual earnings improvements. The five teams identified combined savings of $633,000 per annum earnings improvement, which greatly exceeded the five-team target of $250,000 per annum.

1. The cash processing team identified $55,000 per annum earnings improvement.
2. The home health care patient scheduling team identified over $214,000 per annum earnings improvement net of a one-time investment of $238,000, primarily in scheduling software. In round 1, the disbursements team had identified this team during a review of the root causes of mileage expenses.
3. The inventory team identified $166,000 per annum earnings improvement in just one hospital; to be conservative, the results were not extrapolated to the rest of the system.
4. The patient safety team identified $150,000 per annum earnings improvement.
5. The patient transportation team identified $48,000 per annum earnings improvement.

Positive Outcomes

The next observations were considered benefits of this round and set the stage for expanding the CPM 10-step program system wide.

- The CPM team broadened its participation in the 10-step BI program to a new affiliate beyond the four hospitals, the home health care affiliate. This marked a new milestone in the adoption of the CPM 10-step program.
- The leadership team believed the employees had become so proficient in applying the 10-step BI method that they elected to expand its application from a process or SBU level to an entire hospital. This optimization is discussed in the next section.
- MidMichigan Health had trained over 200 unique people, identified future team leaders, refined problem-solving skills, and created CPM organizational capability across its system.

Opportunities for Improvement

These observations led to adjustments in the 10-step program design that would be incorporated into subsequent rounds of teams to enhance the program.

- At the end of the 10-step process or 12-week cycle, the team leaders turn the To-Be process over to the process owners. In a few cases, the process owners were not members of the 10-step team so this transition was not as smooth as planned. The leadership team decided to include team leaders and process owners on future teams.
- The new system-focused teams covered organizations not represented by the initial steering committee. Representatives from this steering committee and project sponsors successfully presented system recommendations to the corporate level for approval and adoption.
- The solution for the transportation team was not as readily applicable to another affiliate hospital, which approached staffing and scheduling of patient transportation using a different model. For this reason, the $48,000 in results at one affiliate could not be multiplied to other affiliates.

Innovation distinguishes between a leader and a follower.

—**Steve Jobs**

To summarize the chapter thus far, MidMichigan Health leveraged the first five rounds of teams to advance and mature its CPM capabilities from level 1 through level 5 of the CMU model. This enabled MidMichigan Health to apply its level 5 optimized CPM capabilities to an entire hospital in round 6 and to true system-wide teams in rounds 7, both of which are discussed next.

Optimized for a Business Unit, Hospital (Round 6)

Based on the successful maturation of the 10-step program during the prior five rounds of teams, the system CEO determined that the approach could be applied effectively to an entire SBU affiliate hospital. This section describes this novel application to an entire organization.

Leadership Rationale

The system leadership team recognized that one affiliate medical center was experiencing market and competitive pressures, including:

- Expansion of competitors in its service territory
- Reduction in government reimbursement rates
- Change in the mix of inpatient and outpatient resulting in less revenue
- Reduction in the volume of inpatients
- Adoption of numerous new system-led information technology (IT) applications including electronic medical records (EMR) and computerized physician order entry (CPOE), a process of electronic entry of medical practitioner instructions; both required significant overtime and changes to core processes

System leadership team had built confidence in its people and their application of the 10-step problem-solving approach to innovate and apply it holistically to one of its hospitals. This was by far the largest scope application, far exceeding the teams chronicled earlier.

This effort was referred to as round 6, the operational assessment team (OAT). Midland's Diane Nold and the affiliate's chief financial officer Vic Morgan co-led this effort. Nold and CPM director Deb Mills relocated from Midland to the affiliate for the duration of the project and continued for an additional three months to lead this complicated and broad-based business improvement effort. Overall system corporate CEO Rick Reynolds sponsored the 10-step program, a system-level steering committee was formed and OAT leaders Nold and Morgan regularly presented team progress. Nold and Mills were supported by seven active team leaders and well-educated and energetic

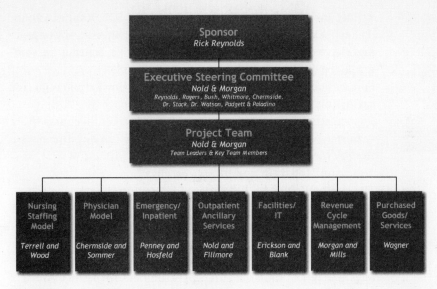

EXHIBIT 4.1 10-Step Program Structure

local professionals and support personnel. The 10-step program structure is shown in Exhibit 4.1.

The OAT, replicated governance experience with prior rounds of teams, was further broken down into seven 10-step teams and numerous goals per team. Notice the realization of quick wins early in team fieldwork phase, which evidenced the teams' advanced problem-solving skills.

Teams Areas of Focus

The seven 10-step teams identified several subgoal statements.

1. The nursing team focused on these key areas:
   a. To improve efficiency in the nursing department by the realignment of nurse manager responsibilities and span of control in six months, which will:
      ▪ Reduce denials for bariatric cases by improving insurance verification/authorization and medical necessity process to increase revenue by $57,500. (Quick win—immediate)

- Reduce incidental nursing overtime costs by $20,000 per annum (following EMR electronic medical records; stabilization) by improving/increasing the nurse manager involvement in scheduling, staffing, and payroll responsibilities. (Post-EMR go-live)
- Elimination of personal vacation days for nursing for potential cost savings on $11,000 per year. (Quick win in month 3)
- Reduce nursing first-year turnovers by 50 percent (equates to six turnovers, or 16.7 percent of total voluntary nursing turnovers), thereby reducing annual orientation costs by $108,615

b. To reduce nursing training delivery costs by:
  - The elimination of 1.5 full-time equivalents in the nursing education department, now provided centrally by system, for $160,681 per annum. (Quick win—immediate)
  - The reduction in staff instruction/training costs by $40,000 per annum by month 4 by providing additional Internet learning, skills days, and other online learning opportunities (American Council of Learned Societies (ACLS)) to nurses, resulting in continuing certification and maintaining or improving patient and physician satisfaction. (Quick win—immediate)

2. The physician team focused on these key areas:
  a. Increase referrals resulting in market share growth in the next areas by streamlining the referral process and fostering relationships using the physician liaison program:
    - Increase orthopedics market share in a specific quadrant by capturing 20 percent (by end of 24 months) of the patients traveling to contiguous cities ($275,000), through the addition of specialty clinic(s) in this area.
    - Grow the ear, nose, and throat market share in a local town by capturing 25 percent of a competitor's business ($42,000) through employment of a specific physician.
    - Recapture lost medical cardiology market share (10 percent) from a competitor and grow by capturing 25 percent of patients traveling to a local town and 15 percent traveling to a local city by including diagnostics in our cardiology group.
    - Grow the ophthalmology market share 6 percent lost market share $20,000 by exploring using operating room capacity, improving provider access, and increasing optometrist referral patterns.
  b. Increase access and market capture in 10 named local markets through the employment of midlevel providers. (All quick wins)

- Specific practice groups and named midlevel providers were identified for each to expand service capabilities and address volumes.

   c. Identify opportunities to improve provider practice efficiencies by analyzing productivity, staffing, and practice costs by office by four months, which will reduce expenses by $100,000 and maintain satisfaction for patients, physicians, and employees.

3. The ED and inpatient IP team focused on these key areas:

   a. Increase overall ED efficiency through revenue enhancement, expense reduction, and patient satisfaction.

- Increase ED copay billings from $900 per month to $5,000 per month by month 5 to provide revenue enhancement of $49,200 per annum.
- Leverage prior 10-step team, ED patient satisfaction working papers.
- Develop an ED efficiency plan by working collaboratively with the nursing team.
- Reduce patients who leave before treatments to the advisory board benchmark of 0.5 percent.
- Reduce ED throughput by 30 minutes (from admission to discharge).

   b. Modify usage practice of high-ticket supply items in ED and inpatient units, which provides savings of $50,000 per annum.

- Medications. Thrombolytic savings of $200 per dose by converting from one drug to another.
- Supplies. Collaboratively evaluate and manage wound care products.
- Supplies. Use subject matter experts to further evaluate analgesic pumps, lifts/slings/mobility devices, external orthopedic devices, and cardiac pacemakers.

   c. Decrease total inpatient length of stay (LOS) for the top three diagnosis-related groups (DRG is a system to classify hospital cases), which results in savings.

- DRG 057—Degenerative Nervous System Disorders
  - a. Decrease LOS by 2.9 days resulting in a total savings of $400,000 per annum (net of adjusted reimbursement).
- DRG 470—Major Joint Replacement
  - a. Decrease LOS by 0.5 days, resulting in a total savings of $184,000 per annum.
  - b. Recommend review of joint camp.
- DRG 392—Esophagitis, Gastroenteritis, and Miscellaneous Digestive Disorders
  - a. Decrease LOS by 0.5 days, resulting in a total savings of $135,000 per annum.

   b.   Work in tandem with hospitalist program (in six months) and review prior CPM Care Coordination 10-step team working papers. The ED/inpatient team also included the $100,000 expected positive impact from properly classifying patients.

4. The outpatient ancillary services team agreed to establish a plan in five months to improve profitability in the areas of cardiac/pulmonary/sleep, imaging services, laboratory services, and rehab services by $2,076,000. This would be accomplished by identifying opportunities for volume growth with a positive contribution margin, expense reduction, and efficiency and productivity maximization while maintaining or improving physician and patient satisfaction and improving employee morale and ambassadorship. The specific goals include:

   a. Establish a wound care program and realize volume growth and subsequent net revenue gain by $270,000 in 13 months.
   b. Purchase an additional computed tomography scanner for one site to address increased volumes. The business case showed net contribution of $243,700 per annum.
   c. Grow volume in rehab services by expanding the physician liaison position to a system focus to promote services to targeted primary care and specialist positions for $266,600 net revenue gain.
   d. Expand services through purchase of a balance system for a clinic for an increase in net revenue by $431,300 in 13 months.
   e. Grow volume in nuclear medicine by capturing referrals for a realization of $43,760 in net revenue for a stress testing component and $162,687 for an imaging component in 13 months.
   f. Realize revenue recovery in cardiac catherization volume for a $131,846 increase in net revenue in 13 months.
   g. Grow the volume of pulmonary function testing by 182 tests with a subsequent revenue increase by $115,400 in 13 months.
   h. Pursue substantial portion methodology billing in rehab services for a 6% increase in revenue capture for a revenue gain of $131,600 in 13 months.
   i. Pursue the establishment of an inpatient utilization review in order to shift appropriate outpatient testing to the most appropriate treatment setting for a net revenue gain of $200,000 in 13 months.
   j. Develop a system physician liaison approach for lab promotion to maintain volumes and physician relationships in 13 months.
   k. Negotiate a lower pricing contract with the blood supplier for a cost savings of $76,732 in 13 months.

l. Explore an automated appointment reminder process to decrease no-shows and last-minute cancellations in rehab services by 2 percent for $2,060 net revenue gain in 13 months. Imaging and cardiopulmonary opportunities to be determined.

5. The facilities and IT team focused on these key areas:

   a. Reduce maintenance system service contract costs on existing biomedical contracts by $42,700 with process changes.

   b. Reduce costs by consolidating/standardizing consumable product supplies and services across system by $40,000.
      - Verify pricing with current vendors through a third-party benchmark service.
      - Assess group purchasing organization contract list for vendors we may not be using today with discounts.

   c. Reduce plant electricity and gas costs by $136,000 in total in seven months.
      - Realize $136,000 if energy conservation scores move to median energy efficiency (38 percentile to 50 percentile), although this may require capital investment to achieve operational improvement.
      - Evaluate local utility energy credits.
      - Establish a consolidated energy purchase strategy for health system.

   d. Reduce laundry costs outsourcing.
      - Operating expense and capital depreciation reduction: $35,000 annual impact.

   e. Evaluate IT costs.
      - Patient billing software and staffing reduction of 1.0 full-time equivalents; year 2 savings of $332,132.
      - Lab systems one-time savings of $260,519 in year 2; ongoing savings 43,621 starting in year 2.

6. The revenue cycle management team focused on these key areas:

   a. Hospital revenue cycle management.
      - Eliminate the practice of providing prompt pay discounts for copays and deductibles to save $106,000 per annum in two months. (Quick win)
      - Reduce controllable write-offs by 50 percent, or $171,100, by improving advance beneficiary notice (ABN) processes by six months:
        1. Lab walk-in ABNs
        2. Physician office network ABNs
        3. Scheduled outpatient diagnostic ABNs

▫ Improve clinical documentation to appropriately report case mix index to generate $1 million from the clinical documentation improvement team.

b. Physician revenue cycle management.

▫ Reduce controllable write-offs of accounts "too old to bill" via billing process improvements implementation starting in three months. This represents an impact of $120,000 annually.

▫ Reduce software fees by $53,000 in three months.

7. The supply chain team focused on these key areas:

a. Products. Deploy supply chain management best practices:

1. Optimize supply contract pricing $250,000 of a total of $1,375,000 identified by benchmarking of cost per adjusted discharge; an industry wide standard measure.

2. Utilization (use of products and services) including price changes, quantities, and procedures of $50,000.

3. Physician preference items of 4.1 percent of $600,000, or $25,000.

4. Pharmacy/intravenous chemotherapy drugs annual savings of $225,000.

5. Pharmacy nonchemotherapy drugs annual savings of $129,000.

6. Pharmacy nonchemotherapy drugs reduced by 1.5% equating to $20,000.

b. Services. Reduce costs for nonbiomedical service contracts by $5,000 per annum by five months while maintaining physician and patient satisfaction levels.

c. Services. Reprocessing of surgical products opportunity 15 percent to 30 percent of $500,000 that could be reprocessed.

During the 10-week cycle, the leadership team engaged an outside benchmarking service to evaluate performance against a peer group of hospitals. This effort cut across several of the previously named teams and helped them to focus on benchmarking two spend categories:

1. Direct and indirect labor across several departments, such as radiology, facilities, laundry, finance, and numerous others.

2. Supply across the hospital focused on the weighted average cost per adjusted discharge not included above.

Team Results

The seven 10-step teams in turn focused their efforts during a shortened 10-week cycle, due to systems go-live projects, and identified $8,560,000 per annum earnings improvement, as shown in Exhibit 4.2. Ongoing results were also communicated to system and hospital boards of directors for advice and counsel.

Positive Outcomes

These observations were considered benefits of this round and set the stage for further leveraging the CPM 10-step program to improve system performance:

- The system executive and leadership teams, armed with the accumulated knowledge of five rounds of 10-step teams, optimized and innovated the method and applied it very successfully to an entire medical center in round 6.
- MidMichigan Health leveraged the CPM experience of Nold and Mills and temporarily loaned them to this hospital to assist a fellow affiliate; they transitioned team work papers to the affiliate and reverted back to their regular roles.
- Affiliate personnel effectively mobilized to function as one optimized and integrated program team.

Opportunities for Improvement

The next observations led to adjustments in the 10-step program design that would be incorporated into subsequent rounds of teams to enhance the program.

Work Thread	FY 2012 Impact				Annual Net Impact Future Years	Net Impact over 5 Years
	Implementation Cost	Net Revenue	Net Expense	Net Impact		
Nursing	$0	$58,000	($196,000)	$254,000	$298,000	$1,444,000
Physicians	0	42,000	7,000	35,000	437,000	1,783,000
Emergency Department, Inpatient	0	76,000	(114,000)	190,000	918,000	3,862,000
OP Ancillary Services	30,000	640,000	190,000	420,000	2,036,000	8,563,000
Facilities/IT	0	0	46,000	(46,000)	631,000	2,740,000
Revenue Cycle Management	0	876,000	285,000	591,000	1,459,000	6,429,000
Purchased Goods and Services	68,000	0	(656,000)	588,000	849,000	3,983,000
Work Thread Total	**98,000**	**1,692,000**	**(438,000)**	**2,032,000**	**6,628,000**	**28,804,000**
Benchmarking—Labor	0	0	(77,000)	77,000	932,000	8,002,000
Benchmarking—Supply	0	0	(298,000)	298,000	1,100,000	13,398,000
Total	**$98,000**	**$1,692,000**	**($812,000)**	**$2,406,000**	**$8,660,000**	**$50,204,000**

EXHIBIT 4.2   Innovative Application of 10-Step Teams to an Entire Hospital

- Due to the short cycle application of the method over 10 weeks, the CPM team departed from the 12-week cycle, it compressed the proven four days of training; this resulted in some team members not fully understanding the approach. The leadership team agreed to revert to the 12-week format for future rounds of teams.

The price of greatness is responsibility.

—Sir Winston Churchill

Building on prior successes, the system leadership team now turned its attention to round 7 and applied the approach to five new system teams to optimize the enterprise. This round is described in the next section.

Optimized for the Enterprise (Round 7)

Given the depth and breadth of trained leaders and system-wide adoption by leaders and managers, round 7 was the first explicitly defined set of five system teams chartered to address five system opportunities.

Leadership Rationale

In round 7, the leadership team identified five enterprise- or system-level teams that would have a multimillion-dollar impact on enterprise earnings. The leadership team identified team members from throughout the system and ensured that teams would be made up of experienced CPM members (those who participated on at least two prior rounds of teams). MidMichigan Health was now optimizing and leveraging its experienced resource pool of CPM professionals.

Team Areas of Focus

The seventh round contained five teams of about ten participants each with representation from multiple disciplines and affiliate locations.

1. The patient schedule team focused on reducing customer (patient) scheduling delays and errors by providing schedulers up-to-date tools and resources. This team aligned with Strategic Goal E: Operational excellence.
2. The lab integration team focused on consolidating lab operations across four hospitals. This team aligned with Strategic Goal E: Operational excellence. This team and its work papers will be discussed in greater detail in Chapter 7.

3. The meaningful use team created a process that leverages technology to report core measures to the federal government in a timely manner. This team aligned with Strategic Goal E: Operational excellence.
4. The HIPAA (Health Insurance Portability and Accountability Act) and security team reduced the risk associated with noncompliance in HIPAA privacy and security regulations. This team aligned with Strategic Goal E: Operational excellence.
5. The pharmacy team focused on consolidating pharmacy operations and spending costs. This team aligned with Strategic Goal E: Operational excellence. This team and its working papers will be discussed in greater detail in Chapter 7.

Team Results

In addition to the customer, process, and people results described in the selected case studies later in this book, the teams identified significant annual earnings improvements. The five teams identified $26,400,000 in a one-time cash flow and $2,318,000 per annum earnings improvement, which greatly exceeded the five-team target of $250,000 per annum:

1. The patient scheduling team identified $80,000 per annum earnings improvement.
2. The lab integration team identified $1,700,000 per annum earnings improvement.
3. The core measures, meaningful use team identified $60,000 per annum earnings improvement. Moreover, it confirmed that it could comply with federal government reporting requirements and avoid penalties and fines.
4. The HIPAA and security team identified $26,476,000 in one-time cash flow benefit, securing grant dollars for compliance with programs requirements.
5. The Pharmacy team identified $292,000 per annum earnings improvement.

Positive Outcomes

The next observations were considered benefits of this round and set the stage for expanding the CPM 10-step program system wide:

■ In a first, during the 12-week cycle, the system-level steering committee approved a recommendation for the lab team to name a new director of an integrated system lab SBU. At the onset of the project, all four medical center lab operations reported locally to each of the four medical centers. This centralization was a transformational change that occurred rapidly and gained wide acceptance.

▪ The teams built on prior system teams; however, something was different with this round. Team members fully understood that they were focused on establishing system solutions for each team. The ability to optimize the system and not the local affiliate was now in focus and embraced by employees.

Opportunities for Improvement

The next observations led to adjustments in the 10-step program design that would be incorporated into subsequent rounds of teams to enhance the program.

▪ One team was driven by compliance with federal guidelines; this is not typically a driver for performance improvement. The leadership team rationale for team selection was expanded to consider a risk or compliance team in future rounds of teams.

▪ The process owner for one team was not involved in the team formation; however, she was invited to the join the team during the first day of training. This was not a very productive situation as the process owner was very invested in the As-Is process; it was hard for her to evaluate the issues and root causes objectively. The team, however, continued through the problem-solving approach and identified solutions.

 SUMMARY

This chapter focused on the journey and maturation of the 10-step BI program to address strategic and operational challenges and realized over $450,000 per team in annual earnings improvements while concurrently improving customer satisfaction scores, modernizing dozens of processes, and attaining better employee or people results. It incorporated CMU CCM to frame and chronicle the evolution of MidMichigan Health's use of the 10-step BI methodology. For each level of maturity, we learned six key elements of program design. This maturation enabled MidMichigan Health to apply its level

5 optimized capabilities to an entire hospital in round 6 and true system-wide teams in rounds 7 and beyond.

The gods help them that help themselves.

—Aesop

 NOTE

1. Mark C. Paulk, Charles V. Weber, Bill Curtis, and Mary Beth Chrissis, "Capability Maturity Model for Software, Version 1.1," Carnegie Mellon University, February 1993.

CHAPTER FIVE

Improve Performance Best Practices

To raise new questions, new possibilities, to regard old problems from a new angle, requires creative imagination and marks real advance in science.

—*Albert Einstein*

I N THIS CHAPTER I SHARE the core Principle 4: Improve performance best practices and greatly expand on them, describing 35 new best practices that were identified, deployed, and validated at MidMichigan Health. The 35 new best practices can be readily adapted to your improvement program to realize the enormous results. Combining the maturity model described in Chapter 4 with the best practices in this chapter holds the key to your sustained success.

CORE BEST PRACTICES

Research from my first two CPM books identified essential Principle 4: Improve performance best practices common to dozens of award-winning organizations. The core best practices are listed next.

- **Prioritize improvement projects.** Identify and prioritize strategic and operational initiatives projects to improve the organization's performance along financial, customer or constituent, process, and people dimensions.
- **Leverage customer-facing processes.** Develop and exercise customer- and constituent-facing processes to understand and recalibrate processes around changing customer needs. Gather customer and competitor intelligence using regular customer surveys, focus groups, call centers, and related methods and approaches.
- **Leverage process improvement methods.** Design and maintain ongoing process improvement methods and problem solving to identify and eliminate root causes of issues.
- **Realize value from benchmarking.** Leverage benchmarking and comparative methods to identify and regularly improve core and support processes.
- **Create a performance culture.** Create a virtual community of practitioners to coordinate initiative completion.

In addition to exercising the core best practices, MidMichigan Health leveraged 35 new best practices during its journey from level 1 basic to level 5 optimized.

 35 NEW BEST PRACTICES

At MidMichigan Health, the successive rounds of teams and application of the 10-step approach resulted in the identification and application of new best practices. This section provides and describes these best practices. They have been assembled in *chronological order* approximating the life cycle of successive rounds teams to enable you to realize value as you roll out your business improvement program.

1. **Portfolio management of projects.** The leadership team regularly reviewed the portfolio of enterprise-wide projects against the company

goals, strategic plan, strategy map, and balanced scorecard performance results (red, yellow, or green) for relevancy, impact, and resource allocation. This regular review ensured that projects were meeting changing market conditions and new strategies, and not burdening the organization with too many projects.

For example, the leadership team reviewed over 180 projects and scored them against the system goals and balanced scorecard and decided to cease activity on about 85 to free up organizational capacity and to focus on a new round of 10-step teams to drive meaningful results.

2. **Sponsorship.** Executive, administrative, or department leader sponsorship and participation was continuous throughout the team 12-week cycle during steering committee meetings, the two-day 10-step trainings, and implementation. Some implementations extended beyond the 12-week team cycle, thus requiring continued sponsorship. Frequently teams productively debated issues but required sponsorship guidance to ensure progress. This is of particular importance since the team cycle is merely 12 weeks long prior to being disbanded or turned off.

For example, the chief financial officer's (CFO's) planning and budgeting 10-step team was constructively debating the appropriate scope and time frame for making transformational improvements. The CFO sponsor participated in some weekly team meetings to provide guidance and clarity to support the goal of a 57 percent reduction in complexity and budget line items in the first year.

3. **Myth busting.** Ten-step teams debunked on average one long-held belief during their 12-week life cycle. The myth consisted of the team goal, issue, its root cause, or potential solutions. The teams objectively reviewed data and voice-of-the-customer surveys as they routinely disproved myths or anecdotes that had been repeated often enough to become accepted facts.

For example, specialty practice areas long believed that general practitioners were not referring their patients to them. However, in fact, the 10-step team survey (step 3 of 10) revealed that consumers (you and me) self-directed to specialists. Consumers actively conducted Web-based research to seek out and visit high-performing specialists, relying less and less on primary physician referrals. Suppose the team had leapt to the solution of training general practitioners on specialty practice services: Wouldn't this have been a wasted effort?

4. **Steering committee: composition.** The steering committee consisted of the chief executive officer (CEO) and his direct report team and was flexed

as needed to include additional leaders functioning as sponsors of the areas being addressed by teams.

For example, the round 6 teams focused on an entire hospital; therefore, the steering committee evolved to include the entire hospital administrative team, physician leadership, as well as the overall enterprise CEO due to the scope and materiality of the dollar savings. Further, the local hospital board and the system board received regular updates.

5. **Steering committee: meetings.** It is vital that the steering committee meet every two weeks during the 12-week cycle to provide milestone meetings or due dates for the team leaders to present team findings. The continuous biweekly review also heightens team expectations and accountability.

For example, the round 6 ancillary services sleep lab (growth) team recognized the importance of the upcoming steering committee meeting. As a consequence, it prepared a decision tree for prequalifying, registering, and scheduling sleep lab patients. This quick win was part of a larger pilot to improve volume and utilization of the sleep lab. The decision tree was readily approved by the steering committee for immediate field deployment.

6. **Steering committee: presentations.** Team leaders present a standard set of five slides to the steering committee with their working papers in the appendix of the steering committee presentation for reference purposes. One of the five slides, called "Permission to Proceed," contains a summary of recommended actions the team seeks immediate approval on. These actions enable the team to maintain momentum inside the 12-week life cycle, demonstrate progress, and test pilots to both risk manage and assess the value of full implementations later.

For example, the emergency department (ED) 10-step team's presentation to the steering committee recommended an investment to hire shift coordinators to address peak demand of patient flow and to reduce cycle time in patient wait time and to improve patient satisfaction. The pilot required an immediate approval due to lead times of hiring personnel inside the 12-week team period. Within 24 hours, the steering committee approved the request. The pilot program generated the targeted results during the first seven days of implementation, week 7 of the team 12-week cycle.

7. **Steering committee: governance.** The steering committee reporter provides clear approval or guidance on each "Permission to Proceed" action item within 24 hours. This enables the team to earn quick wins, create energy, and deal with change management issues during the 12-week cycle.

For example, the finance team requested permission to increase the threshold to $100,000 for making allocations of overhead costs back to the business units and departments. This change in policy reduced both the number and complexity of allocations. This simplification freed up valuable finance team time to focus on business improvement opportunities.

8. **Team roster: behavioral composition.** The most successful teams consist of a balanced set of behavioral types using the Birkman (four-color-based) personality profile model.[1] The four personality profiles improved intra- and interteam communications. Here is a summary of the four profiles modified by successive rounds of teams.

 a. Blue is focused on strategic. The dominant observable behaviors include:
   - Focuses on strategy and innovation.
   - Generates ideas and concepts.
   - Values the welfare of people.
   - Operates with an idealistic outlook.
   - Engages in research and development.
   - Provides vision.
   - Acts sensitive and creative.

 b. Green is focused on people. The dominant observable behaviors include:
   - Focuses on sales and marketing efforts.
   - Influences and motivates people.
   - Seeks recognition.
   - Supports and manages change.
   - Actively communicates with others.
   - Acts independently.
   - Acts outgoing and enthusiastic.

 c. Red is focused on results or tasks. The dominant observable behaviors include:
   - Focuses on tangible projects.
   - Implements the plan.
   - Demonstrates hands-on activity.
   - Makes tough calls.

 d. Yellow is focused on detailed or administrative. The dominant observable behaviors include:
   - Focuses on organizational process/systems.
   - Values accuracy and detail.
   - Analyzes data thoroughly.
   - Is cooperative when working with others.
   - Uses a plan when acting on objectives.

- Appreciates stability in the environment.
- Acts cautious and consistent.

For example, one team leader was a very strong red (or task-oriented) personality. The team, however, was comprised mostly of many green (or people-oriented) members. Consequently, the initial team meetings were not very productive; the team leader dominated the agenda and speaking time. The CPM facilitator intervened and brought this dysfunctional team dynamic to the attention of the full team in a humorous and educational way. The team members responded and had fun highlighting their behavioral differences and developed into a high-performing team.

9. **Team roster: CPM experience.** The configuration of team rosters later in the quarterly cycles of teams included at least two members who had participated in prior rounds of CPM teams. These 10-step alumni provided valuable insights for rookie team members and helped the teams to mature rapidly during their 12-week cycle to realize significant financial and nonfinancial results.

   For example, round 8 teams each had team members with at least one, in some cases two to four, prior team experiences. This depth of experience accelerated productivity during team breakout sessions and enabled the rest of the team members to move rapidly up the learning curve.

10. **Team roster: high-potential team members.** The leadership team offered high-potential employees for consideration as team members but especially for team leadership roles. The 10-step program offered the opportunity for people development. It allowed for a well-defined 12-week cycle to evaluate individuals' leadership skills, analytical capabilities, presentation skills, and specifically ability to deliver team results.

    For example, during regular team meetings, one rather reserved team member participated intermittently. But he demonstrated outstanding analytical skills and took the initiative to prepare advanced process solutions during the fieldwork phases and present back to the team during regular meetings. This was not only a pleasant surprise but also positioned him for a team leader role during the next round of teams. In the subsequent round, this new team leader successfully led a team dealing with an enterprise-wide issue, and his team devised a successful a practical solution.

11. **Team roster: configuration.** The configuration of teams included a cross-functional set of personnel. These included:
    - Process or topic participants
    - Internal or external customers of the focus area or process
    - Finance subject matter expert (SME)

■ SMEs as needed from human resources and information technology (IT)

For example, starting in round 3, the steering committee identified teams and required the rosters to include members from the four groups just described. Inclusion of the standard experts provided know-how and alleviated complexity and possible team delays from onboarding one or more SMEs during the tight 12-week team cycle.

12. **Team roster: pre-reading.** Provide the team with pre-reading so members have the strategic context, basic conceptual understanding of the 12-week cycle, key dates, team area of focus or topic, and team member roster.

For example, starting in round 2, pre-reading materials consisting of 20 PowerPoint slides were sent out one week prior to the first two-day training. This pre-reading module included an overview of the 10-step training life cycle and a prior team case study with working papers for each step. The combination of an overview of the 10-step approach and concrete or tangible working papers educated participants and also created trainee confidence in their ability to adopt the program.

13. **Team roster: planning.** Ten-step team members were selected and notified several weeks prior to training in order for them and their colleagues to shift work to accommodate the time commitment for training and team meetings.

For example, starting in round 2, team members were notified at least three weeks prior to the start of the first two-day training. This reduced scheduling concerns and stress on the part of team members. This planning also removed this tension from the step 2 team breakout session that established the team charter and team member commitments to weekly meetings and training days.

14. **Team leader: objectivity.** Assign a capable person as team leader who is not the department head or process owner for the topic of focus. This appointment enabled leader objectivity, removed the opportunity for interference, and provided a fresh set of eyes to lead the effort.

For example, when the 10-step team focused on the financial and management reporting process, the system CFO was not the team leader. Instead, the CFO functioned as an SME and was purposely interviewed by the team. From the 10-step program perspective, most process owners were glad to have the additional assistance of the team and were pleasantly surprised by its objective creativity and solutions.

15. **Team leader: experience.** Assign team leadership to an employee who has participated as a team member on at least one team cycle; two experiences are preferred. Being an experienced trained employee enables the

team leader to focus on team dynamics and subject matter and spend less time learning the 10-step methodology.

For example, armed with experiences from two rounds of prior teams, the patient scheduling team leader developed very advanced facilitation and people management skills. His heightened skills proved invaluable for leading his first team consisting of very intense team members, and it enhanced the enterprise-wide solution.

16. **Team behavioral life cycle.** The 10-step training is designed for the teams to manage themselves through the four stages of group development. During the 12-week team life cycle, the teams will experience forming, storming, norming, and performing stages each with symptoms and countermeasures. These four phases are necessary and inevitable in order for the team to grow, confront their challenges, tackle problems, find solutions, plan work, and ultimately deliver results. The four stages, based on the work of Bruce Tuckman, are described more fully next.[2]

a. **Forming.** In the first stage of team building, the forming of the team takes place. Individual behavior is driven by a desire to be accepted by the others and avoid controversy or conflict. Serious issues and feelings are avoided, and people focus on routines, such as team organization, who does what, when to meet, and the like. But individuals are also gathering information and impressions—about each other and about the scope of the task and how to approach it. This is a comfortable stage to be in, but the avoidance of conflict and threat means that not much actually gets done.

b. **Storming.** Next every group enters the storming stage in which different ideas compete for consideration. The team addresses issues such as what problems they are really supposed to solve, how they will function independently and together, and what leadership model they will accept. The storming stage is necessary to the growth of the team. It can be contentious, unpleasant, and even painful to team members who are averse to conflict. Tolerance of each member and their differences should be emphasized. Without tolerance and patience the team will fail.

c. **Norming.** The team manages to have one goal and come to a mutual plan for the team at this stage. Some may have to give up their own ideas and agree with others in order to make the team function. In this stage, all team members take the responsibility and aim to work for the success of the team's goals.

d. **Performing.** High-performing teams are able to function as a unit as they find ways to get the job done smoothly and effectively without inappropriate conflict or the need for external supervision. By this time, they are motivated and knowledgeable. Team members are now competent, autonomous, and able to handle the decision-making process without supervision. Dissent is expected and allowed as long as it is channeled through means acceptable to the team.

Teams will proceed through the four stages at different rates. For example, one team progressed through all four phases in one 90-minute meeting while another team was stuck at storming for an entire meeting as members constructively debated the scope of the goal statement. Effective team leaders recognize the phase of their team and facilitate it to the next phase.

17. **Team member participation.** Attendance is mandatory for the two two-day training sessions and all weekly team meetings, which typically are between 60 and 90 minutes in length. When a team member misses a training or team meeting, reentry into the team project flow typically results in the team storming.

For example, during the beginning of round 7, two team members who had not been through the training could not participate in the first two-day training sessions. Once the two individuals joined the teams in week 2, the team sponsors and leaders could not prevent the eventual team storming from occurring. The team recovered from this predictable phase; however, it served to reinforce the mandatory attendance rule.

18. **Goal statement: compound elements.** The teams focused on system topics or complex issues would break down their goals statements into multiple subgoals, often called components or elements. Types of subgoals were delineated by geography, financial line items, age groups, customer segments, and other.

For example, the disbursement team (see detailed case in Chapter 6) focused on seven financial elements of value:
a. Implement commercial credit card accounts payable payment program to realize discounts and rebates.
b. Standardize system policy for mileage reimbursement rate to 10 cents less than the Internal Revenue Service standard reimbursement rate.
c. Implement policy change to discontinue mileage reimbursement audits.
d. Implement and standardize system credit card policy to utilize health system's tax-exempt status to not pay sales tax.
e. Implement revenue share program with bank to receive annual rebate.

    f. Implement policy change around airline spend (revenue share opportunity).

    g. Amend existing health system employee reimbursement policy (remove all affiliate policies) leading to research, evaluation, and recommendation of automation options for expense reimbursement.

19. **Goal statement: balanced.** Teams developed balanced goal statements to concurrently optimize several competing outcomes. Teams recognized that they could simply optimize one variable at the expense of others; however, the team focus would be to establish goals to optimize competing variables.

    For example, the care coordination team (described in detail in Chapter 8) created a three-part goal consisting of reducing process cycle time, reducing costs, and improving customer scores. The intent was to consciously set acceptable targets for all three sub goals.

20. **Leadership team collaboration.** The leadership team temporarily assigned senior team members to another affiliate hospital to augment its CPM program and train others to manage a comprehensive program.

    For example, Diane Nold and Deb Mills cited in the previous chapter from one hospital traveled to another hospital affiliate for three months to directly lead and facilitate round 6 10-step teams that identified over $8.5 million in earnings improvements (described in Chapter 4).

21. **Training–adult learning.** The 10-step approach leverages adult learning techniques in four stages in each training module:

    a. Provides an introduction of each step (of 10), its key concepts techniques, tools, and methods.

    b. Shares examples of each step including key deliverables through case examples from award-winning companies.

    c. Conducts team breakout sessions on each step for team members to develop deliverables and apply techniques to their area of focus.

    d. Enables teams to present their work products to the larger group of five teams for question and answer period. The open comments period invariably results in key refinements.

22. **Team member CPE credits.** The participants in the two two-day 10-step training program received Continuing Professional Education (CPE) requirement credits and two certificates of completion from Bob Paladino & Associates, LLC, and a member of National Registry of CPE Sponsors.

    For example, during each two-day training session, participants would sign in and out to earn their CPE training certificate.

23. **CPM certificate of recognition.** The participants on a 10-step team received a Corporate Performance Management Excellence Award Certificate, from the CPM Office, Midland CEO, and Bob Paladino & Associates, LLC.

    For example, the CPM Certificate in round 1 stated: "Teamwork is the fuel that allows ordinary people to achieve extraordinary results. Thanks for being a part of a great team!"

24. **Team technology and tools.** Each team is issued a CPM laptop preloaded with electronic templates to develop team working papers. The technology enhanced productivity and standardized working papers.

    For example, the teams were issued passwords to post their team working papers on a shared drive for their team; this enabled virtual team meetings and information sharing. Subsequent teams regularly retrieved archived working papers to gain insights to their team issue.

25. **Team technology weekly team meetings.** Teams leveraged video and desktop sharing technology for geographically distributed teams. This saved transportation (avoiding up to two lost hours per team member per week for those traveling). This technology also allowed for real-time updates for team working papers and rapid postmeeting distribution of assignments to maintain team momentum.

    For example, the system teams representing the four hospitals communicate during weekly team meetings using video and phone technologies.

26. **CPM leadership: function.** MidMichigan Health established a formal CPM function. This signaled not only the importance of this role to the organization but also MidMichigan Health's commitment to the CPM approach—the 10-step program was not the initiative du jour.

    For example, MidMichigan Health appointed Deb Mills as director of corporate performance management. This created sustained business improvement infrastructure.

27. **CPM leadership: experts.** The organization trained over 250 individuals during the first seven rounds to create legions of CPM-centered problem solvers with representation from all nine affiliates and from corporate. The organization trained numerous people multiple times to create experts.

    For example, these experts were distributed among successive teams to ensure rapid learning and to accelerate results.

28. **Benchmarking and best practices.** Ten-step teams in step 8 of the 10-step approach engaged in several forms of benchmarking and best practice gathering. Examples include:

    a. Formal benchmarking using private services that involved peer group hospitals and shared services functions (e.g., finance, human resources, supply chain) nationwide in cost, service levels, and employee skill mix.

b. Formal benchmarking using government-furnished data for quality measures (e.g., *Hospital Consumer Assessment of Healthcare Providers and Systems)* covering hundreds of hospitals nationwide.

c. Site visits to award-winning hospitals (e.g., Malcolm Baldrige, state quality awards) to compare benchmarks and best practices to support design To-Be state solutions.

d. Conference calls with award-winning hospitals to compare benchmarks and best practices to design To-Be state solutions.

29. **CPM team leader: turnover.** By training a broad base of practitioners, the organization ensured sustainability and that the normal turnover of leaders, managers, and employees would not disrupt momentum toward achieving results. This program therefore is not dependent on a single personality but on the collective skills of multiple leaders.

For example, when a senior IT leader left the organization, the IT function, with deep 10-step bench strength, was able to contribute to teams in the following round without missing a beat.

30. **Implementation: pilots.** The teams identified root causes and creative solutions, although most conducted a pilot at one location before expanding it to multiple locations. This approach enabled teams to work out issues and refine solutions for optimal results.

For example, the care coordination team focused on properly and accurately classifying patients for care at one hospital. As the system team rolled out the solution, it leveraged and applied successive best practices and lessons learned from one location to the next.

31. **Implementation: system.** The teams (step 6) take a holistic view of their topics and optimize up to eight different contributing factors for improvement. These factors include people, procedures, processes, policies, technologies, places or locations, products and services, and pricing.

For example, the financial and management reporting team (see case in Chapter 6) emphasized numerous policy changes, such as raising dollar thresholds for journal entries to bring out meaningful change.

The lab team (see Chapter 8 for detailed case) evaluated these eight elements system-wide and discovered that two primary elements (place) the number of locations and (people) staffing were primary drivers of value.

32. **Team celebration.** At week 12, it is essential to conduct a two- to three-hour final celebration to recognize and thank all five teams in that cycle. During this assembly of 50 professionals, teams present their findings,

share pilot results, receive recognition, and participate in a short reception to bring closure to their efforts. This session officially releases 10-step team members, transfers work products to the recipient process or department owner, and provides executive visibility for all team members (regardless of level in the company).

For example, the CEO and leader of the steering committee provided a keynote address and personally handed each of 50 team members their CPM certificates. The balance of the celebration consisted of an open reception for all team members.

33. **Benefits realization: biweekly reviews.** Teams run in 12-week cycles, resulting in the accumulation of teams from previous rounds; four rounds of five teams can generate up to 20 active team solutions being implemented concurrently. It is crucial to meet with recipient process owners every two weeks for 15 to 30 minutes to gauge their adoption of the newly designed To-Be process. This regularity creates visibility and expectations for continuing results and alerts the standing steering committee of any issues or new permission needed to proceed actions to realize value (see best practice #7).

For example, the disbursement team solution focused on cash rebates by concentrating vendor payments using a corporate credit card. However, the process for issuing requests for proposal and determining the final financial vendor required the process owner to meet with the CPM team every two weeks over a period of several months to monitor progress.

34. **Benefits realization: the handoff.** Experience shows that if the process owner is on the 10-step team, the transition from week 12 to realization of benefits is a seamless continuum. However, if the process owner is not part of the 10-step team or functions as the team sponsor, it is critical that he or she attend the final team meeting and is thoroughly briefed to ensure a seamless handoff and realization of benefits.

For example, the safety team investigated severe adverse events and designed a new To-Be process for preventing them. However, a new director of safety was named toward the end of the project; she had not been part of the 10-step team or steering committee. Therefore, the CPM director and project team leader provided the new safety director with a complete briefing on the team results. The director of safety appreciated the team's efforts and thoughtful solutions.

35. **Change management: communications.** Regular CEO town hall meetings, newsletters, and monthly executive meetings create opportunities to

share 10-step team success stories and to duly recognize high-performing teams.

For example, the system CEO authored an article called "Corporate Performance Management, 10-Step Team Approach Improves Patient, Employee, Process and Financial Outcomes" in the enterprise-wide newsletter, This article provided an executive summary of the 18 teams to date, short summaries of five teams, and specific recognition of team members for their contributions.

Necessity is the mother of invention.

—**Plato**

 ## SUMMARY

This chapter shared the core Principle 4: Improve performance best practices and built on them with 35 new best practices identified, deployed, and validated at MidMichigan Health. These 35 new best practices can be readily adapted to your improvement program to realize enormous results. Combining the maturity model described in Chapter 4 with the best practices in this chapter holds the key to your sustained success.

 ## NOTES

1. *Birkman Pocket Guide* (Houston, TX: Birkman International, 2004).
2. Bruce Tuckman, "Developmental Sequence in Small Groups," *Psychological Bulletin* 63, no. 6 (1965): 384–399.

6

Shared Services: 10-Step Team Best Practice Cases

Pleasure in the job puts perfection in the work.

—*Aristotle*

THIS CHAPTER DESCRIBES FINANCE, human resources (HR), and supply chain management shared services teams from a practitioner's perspective by walking through the 10-step teams' working papers in narrative form. The formal team titles are followed by two words that capture the strategic intent of that team. The cases include:

- Finance: Accounts Payable and Disbursements, *Smart Spending*
- Finance: Financial and Management Reporting, *Streamline Information*
- Human Resources: New Employee Requisitions, *Simplify Hiring*
- Supply Chain Management: New Product Requisitions, *Manage Innovation*

In Chapter 3 I introduced the 10-step improvement program in summary form; the case studies in the balance of the book provide a more in-depth use of the method and content. I thank the dozens of team leaders and several hundred team members for their massive efforts, innovative solutions, and pride and passion of ownership. Ten cases have been selected for a more expanded discussion in this book. Unfortunately, space limitations prevent sharing all of them.

> Everything that is really great and inspiring is created by the individual who can labor in freedom.
>
> **—Albert Einstein**

FINANCE: ACCOUNTS PAYABLE AND DISBURSEMENTS 10-STEP TEAM CASE STUDY, *SMART SPENDING*

> I was impressed with the evolution of this team. The team dynamics were quite diverse contributing to many "storming" sessions, but once we established our goal we truly performed as a unit with a common purpose. We exceeded my expectations.
>
> —Kevin Wing, Pay Management Manager
> (team leader)

Strategic Context

MidMichigan Health system chief financial officer (CFO) Francine Padgett cosponsored the corporate performance management (CPM) 10-step program.[1] She dedicated one of her senior finance team members to the newly created position of CPM director. Other finance function members participated as team leaders, subject matter experts, or team members.

The accounts payable and disbursement team aligned with Strategic Objective E: Operational excellence. The genesis of this team was a prevailing view that employee expense reporting process was cumbersome, contained unnecessary steps, and delayed reimbursement checks to employee travelers. The team busted some myths and identified significant value creation opportunities.

This case study consists of these sections:

- **Steps 1–5 Training** encompasses developing team working papers and content during the first two-day training team breakout sessions.

- **Steps 1–5 Fieldwork** shares key findings primarily from voice-of-customer surveys, data review, and analytics.
- **Steps 6–10 Training** consists of working papers and content developed during the second two-day training breakout sessions.
- **Improve performance** shares the financial and nonfinancial team findings to improve performance.

Steps 1–5 Training Days 1–2

Step 1: Have We Identified the Right Areas of Focus?

Since teams (by design) consisted of representatives from different functions that possessed varied understanding of the current process, step 1 focused the team to establish a baseline or common understanding of the current situation.

The team spent considerable time and identified several customers of the process, who were discussed and debated. These customers included (1) employees (also referred to as travelers), (2) department heads who approved employee travel, (3) vendors who provided the travel services, and (4) accounting department employees who facilitated and participated in the processes. Since the team only had 12 weeks to establish and complete its goals, primary customers had to be selected carefully. In light of the strategic context provided, the team decided to focus on two primary customer groups: travelers and accounting personnel.

The team brainstormed the customers' requirements, prioritized them through voting, and drafted the Five Ups (standard reference to the top five requirements for a customer group and also described in Chapter 3) charts for each customer group.

The team concurred that the first customer group, *employees*, had three primary requirements:

1. Cycle time to reimburse, from the time the report is submitted by the employee to when employees receive their reimbursement checks.
2. Average preparation time for each expense report, from downloading the expense report, filling it out, and submitting it to the department head for approval.
3. Percentage of dissatisfied employees who would negatively rate the current process. Based on its experience and estimates, the team established As-Is and To-Be targets for each of the three requirements. The As-Is cycle time was 21 days; the To-Be cycle time target was set at 14 days, a 33% reduction. The As-Is average preparation time of 30 minutes and the To-Be

target was set at 15 minutes, a 50% reduction. The As-Is percentage dissatisfied of 80% and the To-Be target was set at 40%, a 50% reduction.

The team recognized the significance and implications of establishing aggressive reductions or improvements in the three requirements of 33%, 50%, and 50%. The team discussed the importance of a balanced set of targets that concurrently solved for multiple aspects of this process.

The team agreed that the second customer group, accounting department personnel, had three primary requirements:

1. Number of touches, essentially steps in the process involving accounting department actions or inputs for each expense report
2. Percentage of audits, representing the percentage of employee expense reports that are audited by accounting personnel either once or twice during the process
3. Cycle time to processing, or the elapsed time from when the report is received in accounting to when the reimbursement check is disbursed to the employee

The As-Is number of touches was 20; the To-Be target was set at 15, a 25% reduction in effort. The As-Is percentage of audits was 125%; the To-Be target was set at 75%, a 40% reduction. The As-Is cycle time for processing was 14 days; the To-Be target was set at 10 days, a 29% reduction.

The team recognized the significance and implications of establishing aggressive reductions or improvements of 25%, 40%, and 29% in the three requirements. The team discussed the importance of a balanced set of targets that concurrently solved for multiple requirements. It consciously decided to make more significant improvements in those requirements for the traveler customer group rather than the accounting department personnel customer.

The team brainstormed causes for the current performance and identified 18 reasons. The team the categorized these causes by six factors (in parentheses), including process, policy, people, materials, technology, and environment:

1. Multiple processes (Process)
2. Multiple forms (Material)
3. Manual process (Process)
4. Redundant steps (Process)

5. Minimal level for receipts (Policy)
6. Minimal level for check requirement (Policy)
7. Inaccuracies (People)
8. Missing accountability (People)
9. Lack of training (People)
10. Lack of education (People)
11. Duplicate requests (People)
12. Lack of documentation tracking (Technology)
13. Batch handling versus continuous process (Process)
14. Too many touch points (Process)
15. Low priority (People)
16. Lack technology (Technology)
17. "Excessive" approval/audit 100% (Environment)
18. Auditor tweaking data instead of returning (Environment)

Data Sets. The team identified key data sets to better understand the As-Is situation and avoid basing discussions on anecdotes. (The anecdotes later were called myths for many of them were busted.) Data sets would provide insights and facts to better analyze and validate and refine the goal statement. Data sets also provided the basis to refine project scope, goals, and selection of subject matter experts (SMEs). The team determined that the next data sets would be useful to gather to during the ensuing four weeks of fieldwork:

- Number of time and expense reports by month and one full year
- Number of time and expense reports by enterprise location/entity
- Travel expenditures by month and one full year
- Category of travel expenditures (e.g., air, hotel, mileage) by month and one full year
- Travel expenditures by physician and nonphysician employees for a full year
- Travel expenditures by credit card andaccounts payable checks for one full year
- Travel expenditures by category and by enterprise location/entity
- Given the materiality, the travel mileage reimbursed by enterprise location/ entity
- Number of touches for time and expense reports

Next the team defined the background, preliminary problem statement, and preliminary goal statement.

Background   Employee reimbursement consists of business travel (mileage), seminars, catered meals, and various supplies. The employee is required to submit an employee reimbursement form for these expenses and include receipts as appropriate; this is a manual process. The reimbursement is approved by the employee's manager and sent to the pay management department for payment. Once the document is received in pay management, it is placed in an audit basket for review. Once the audit has been completed, the form is returned to pay management, where it is then checked to see if it consists of mileage only or other expense reimbursement. If it is mileage only, the form is processed through the next payroll cycle. All other reimbursements are processed within the next accounts payable cycle. Due to the number of touches, reviews, and multiple processing types, it takes 14 to 21 days to process employee reimbursements. Due to the delay, pay management receives multiple phone calls from employees asking the status of their reimbursement. Due to the manual process, it is time consuming for pay management to determine where the form is in the process.

Preliminary Problem Statement   Multiple manual processes result in prolonged cycle time and higher costs.

Based on the insights derived from the prior activities, the team was positioned to establish a preliminary goal statement. Clearly the team is only in step 1 of 10, so the goal statement will be continuously refined and updated as more evidence and data become available.

Preliminary Goal Statement   Reduce payment cycle time for employee reimbursement by 7 to 14 days in three months, which increases employee satisfaction by 40%, results in cost savings of $75,000, allows for document tracking, and reduces the number of touch points.

The preliminary goal statement included multiple elements and therefore is considered a compound goal statement.

Step 2: What Is the Initial Goal Statement? Team Charter?

Team Roles   Team member use of roles during break-out sessions during the two-day training has supported improved team dynamics and performance. The 10-step team's sponsor and team leader roles were determined prior to the start of the project. However, remaining team members volunteered for the balance of the roles; brief descriptions are provided.

- Sponsor (oversees teams, reviews work, owns results): Liz Minbiole
- Team leader (sets guidelines, goals, weekly meetings): Kevin Wing
- Timekeeper (ensures deadlines are met): Cinthia Brooks
- Recorder (takes notes): Jon Athey
- Scribe (makes ideas visible in meetings): Ann Archuleta
- Monitor (adheres to methodology): Tara Schmitt
- Process observer (ensures participation): Tara Schmitt
- Spokesperson (reports to other groups): Rachelle Druelle

Code of Conduct   The team established a code of conduct to be observed during team meetings and phone calls in order to remain highly productive and meet its ambitious goals. The code of conduct incorporated cultural dimensions the team believed to be important to maintain good morale and working relationships. The code of conduct included these elements:

- Meet once per week for 1.5 hours (Wednesdays 8:30 a.m.–10:00 a.m.).
- Meeting agenda required.
- Team members are prepared for meeting.
- Majority voting (team leader get two votes in case of tie).
- Sponsor provides dinner for successful completion of project.
- Open roundtable discussion.
- Minutes distributed by notes taker by end of week.
- Agenda for next meeting set at end of prior meeting.
- Be respectful.
- Attendance required.

These items were consolidated with modifications into a more complete team charter, which formed a team agreement.

Team Charter

- Issue/Problem
  - Multiple manual processes results in prolonged cycle time and higher costs
- Goal Statement (revised)
  - Reduce payment cycle time for employee reimbursement by 7 to 14 days in three months, which increases employee satisfaction by 40%, results in a cost savings of $75,000, allows for document tracking, and reduces the number of touch points

- Constraints
  - Team members off for vacations or other commitments
  - Time
  - Regular job responsibilities
  - Team members committed to other teams
  - Family/medical
  - Technology
  - Multiple processes and multiple policies within the hospital system
  - Forms
  - Training
  - Customer resistance to change
- Assumptions
  - Average minutes for employee, pay management, and audit
  - Cycle time measured in days
  - Average hourly rates to calculate cost savings
- Team Guidelines (included in code of conduct)
- Resources (included in roles and additional SMEs not considered during the project planning phase)
- Preliminary Project Plan (10-step milestone level)
  - Steps 1–5 Training: Week 1
  - Steps 1–5 Fieldwork: Weeks 2–4
  - Steps 6–10 Training: Week 5
  - Steps 6–10 Fieldwork: Weeks 6–10
  - Celebration and Team Turnoff: Week 11 or 12

Step 3: What Are Three to Five Customer Requirements/Complaints?

Voice of the Customer. The purpose of the customer survey, consistent with step 1, was to secure input from the customer segments to validate and in some cases refine key requirements, modify As-Is baselines, recalibrate To-Be performance targets, and provide valuable text responses. The team designed a voice-of-the-customer (VOC) survey to be deployed early in fieldwork. The draft survey is presented on the next page.

Step 4: What Are the Current Process (Map) and Issues?

The team developed a high-level process map consisting of 20 steps and decision points. The scope of this process started from the point that the employee incurs expenses to when he or she submits the report to the approver and from

- Have you been reimbursed for business expenses in the past year?
- Do you know where to find the Travel and Expense policy for your affiliate?
- How satisfied are you with the current reimbursement process?
- In general, how long does it take you to receive your expense reimbursement?
- How many days after the expense occurrence do you complete and turn in the form to your approver?
- What payment method do you prefer for your expense reimbursement?
- Would you prefer submitting for expense reimbursement electronically?
- Would you prefer an electronic approval process?
- What can be done to improve the expense reimbursement process?
- My primary MidMichigan Health employer is: _____.
- Do you receive expense reimbursement checks from more than one affiliate?
- Do you approve expense reimbursements?
- If so, how long does it take you to approve them?
- We welcome your feedback.

when the approver submits it to payroll or accounts payable to when the travel reimbursement check is distributed to the employee. The team reviewed the 20-step and decision points map and highlighted and numbered those that contained choke points or produced issues. The step numbers and short descriptions of the issues, with some steps containing multiple issues, appear next. Notice the first three steps contained nine unique choke points early in the employee experience of using the time and expense reporting process.

    1a   What form? Access to forms
    1b   Submission timing (lag from expense incurred)
    1c   Accuracy & Complete
    1d   Form version correct?
    2a   Approval time
    2b   Accuracy review
    2c   Completeness review
    3a   Large batches

3b   Competing priorities

4   Hard to find/contact traveler; requires back track

5a   Duplicate handling by pay management

5b   Large batches

6   Potential mis-sorts causing shuffling form

7a   Waiting vendor add causes delay (hold/set aside)

7b   Potential misprocessing

8a   Too much to key by deadline

8b   Given to wrong person

9a   User error

9b   System error

9c   Misfiled/misplaced paperwork

10a Machines working?

11a If not approved, checks do not go out

12a If delayed, must research

13a Forms submitted correctly?

13b If not, do we need to contact employee/manager?

13c Errors may delay payment, which may lead to more research because of inquiries

14a Was it keyed correctly?

14b If not, did you catch it before it was paid out or after?

14c Look up employee numbers

14d Look up affiliate

14e Is the position number correct?

14f If the position isn't correct must key to expense code.

15a User error?

15b System error?

16   Equipment working?

17a Post office delivers timely?

17b Does it fall on/near holiday?

The team felt it had identified an overwhelming list of choke points or problems to address; however, step 4 positioned the team for step 5: to prepare a root cause diagram, which categorized and prioritized these issues and identified new ones.

Step 5: What Are the Prioritized Choke Points, Issues, and Root Causes?

In this step, the content developed in prior steps is further analyzed by the team to better understand the causes of issues. The primary tool in this step is the fishbone diagram.

The 10-step team initially used the 6Ms fishbone model and produced this problem statement for the head of the fish: "Multiple manual processes results

Ishikawa (Fishbone) Diagrams

Ishikawa diagrams are also called fishbone diagrams, herringbone diagrams, cause-and-effect diagrams, or Fishikawa diagrams. They are based on a diagram originally developed by Kaoru Ishikawa, which showed the causes of a specific event. Ishikawa diagrams commonly are used in product or service design and quality defect prevention, to identify potential factors causing an overall effect or problem. Each cause or reason for imperfection is a source of variation. Visualize a fish with the problem statement at its head (on the right-hand side of a page) and the categories of causes as bones protruding to the left of the page. The large fish bones are categories of issues where causes can be grouped to identify the true reasons or causes of service or product variation. The fishbone categories include three basic models: the 6Ms, 8Ps, or 5Ss. At MidMichigan Health, initially 10-step teams used the 6Ms. However, teams later adopted the 8Ps as more suitable for the health care service model.

1. The general model, initially referred to as the 6Ms, developed in the manufacturing sector but is now adapted and leveraged across sectors. It includes:
   a. Manpower, People, Skills: Anyone involved with the process
   b. Methods: How the process is performed such as policies, procedures, rules, regulations and laws
   c. Machines, Technology: Any equipment, computers, tools, and so on, required to accomplish the job
   d. Materials: Raw materials, parts, pens, paper, and the like used to produce the final product
   e. Measurements: Data generated from the process that are used to evaluate its quality

(Continued)

f. Mother Nature, Environment: The conditions, such as location, time, temperature, and culture, in which the process operates
2. The 8Ps (plus information technology [IT]) used in service industry include:
   a. Product or service
   b. Price
   c. Place or location
   d. Promotion/marketing
   e. People or skills
   f. Process
   g. Policy
   h. Procedures
   i. Technology
3. The 5Ss also used in service industry include:
   a. Surroundings
   b. Suppliers
   c. Systems
   d. Skills
   e. Safety

in prolonged cycle time and higher costs." The 6M categories and their root causes or bones of the fish are listed next.

- Manpower (people) category root causes included lack of accountability; lack of user training and education; low priority for employees, managers, and auditors; and minimal review by approvers.
- Method (process) category root causes included redundant multiple processes, manual processes, multiple batches, strict traveler receipt thresholds, and multiple review points.
- Machines (technology) root causes included low use of technology, not using current technology, lack of document tracking, limited employee access to technology, and manual not automated steps.
- Materials category root causes included lack of standardization, multiple policies and forms, multiple process including accounts payable and payroll, multiple travel agents, lack of enforcement of rules, lack of alternative printing methods for travelers.

- Measures root causes included no cycle time performance history, no cost per report history, and no volume history.
- The team voted on those most important root causes.

At the conclusion of step 5, the team evaluated its performance across multiple attributes. The focus and intent of this exercise contributes to self-correcting teams that can weather challenges during their life cycle. The team voted using a 1–5 scale, with 5 being the highest grade, on five key factors of team performance. These included:

1. Established goals/agenda scored 4.
2. Used code of conduct and group roles scored 4.
3. Used tools/methods scored 3.
4. Freedom to participate (captured brain power) scored 4.
5. Overall meeting effectiveness scored 4.

As the facilitator and trainer of the teams, I observed that this team developed extensive working papers in just two days. The self-scores indicated that members had started to function as a high-performing team and had some fun. These accomplishments are notable. It is also important to recognize that if the team was dealing with an easy issue, it would have been solved already.

Steps 1–5 Fieldwork

The fieldwork contained key findings that updated hypotheses developed during the two-day training and contained in the working papers. During fieldwork, the team deployed the internal customer (traveler) survey and gathered a significant amount of data, which it then analyzed. The team was initially launched based on a long-held belief that the time and expense reporting process functioned poorly and resulted in widespread employee dissatisfaction. *These two myths could not be further from the truth.*

Survey Results

Traveler survey results were quite unexpected. Here are two key survey questions and results:

1. How satisfied are you with the current reimbursement process?
   - 82% in total ranged from neutral to very satisfied: 44% were neutral, 30% were satisfied, and 8% were very satisfied.

2. In general, how long does it take you to receive your expense reimbursement?
   - 81% of the total received their checks between 0 and 3 weeks: 6% in 0 to 1 weeks, 45% in 1 to 2 weeks, and 30% in 2 to 3 weeks.

Travelers volunteered dozens of comments that provided the team with potential areas of focus. When asked what can be done to improve the expense reimbursement process, highlights of the responses included:

- The *approver part is what seems to be the kink* in the process.
- I think that the *electronic approval for expenses would be great*, Also, if you could investigate an electronic time-off request. My old employer had this system in their labor management system. It was an approval process. When the manager was sent a notification, I would get a response with details if I did not get the request. To me the blue piece of paper seems dated and a waste of time if you could get the time off request to be on the IT system Lawson Employee direct access screen. There has to be a cost savings to the above process. Plus I could trend time off request, look at balances of employees, and approve or deny from home.
- A credit card *"loaded" with the set preestimated, approved, amount* so we wouldn't have to use our own resources.
- *Standardization* . . . sometimes I receive reimbursement for travel in an AP [accounts payable] check sometimes in a PR [payroll] check. Most recently it's been through PR.
- *Faster turnaround* between submission of the travel and expense voucher and approval. It used to be faster, but now I understand it goes to an auditor and is much slower.
- *Eliminate paper, make online availability from home,* have help boxes for the various areas that need to be filled out citing policies or procedures to help with the process. Require employees to keep receipts, audit occasionally. The approval process should really be the accountability portion of the process. If the approver is not accountable, perhaps they should not be in that position.
- Since these forms are modified by each affiliate, I have run into problems where I work for one affiliate but my office is at another, so when I grab the form, payroll tends to give grief because the affiliate has modified it or it is not current. Why do we give the affiliate the option to modify this form? Why does payroll create forms and not post them for all to use? I find it frustrating when I am told I have not used a current form but it is the only

form at the affiliate. *Create one master form* with payroll controlling and create an online process and electronic approval process.

- Sometimes it's hard to get receipts for certain things, like taxis.
- Education should always be reimbursed so as to improve and provide good care to our patients.
- Currently I complete monthly due to the process time. I have assumed it is easier on everyone to process monthly rather than weekly—try to cut down on some of the paperwork.
- My main expense is mileage reimbursement. At one time when we were having problems with getting our mileage checks, it was supposed to have been that if you turned in your mileage request by Monday 12 noon after being paid on Thursday, the week before it would be on the next check. This has worked quite well for a long time. But the last two times I have submitted for mileage reimbursement, this has not been the case. Instead it has come on the check after, and this is 3 to 4 weeks after the mileage form has been submitted. I also liked getting the mileage reimbursement in a separate check.
- Offer more continuing education seminars.
- Move to an online entry/approval process. Receipts should be provided for items greater than $25 instead of $10 to cut down on time/paperwork associated with expense reports.
- For the people who are constantly traveling between units, it would be easier if we could go online (intranet) and had preapproval for a certain amount. This would eliminate the extra step of filling out the form, getting a signature from our clinical coordinators, then faxing to pay management. After the preapproved amount had been reached for an employee (in a month), then it would have to be sent to management for approval via e-mail.
- I thought the reimbursement process was great.
- I think the electronic thing might be a step in the right direction.
- No complaints.
- This system works fine for me. I would like to see everything done electronically.
- Higher mileage pay (gas prices are going up).
- Does this include education reimbursement? Because I was told there is no more education reimbursement, but then other departments are receiving it. It should be equal across the hospital.
- Speed. I want my money back ASAP. I am not in the business of loaning money for free.

- It would be nice to submit these forms online if possible. It would also be nice to receive the reimbursement as a direct deposit, either as a separate check or part of your paycheck.
- I normally go to my manager to fill out an expense reimbursement request usually only for mileage. I do not use it enough to be able to give more feedback.
- Eliminate the paper. However, it sounds like this is what you are striving for.
- I would like it to not be included with my paycheck. It would be better to get it separate so less tax is taken.
- All expense/travel reimbursement should be paid out on a weekly basis. This way you are not waiting 2 or 3 weeks to get reimbursed.

Data Analysis

While survey results presented opportunities for improvement, the overarching facts refuted the two myths, so the team asked the steering committee to allow them to refocus their efforts to evaluate the spending categories for possible savings. The data revealed some interesting trends:

- Spending on mileage was $1,400,000 per year with nearly $1,000,000 being incurred in the home health care unit.
- The top 100 travelers in the home health care unit accounted for 85% of the mileage.
- The $500,000 per year AP checks paid to vendors did not take advantage of credit card rebates.
- The system paid $75,000 in sales tax on purchases; due to its nonprofit status, the system is not required to pay sales tax.

Steps 6–10 Training Days 3–4

During the two-day 10-step training, the team created solutions, a To-Be design, and implementation plans to realize value.

Step 6: What Are Future State or Desired Process Attributes?

The team engaged in a breakout session designed to leverage both creative and analytical thinking to develop a To-Be design for the core process.

The *creative* exercise resulted in these To-Be design elements:

- Research revenue share possibilities and discounts; utilize tax exempt status.
- Prepare requests for proposal and requests for information for credit card vendors.

- Identify desired technologies, processes, and best practices.
- Review and improve all policies.
- Standardize to one system reimbursement policy (includes all reimbursement types).
- Brainstorm solutions for reimbursement tools/options.
- Analyze new technologies and processes.
- Identify quick wins—eliminate finance audit; nonexempt personnel should enter mileage at time clock.
- Select vendors, processes, and technologies; negotiate.
- Develop implementation plan.
- Administrative approval for travel
- Train managers and end users.
- Follow implementation plan.
- Enforce new processes, policies, and procedures.
- Leverage scorecard.

During the analytical exercise, the team reviewed the As-Is issues contained in the choke point tables and root cause diagrams, and developed To-Be Solutions for each (see Exhibit 6.1).

Step 7: What Improvement Level Is Expected—Final Goal Statement?

Based on the cumulative learning from the prior steps, the team revisited its initial goal statement and identified several new components to create significant value. The new targets also factor in benchmarks and best practices.

Initial Goal Statement (from steps 1–5) Reduce payment cycle time for employee reimbursement by 7 to 14 days in three months, which increases employee satisfaction by 40%, results in a cost savings of $75,000, allows for document tracking, and reduces the number of touch points.

The field work on steps 1–5 and breakout for step 6 enabled the team to more fully understand the issues and create a refined goal statement below.

Refined, Compound Goal Statement (through step 7) Achieve $750,000 per-annum savings from these six areas:

1. Policy savings on mileage, reimburse at 10 cents below Internal Revenue Service (IRS) rate: $212,000 annual savings
2. Sales tax savings: $75,000 annual savings

EXHIBIT 6.1 Step 6 To-Be Design Elements

As-Is Design	To-Be Design
Process—Manual	Automation
Process—Receipt threshold	Increase dollar threshold
Process—Multiple reviews	Manager review only
People—Training	Net learning/MAP training
People—Low priority	Move accountability to manager/employee
Materials—Multiple policies/forms	System level forms only
Materials—Travel agent	Retain one system travel agent
Materials/Technology	Input mileage at clock/all other reimb is AP
Technology	Increase use of P-Cards/T&E Cards
Technology	Electronic forms
Technology	T&E system
Technology	Leverage Lawson T&E program
Environment—Audit	Eliminate 100% audit-only random spot audit
Measures—Lack of	Add technology

3. Policy change for mileage audit, discontinue audits: $56,000 annual savings
4. Policy change saving rebate on current purchase card usage: $5,000 annual savings
5. Policy change around airline spend, revenue share opportunity: $2,000 annual savings
6. Commercial credit card AP payment: $400,000 annual savings

Notice that the team's scope changed significantly. It shifted away from time and expense reporting process to spending based on the facts secured during fieldwork. The earnings improvement dollar value increased tenfold from $75,000 to $750,000.

Step 8: What Should the Future Process Be (New Map)?

Based on the preceding design elements and compound goal statement, the existing process was not changed significantly. The majority of the value resulted from revised policies on mileage, payment of sales tax, and use of credit cards in place of checks. The team revised its step 4 process map to reduce the number and percentage of reports being audited.

Step 9: What Are the Barriers to Improvement? Countermeasures?

The 10-step team completed two analytics in step 9 to deal with two change management issues: force field analysis and a stakeholder map and communications plan.

Force Field Analysis   The first exercise focused on preparation of a force field analysis. The purpose of this tool is for participants to think together about all the aspects of a desired solution. It is particularly useful for analyzing how to deploy change initiatives. A force field analysis is a structured approach to generating supports for and barriers to implementing a particular solution. The key steps in a force field analysis include:

1. Define the ideal state on the top right of the team template.
2. Prioritize driving forces of those than can be strengthened.
3. Prioritize the restraining forces that can be removed or reduced.
4. Brainstorm force field actions to enhance driving forces and/or mitigate restraining forces.

The team modified this approach by applying the first three steps to each element of its goal statement, outputs included.

1. **Ideal State.** Policy savings on mileage, reimburse at 10 cents below IRS rate: $212,000 annual savings.
   - Prioritize the driving forces of those than can be strengthened (pros):
     - Establishes a system-wide policy and reimbursement rate.
     - Establishes a standardized form.
     - Educates employee on tax process.
   - Prioritize the restraining forces that can be removed or reduced (cons):
     - Employee dissatisfaction with new rate.
     - Not electronic or automated solution.
2. **Ideal State.** Sales tax savings: $75,000 annual savings
   - Prioritize the driving forces of those than can be strengthened (pros):
     - System-wide policy that will enforce consistent usage procedures by expense category.
     - Reduce check payments to infrequent vendors.
   - Prioritize the restraining forces that can be removed or reduced (cons):
     - Vendor may not accept credit cards.

3. **Ideal State.** Policy change for mileage audit, discontinue audits: $56,000 annual savings
   - Prioritize the driving forces of those than can be strengthened (pros):
     - Increase employee satisfaction.
     - Educate and hold approver accountable.
     - Reduce touch points.
     - Reallocate audit full-time equivalent resource (soft cost).
   - Prioritize the restraining forces that can be removed or reduced (cons):
     - Potential for overpayment on miles.
     - Approver dissatisfaction from delay.
     - Not electronic or automated.
     - Miles tally put on pay management.
4. **Ideal State.** Commercial credit card AP payment: $400,000 annual savings
   - Prioritize the driving forces of those than can be strengthened (pros):
     - Gain rebate on purchases.
     - Reduce check stock.
     - Reduce postage.
   - Prioritize the restraining forces that can be removed or reduced (cons):
     - Vendor acceptance for payment.
     - Impact on pricing.

Stakeholder Map and Communications Plan   The team leveraged the force field analysis and built a stakeholder map that identified the anticipated roles each stakeholder group would play during deployment of solutions. The stakeholder roles included:

- Change sponsors
- Change originators
- Change agents responsible for deploying or implementing the changes
- Change advocates
- Change blockers
- SME informants to provide information on the change

The stakeholder map provides insights into key constituencies. From the map, the team developed a summary communications plan that contained key actions that will enable the primary elements of the To-Be solution to gain traction in the organization. The team also developed specific messages for each stakeholder group.

Step 10: What Do We Pilot? Results? What Is the Full Implementation Plan?

The team developed an action plan that contained over 30 specific steps in three categories:

1. Quick wins that could be deployed inside the team's 12-week life cycle
2. A pilot program to test changes and prepare for full implementation
3. To-Be changes that would be handed off to the process owner after the 12-week team cycle

Improve Performance

The team identified financial opportunities of $750,000 per annum savings ($3,750,000 over five years) from six areas:

1. Policy savings on mileage, reimburse at 10 cents below IRS rate: $212,000 annual savings
2. Sales tax savings: $75,000 annual savings
3. Policy change for mileage audit, discontinue audits: $56,000 annual savings
4. Policy change saving rebate on current purchase card usage: $5,000 annual savings
5. Policy change around airline spend, revenue share opportunity: $2,000 annual savings
6. Commercial credit card AP payment: $400,000 annual savings

All great things are simple, and many can be expressed in single words: freedom, justice, honor, duty, mercy, hope.

—Winston Churchill

FINANCE: FINANCIAL AND MANAGEMENT REPORTING 10-STEP TEAM CASE STUDY, *STREAMLINE INFORMATION*

Strategic Context

The financial and management reporting team aligned with Strategic Objective E: Operational excellence. The CFO's intent was to reduce complexity, improve information value, and reduce cycle time to provide information to managers to improve decision making.

This case study consists of these sections:

- **Steps 1–5 Training** encompasses working papers and content developed during the first two-day training team breakout sessions.
- **Steps 1–5 Fieldwork** shares key findings primarily from voice-of-customer surveys, data review, and analytics.
- **Steps 6–10 Training** consists of working papers and content developed during the second two-day training breakout sessions.
- **Improve performance** shares the financial and nonfinancial team findings to improve performance.

Steps 1–5 Training Days 1–2

Step 1: Have We Identified the Right Areas of Focus?

Since teams (by design) consisted of representatives from different functions that possessed varied understanding of the current process, step 1 focused the team to establish a baseline or common understanding of the current situation.

Customer Segments and Requirements   Since the team had only 12 weeks to establish and complete its goals, it carefully selected its primary customers. In light of the strategic context provided, the team focused on two primary customer groups: departmental managers and directors; and executives, administrators, and board of directors.

The team brainstormed customer requirements, prioritized them through voting, and drafted the Five Ups charts for each customer group.

The first customer group consisted of departmental managers and directors. Their primary requirements included: (1) percentage not trained, (2) percentage lagging information, (3) irrelevant information, (4) nonstandardized reports, and (5) number of sources.

The second customer group consisted of executives, administrators, and board of directors. Their primary requirements included: (1) cycle time, (2) nonstandard core reports, (3) number of reports and pages, (4) detail provided, and (5) percentage of time on non-value-added activities.

Based on experience, the team estimated As-Is and To-Be targets for each requirement.

Causes of Issues   The team brainstormed causes of issues for the two customer segments. For the first customer segment of departmental managers and directors, the issues were ranked; items 1 to 5 received the top number of votes for being the most impactful:

1. Easy access to systems/data
2. Lag time
3. Number of source systems
4. Lack of thresholds
5. Clearly defined expectations
6. Lack of ongoing training
7. Combined cost centers
8. Overtime report before it happens
9. Accountability
10. Appropriateness of variance questioning
11. Communication

For the second customer segment of executives/administrators/board of directors, the issues also were ranked; items 1 to 5 received the top number of votes:

1. Too much detail
2. Non-value-added reporting
3. Timeliness
4. Lack of standardization
5. Excessive reporting
6. Undefined needs/demand
7. Useless information
8. Manual processes
9. Communication
10. Adapting to needs
11. Different levels of expectations
12. Support from administration
13. Leading indicators

Data Sets. The team identified key data sets to better understand the As-Is situation and avoid basing discussions on anecdotes. Data sets would provide insights and facts to better analyze and validate and refine the goal statement. Data sets also provided the basis to refine and adjust the scope of the project. The team determined that the next data sets would be useful to gather during the ensuing four weeks of fieldwork.

- Catalog all reports.
- Count the pages of all reports.
- Review and identify similarities or common data sets by customer segment.
- Review and identify unique or different data sets by customer segment.

During the next set of activities, a common understanding of the background on the issue being addressed and a problem statement and a preliminary goal statement were drafted.

Background   The background to this topic consisted of multiple key points:

- Multiple reporting for various customers
- Not currently considered world-class reporting or using benchmarking
- Varied levels of detail
- Varied demands based on user requests
- Multisource systems are not user friendly
- Unclear and unrealistic expectations

The team's preliminary problem statement identified several components:

- High volume of reporting
- Producing non-value-added reports, not used for decision making
- Lack of standardized core reporting
- Inappropriate levels of detail
- Long cycle time for report production
- Excessive reporting that diverts resources from value-added activities
- Shifts employee focus away from core operations

Preliminary Goal Statement
Identify opportunities to reduce cycle times and volumes using standardized financial and management reporting by February. The changes will provide time savings and eliminate non-value-added reporting. The primary goal is to meet the needs of management and administration through delivery of world-class reporting.

Step 2: What Is the Initial Goal Statement? Team Charter?

Team Roles   Team member use of roles throughout the 12-week life cycle has supported improved team dynamics and performance. The 10-step team's sponsor and team leader roles were determined prior to the start of the project. However, remaining team members volunteered for the balance of the roles; brief descriptions are provided.

- Sponsor (oversees teams, reviews work, owns results): Jeff Wagner
- Team leader (sets guidelines, goals, weekly meetings): Judi Graves
- Timekeeper (ensures deadlines are met): Ben Faulk
- Recorder (takes notes): Jason Hunt
- Scribe (makes ideas visible in meetings): Heather Wager
- Monitor (adheres to methodology): Jeramie Soderberg
- Process observer (ensures participation): Tonia VanWieren, Mike Bersani, and Randy Wyse
- Spokesperson (reports to other groups): Kari McDowell, Beau Hultquist

Code of Conduct   The team established a code of conduct to be observed during team meetings and phone calls in order to remain highly productive and meet its ambitious goals. The code of conduct incorporated cultural dimensions the team believed to be important to maintain good morale and working relationships. The code of conduct included these elements:

- Weekly meetings Tuesdays at 8:30–10:00 a.m. (Monday 6th exception).
- Attendance required.
- Agendas will be set at the end of each meeting.
- Be courteous . . . show respect.
- Obtain consensus.
- Prepare before meeting.
- Foster honesty, openness, trust (no ridicule for throwing out idea).
- Have fun.
- Clearly define goals—get agreement.
- SMEs are not team members.

These exercises were consolidated with modifications into a more complete team charter that formed a team agreement.

Team Charter

- Issue/Problem
  - High volume of detailed, nonstandard, and non-value-added reporting that results in excessive cycle time and management dissatisfaction
- Goal Statement

- Identify opportunities to reduce cycle times and volumes using standardized financial and management reporting by February. The changes will provide time savings and eliminate non-value-added reporting. The primary goal is to meet the needs of management and administration through delivery of world-class reporting.
- Constraints
  - Buy-in by management and preparers
  - Technology (multi-dimensional data base) delivery)
  - Resources to implement change
- Assumptions
  - Not delivering world-class reporting
  - Dissatisfaction with current reporting
  - Data in reports not utilized
- Team Guidelines (included in code of conduct plus these new ones)
  - Roles defined and followed
  - Decisions made by consensus
  - Define opportunities that can be used to move toward world-class reporting
- Resources (included in roles and additional SMEs not contemplated during the project planning phase)
- Preliminary Project Plan (10-step milestone level)
  - Steps 1–5 Training: Week 1
  - Steps 1–5 Fieldwork: Weeks 2–4
  - Steps 6–10 Training: Week 5
  - Steps 6–10 Fieldwork: Weeks 6–10
  - Celebration and Team Turnoff: Week 11 or 12

Step 3: What Are the Three to Five Customer Requirements? Complaints?

Voice of the Customer. The purpose of the customer survey, consistent with step 1, was to secure input from the customer segments to validate and in some cases refine key requirements, modify As-Is baselines, recalibrate To-Be performance targets, and provide valuable text responses. The team designed a VOC survey to be deployed early in fieldwork.

- Developed VOC survey for managers and directors.
  - Sent 15-question survey via internal survey tool.
  - Allowed one week for responses.

- Responses were charted and will be used in next steps for future state of management reporting.
- Developed VOC survey for financial executives.
  - Developed 9-question survey and distributed to accounting staff for face-to-face interviews.
  - Allowed 10 days for responses.
  - Responses are being collected and will be used to develop standardized, value-added financial reporting across MidMichigan Health.

Step 4: What Are the Current Process (Map) and Issues?

Since the financial and management reporting processes were so complex, the 10-step team decided to divide its process mapping exercise into two primary groups to enable more in-depth analyses:

- The primary steps associated with financial reporting in the finance department brought a clear focus on source systems and external data sets that contribute to the financial closing process. The financial statement closing process steps included consolidations, eliminations, allocations, and all the attendant approvals.
- The primary steps associated with the management reporting leverage those from the financial reporting process but also included numerous other key inputs and data warehouses. These inputs included more detailed information on key operating measures, payroll, strategic business units, productivity, income, and volume reports.

The visual rendering of the two primary processes aided the team in identifying comprehensive list of choke points factors that had been driving the issues.

The team reviewed the two process mapping and choke point outputs and prioritized them into five key groups:

1. **Volume** of reports and pages within reports
2. **Level of detail** requested or supplied within multiple reports
3. **Lack of standardization** between affiliates and reporting systems
4. **Too many systems** for managers to learn and use to retrieve all needed information
5. **No training policy** for training of new or reassigned managers

Step 5: What Are the Prioritized Choke Points, Issues, and Root Causes?

The team further analyzed the content developed in step 4 to better understand the causes of issues. The team used the fishbone diagram described earlier in this chapter. The head of the fishbone captured the problem statement, and the body of the fish (and bones) captured its root causes.

The 10-step team initially used the 6Ms fishbone model and produced this problem statement for the head of the fish: "High volume of very detailed non-value-added reporting from multiple source systems." The 6M categories and their root causes or bones of the fish were modified and are listed next.

- Machines (technology) root cause included multiple systems, lack of user training on technology, lack of daily dashboards, and lack of real-time data availability.
- Manpower (people) category root causes include lack of training, lack of empowerment, lack of manager support, and a culture of expectations to produce all the reports.
- Method (process) category root causes included too many manual processes, numerous outside inputs and interfaces, and too much detail.
- Policies and procedures category root causes included lack of standardization, lack of formal policies, no policy on reclassifications, the number of meetings using draft reports, multiple approval levels, multiple reviews for each report, irrelevant information not removed, old habits, lack of report structure, and low materiality for variance explanations.

At the conclusion of step 5, the team evaluated its performance across multiple attributes. The focus and intent of this exercise contributes to self-correcting teams that can weather challenges during their life cycle. The team voted using a scale of 1 to 5, with 5 being the highest grade, on five key factors of team performance. These included:

1. Established goals/agenda scored 4.
2. Used code of conduct and group roles scored 4.
3. Used tools/methods scored 3.
4. Freedom to participate (captured brain power) scored 5.
5. Overall meeting effectiveness scored 5.

Steps 1–5 Fieldwork

The fieldwork contained key findings that updated hypotheses developed during the two-day training and contained in the working papers. During fieldwork, the team deployed its internal customer survey and gathered significant amount of data to analyze.

Data Analysis

The 10-step team conducted an in-depth review of existing financial reports. This review revealed that the number of pages in monthly reports for affiliates ranged from a low of 6 pages to a high of 166 pages. A further stratification revealed:

- Reports for eight affiliates consisted of between 6 and 13 pages
- Reports for four affiliates consisted of between 25 and 50 pages
- Reports for the top two affiliates consisted of 82 and 166 pages

The 10-step team reviewed journal entries requested by the affiliate with the top page count (166 pages). The team discovered that 56% of the journal entries for this affiliate were for less than $5,000 and that none of the journal entries impacted overall system earnings.

Clearly the root causes contributed to wide variation in reports and a significant percentage of non-value-added steps (e.g., journal entries).

Steps 6–10 Training Days 3–4

During the two-day 10-step training, the team created solutions, a To-Be design, and implementation plans to realize value.

Step 6: What Are Future State or Desired Process Attributes?

The team engaged in a breakout session designed to leverage both creative and analytical thinking to develop a To-Be design for the core process.

The *creative* exercise resulted in these To-Be world-class reporting design elements:

- Efficiency, focus on core operations.
- Surveys with users.
- Top management support and communication to other executives and managers.

- Meet with data warehouse specialist to see software capabilities.
- Find appropriate timing to implement changes.
- Eliminate non-value-added processes and inputs.
- Quick wins, making room for change.
- Get management buy-in; utilize technology
- Narrow scope and focus on goals we can accomplish in time frame; quick wins.
- Further evaluate survey data to focus key issues.
- Stop producing reports; make drastic changes resulting in feedback.
- Find new technology for one-stop reporting tool.
- Utilize available resources.
- Benchmarking; meet with steering committee.
- Staff and management incentives for change (scorecards); training incentives for manager reporting.
- Changing mind-sets, culture.
- Change to dashboard, PDF-based files, real-time information.
- Communicate after implementation to evaluate process.
- Let go of the old and embrace the new formats.
- Implement change.
- Standardization; fit old valued information into new format.

The *analytical, structured* exercise resulted in several To-Be process design elements:

- Process
  - Daily interfaces for revenue
  - System prompting review for managers
  - Standardized financial process and reports
  - Fewer manual journal entries
  - Exception-based detail reporting
  - Process to train new managers on manager reporting tool
  - Timeline approval process
- Policies and Procedures
  - Formalized policies for future changes and status quo
  - Threshold policy with criteria for determining accounting system entries and adjustments
- Technology
  - One-stop manager reporting tool
  - Flexible /user-friendly tool

- ■ Real-time information
- ■ Executive use of technology for variance analysis
- ■ Manage from scorecards, not financial statements
- ■ People and Skills
  - ■ Training for managers
  - ■ Executive buy-in and follow-through for changes
  - ■ Accountability at appropriate place
  - ■ Empowerment of staff
- ■ Partners and Vendors
  - ■ Remote hosting
  - ■ More input from internal IT
  - ■ Solutions from software vendors

The 10-step team merged these two exercise outputs to define a comprehensive To-Be solution.

Step 7: What Improvement Level Is Expected—Final Goal Statement?

Based on the cumulative learning from the prior steps, the team revisited its initial goal statement and identified several new components to create significant value. The new targets also factor in benchmarks and best practices.

Preliminary Goal Statement from steps 1–5   Identify opportunities to reduce cycle times and volumes using standardized financial and management reporting by February. The changes will provide time savings and eliminate non-value-added reporting. The primary goal is to meet the needs of management and administration through delivery of world-class reporting.

Please notice the clarity and separation of financial and management reporting into two separate sets of goals.

Goal Statement Financial Reporting   Reduce the number of pages in monthly financial reports by 35%, and reduce total number of reports generated by 25% using standardized financial reporting by June. The changes will provide time savings and create value-added reporting that will facilitate informed decision making by administration through delivery of world-class reporting.

Goal Statement Management Reporting   Identify opportunities to increase manager use of reporting tool by 25% using training on a one-stop user-friendly tool (queries) and providing value-added information over the next 12 months. The changes will eliminate non-value-added/duplicate reporting, saving $300,000 per year through terminating a redundant software license. The primary goal is to meet the critical needs of management through delivery of world-class reporting.

Step 8: What Should the Future Process Be (New Map)?

The 10-step team incorporated design elements from step 6 and the refined goal statement elements from step 7 to design new reporting processes. The new process maps observed these key parameters:

- Five standardized pages, focus on key indicators
- Condensed financial reports
- Self-service through portal
- Portal to have drill-down capabilities and variance alerts
- Eliminated affiliate approval meetings and individual issuance
- Cycle time and accountability deadlines
- Daily revenue interfaces

Step 9: What Are the Barriers to Improvement? Countermeasures?

The 10-step team completed two analytics in step 9 to deal with change management issues: force field analysis and a stakeholder map and communications plan.

Force Field Analysis   The first exercise focused on preparation of a force field analysis. The purpose of this tool is for participants to think together about all the aspects of a desired solution. It is particularly useful for analyzing how to deploy change initiatives. A force field analysis is a structured approach to generating supports for and barriers to implementing a particular solution. The key steps in a force field analysis include:

1. Define the ideal state on the top right of the template.
2. Prioritize driving forces of those than can be strengthened.
3. Prioritize the restraining forces that can be removed or reduced.
4. Brainstorm force field actions to enhance driving forces and/or mitigate restraining forces.

The team followed the four steps, outputs included.

1. **Ideal State.** Value-added strategic reporting
2. Driving forces that can be strengthened included:
   - Health care environmental and government changes

- New technology
- Standardization of reports
- Customer demand for one-stop reporting
- Simplification of general ledger (GL) structure
- Optimize financial staff resources

3. Restraining forces that can be removed or reduced included:
   - Culture (old habits, perceived needs)
   - User training, new technology limitations
   - Variation by affiliate; user expectations
   - IT capabilities
   - Timing, resources
   - Detailed requests due to unclear expectations

4. Brainstorm force field actions to enhance driving forces and/or mitigate restraining forces presented with team votes in parentheses:
   - Eliminate level of detail in reports (8).
   - Executive and management buy-in for new standardized format (4).
   - Discover capabilities and limitations of new tech (2).
   - Eliminate issuance of financial packets (2).
   - Establish policies for clearly defined expectations of financial services and operational managers (2).
   - Implementation training on new report structure (1).
   - Incentives (1).
   - User training on new tech.
   - Look at current software capabilities to use for dashboard.
   - Initiate communication with previous budget team for GL changes to be completed.
   - Use of experts on new tech.
   - Top-down ambassadors for reporting change.
   - Support team to address concerns.
   - Discover IT capabilities for internal dashboard.

Stakeholder Map and Communications Plan   Building on the force field analysis, the team built a stakeholder map that identified the anticipated roles people would play during deployment of solutions. The roles included:

- Change sponsors.
- Change originators.
- Change agents responsible for deploying or implementing the changes.
- Change advocates.

- Change blockers.
- SME informants to provide information on the change.

The stakeholder map provides insights into key constituencies. From the map, the team developed a summary communications plan that contained key actions that will enable the primary elements of the To-Be solution to gain traction in the organization. The team also developed specific messages for each stakeholder group.

- Steering committee: Ambassador request.
- CPM team: Scorecard models by affiliate and scorecard software.
- Financial analysis and planning: Questions related to the 10-step initiative.
- Data warehouse and reporting representative: Product capabilities.
- IT: Lawson dashboards.
- MidMichigan Health managers: Training plan for reporting tool.
- MidMichigan Health executives: Standardized reporting.

Step 10: What Do We Pilot? Results? What Is the Full Implementation Plan?

The team developed an action plan that contained over 30 specific steps in three categories:

1. Quick wins that could be deployed inside the team's 12-week life cycle
2. A pilot program to test changes and prepare for full implementation
3. To-Be changes that would be handed off to the process owner after the 12-week team cycle

Three quick wins, approved by the 10-step steering committee, enabled the team to demonstrate value prior to pilot or full implementation of the To-Be solutions.

Quick Win 1: Draft Policy for Materiality Limits on Transactions

- **Purpose.** This policy establishes the standards and procedures for ensuring that the MidMichigan Health and related affiliates account for intercompany and interdepartmental transactions in compliance with management's objectives. The purpose for intercompany accounting is to reasonably allocate assets, liabilities, revenues, and expenses to the appropriate legal entity in relation to the material economic benefits and obligations associated with the operational activity incurred.

- **Definitions.**
    - Intercompany transactions: Transactions occurring between two or more affiliates
    - Interdepartmental transactions: Transactions occurring between two or more departments of the same affiliate
- **Procedures.** These procedures pertain to all intercompany and interdepartmental transactions throughout MidMichigan Health. For purposes of this policy, transactions include allocations, chargebacks (for products and/or services), adjustments, and reclassifications.
    1. The minimum dollar threshold for each intercompany or interdepartmental request must total at least $5,000 per month or $60,000 annually unless legally required (i.e., risk management, IRS, or Medicare reimbursement requirements).
        - In the case of a request that would normally be a budgeted allocation, the threshold is $100,000 annually to comply with the budget policy.
        - Transactions may not be combined solely to meet the minimum dollar threshold.
    2. It is the responsibility of the manager initiating the request to obtain all required information including GL account numbers to complete the entire transaction.
    3. All intercompany entries must be entered into the accounting system by the end of normal business hours on Workday 3. No intercompany entries will be permitted after Workday 3. Any entries booked after Workday 3 resulting in an intercompany out-of-balance situation will be reversed by corporate accounting.
    4. Any exceptions to these procedures must be approved by MidMichigan Health's CFO prior to being entered into the accounting system.

Quick Win 2: Standard Financial Report Elements for a Major Hospital Affiliate
The team standardized data sets to streamline reports. An example report includes eight elements:

1. Provider financial statement
2. Provider financial profile
3. Provider volume graphs
4. GL detail (selected accounts)
5. Procurement detail (selected accounts)
6. Gross revenue graphs
7. Revenue and volumes by current procedural terminology (CPT)
8. Departmental responsibility reports

Quick Win 3: Internal and External Financial Reporting Classification Table
To standardize and simplify preparation and understanding of internal and external financial reports consisting of balance sheets and income statements, the team devised a mapping table of common data elements. The table standardized all internal descriptions of accounts to the external terminology so the terms were consistent. For instance, if the income statement item is "Self-Insurance Income," and it was formerly called "Other Operating Income" for internal reporting and "Investment Income" for external reporting, it would be called "Investment Income" for both internal and external reporting going forward (see Exhibit 6.2).

EXHIBIT 6.2 Internal and External Financial Reporting Classification Table

Balance Sheet	Internal Classification	External Classification
Trading securities	Self-insurance and other	Trading securities
Market valuation	Market valuation allowance	Same balance sheet line as related asset
		Current portion of assets limited as to use
		Investments
		Assets limited or restricted as to use, non current
		Capital acquisition
		Self-insurance, deferred compensation, and other
Income Statement		
Medicaid assessment fee	Provision for contractual	Fees
Health plan funding	Provision for contractual	Purchased services and other
Self-insurance income	Other operating income	Investment income
Amortization	Fees	Depreciation and amortization
Expense and income	Expense offset against income to have zero impact on both lines	Proper expense category and other operating income

Balance Sheet Income Statement	Internal Classification	External Classification
Restricted released for operations	Release (revenue) never booked, hits restricted funds directly	Net assets released from restrictions for operations (revenue)
	Expense never booked, hits restricted funds directly	Expense—supplies, but could be other expense line
Gain/loss on disposal of capital assets	Depreciation	Purchased services and other

Improve Performance

The team identified financial opportunities of $300,000 per annum savings through termination of software licenses ($1,500,000 over five years). The nonfinancial opportunities are described next.

Financial Reporting
■ Reduce the number of pages in monthly financial reports by 35%.
■ Reduce total number of reports generated by 25% using standardized financial reporting.

Management Reporting
■ Increase manager use of reporting tool by 25%.
■ Meet the critical needs of management through delivery of world-class reporting.

   Perfection is not attainable, but if we chase perfection we can catch excellence.

   —**Vince Lombardi**

HUMAN RESOURCES: NEW EMPLOYEE REQUISITION 10-STEP TEAM CASE STUDY, *SIMPLIFY HIRING*

I believe the CPM training provided our staff with the tools and clarity to really focus on results/outcomes that aligned with our system strategic goals and objectives. Once the team was selected and team roles were identified, the team followed the code of conduct and quickly gathered a tremendous amount of information which was then used to make decisions on our new process. The 12-week deadline at first seemed impossible but the team bonded quickly and came to a solution that we knew would create efficiencies and cost/time savings for our facility.

—Lorie Mault, MSA, PHR, Director of
Labor Relations, (team leader)

Strategic Context

The human resource (HR) requisition team aligned with MidMichigan Health system Strategic Objective E: Operational excellence. The existing new employee requisition processes varied greatly by affiliate (entity), contained many manual steps, and caused long delays and missed opportunities to interview desired candidates.

The case study consists of these sections:

- **Steps 1–5 Training** encompasses working papers and content developed during the first two-day training team breakout sessions.
- **Steps 1–5 Fieldwork** shares key findings primarily from voice-of-customer surveys, data review, and analytics.
- **Steps 6–10 Training** consists of working papers and content developed during the second two-day training breakout sessions.
- **Improve performance** shares the financial and nonfinancial team findings to improve performance.

Steps 1–5 Training Days 1–2

Step 1: Have We Identified the Right Areas of Focus?

Since teams (by design) consisted of representatives from different functions that possessed varied understanding of the current process, step 1 focused the team to establish a baseline or common understanding of the current situation. The team consisted of HR representatives, internal department hiring managers, and SMEs from finance and IT.

Customer Segments and Requirements The team identified three primary customer segments: hiring managers, HR department employees, and applicants for positions.

Internal customer requirements of hiring managers included:

1. Decrease cycle time.
2. Standardize the request form.
3. Define roles of the pre-employment process.
4. Reduce the number of approval levels for a new hire.

The HR department employee requirements included:

1. Standardize processes and forms.
2. Reduce rework and error rates.
3. Reduce keying into multiple systems.
4. Decrease manager response time on applicants.

Customer segment requirements for applicants included:

1. Decrease cycle time.
2. Communications to applicants.
3. Standardized application form.

Due to the complexity of the process and limited training breakout time, the team agreed to set the As-Is and To-Be measurements for each requirement at a later team meeting.

Causes of Issues   The team brainstormed causes of customer problems and felt it would be important to capture them by customer segment.

Hiring Manager
- Lengthy process with multiple steps, which adds to overtime and to loss of productive time
- Confusing process; is not clear; missing information to fill out form due to:
  - Lack of training to use the system
  - Additional information needed
  - Multiple versions in both paper and electronic form
- Process includes multiple approval levels; many steps (can be multiple weeks for approval); for example:
  - One affiliate requires approvals by the financial director and the vice president
  - Another affiliate requires approvals from an administrative or operations committee
- Length of postings

- Confusion with employees who hold more than one position
- Multiple versions of paper and electronic forms
- Confusion and variation in who performs pre-employment screening, scheduling orientation, checking references, scheduling interviews (multiple rounds), making verbal offers with pay rate, and generating status change forms

Human Resources

- Receiving complete information (i.e., shift, posting preferences)
- Receiving requirements that did not go through the appropriate approval processes
- Received multiple ways (paper versus electronic)
- Keyed into multiple systems (position manager versus electronic submittal system developed for some but not all affiliates)
- Communication to managers over approval
- Who has access to enter requirements into Lawson system:
  - Creating defects
  - Budget issues create new forms, budget, headcount, and justifications
- Inconsistent forms; being able to *free type* allows for inconsistent information
- Status forms used consistently
- Managers not updating applicants in HR information system called position manager in a timely fashion
- Multiple keying of information into multiple databases

Applicants

- Full external hire application versus internal application (limited information to manager on applicant)
- Difficulty with application (i.e., pop-up blocker using Web-based forms)
- Manager may already have applicant in mind
- To change bid hours, employee must create another post (status change)
- Excessive wait time to hear on status
- Confirmation of receipt of application
- Communication vague from position manager

Data Sets. The team identified key data sets to better understand the As-Is situation and avoid basing their discussions on anecdotes. The data sets would provide insights and facts to better analyze and validate and refine the goal statements. Data sets also provided the basis for refined project scope, goals, and selection of SMEs. The team determined that these data sets would be useful to gather to during the next four weeks of fieldwork:

- Cycle time by affiliate for internal hires
- Cycle time by affiliate for external hires
- Third-party benchmark percentiles for cycle time for internal hires
- Third-party benchmark percentiles for cycle time for external hires
- Number of minutes consumed per requisition by hiring managers
- Number of minutes consumed per requisition by HR employee
- Cost per employee requisition

Next the team defined the background, preliminary problem statement, and preliminary goal statement.

Background
- Multiple requisition forms and processes
- Inefficiencies in productive time
- Lack of leveraging technology
- Lack of communication among all users
- Perceived low satisfaction among all users

Preliminary Problem Statement
Our multiple requisition/application processes result in increased cycle time, generating rework and delayed hiring, increasing time to fill and costs.

Based on the foregoing activities, the team was positioned to establish a preliminary goal statement. As the team is only in step 1 of 10, the goal statement will be continuously refined and updated as more evidence and data becomes available.

Preliminary Goal Statement
Reduce average cycle time in the requisition and hiring process by X days by developing a standardized system approach (process, forms, and technology), resulting in increased end user satisfaction, decreased costs of $50,000, and increased service levels.

Step 2: What Is the Initial Goal Statement (Team Charter)?

Team Roles Team member use of roles throughout the 12-week cycle has supported improved team dynamics and performance. The 10-step team's sponsor and team leader roles were determined prior to the start of the project. However, remaining team members volunteered for the balance of the roles; brief descriptions are provided.

- Sponsor (oversees teams, reviews work, owns results): Mike Erickson
- Team leader (sets guidelines, goals, weekly meetings): Lorie Mault
- Timekeeper (ensures deadlines are met): Lisa Weston
- Recorder (takes notes): Kendra Huckins and Rebecca Messing
- Scribe (makes ideas visible in meetings): Kevin Isbister and Sarah Hills
- Monitor (adheres to methodology): Melanie Mickle
- Process observer (ensures participation): Tom Elsen
- Spokesperson (reports to other groups): Kari McDowell, Dave Koutz, and Michael Rogers

Code of Conduct   The team established a code of conduct to be observed during team meetings and phone calls in order to remain highly productive and meet its ambitious goals. The code of conduct incorporated cultural dimensions the team believed to be important to maintain good morale and working relationships. The code of conduct included these elements:

- No cell phones/PDAs, iPads, and so on.
- Set meeting agenda, allocate time.
- SMEs are not team members.
- Ensure timeliness and attendance (calendar integrity—start/stop on time).
- Involve everyone (round robin).
- One idea at a time (no flops).
- No judgment of other's ideas (brainstorm).
- Obtain consensus.
- Prepare before meeting.
- Clearly define goals—get agreement.
- Define roles.
- Define tool to meet objective.
- Be courteous . . . show respect.
- No side discussions.
- Take turns talking.
- Foster honesty, openness, trust (no ridicule for throwing out idea).
- Documents will be saved on shared drive in lieu of e-mailing.
- Two-knock rule.
- Have fun.

These exercises were consolidated with modifications into a more complete team charter that formed a team agreement.

Team Charter
- Issue/Problem
  - Our multiple requisition/application processes result in increased cycle time, generating rework and delayed hiring, increasing time to fill and costs.
- Goal Statement
  - Reduce average cycle time in the requisition and hiring process by X days, by developing an efficient, effective, and standardized system approach (process/ forms/ technology) by April 18, 2011, resulting in increased end user satisfaction, decreased costs of $50,000, and increased service levels to achieve MidMichigan Health's levels of operational excellence.
- Constraints
  - Availability of quantitative data, requiring manual gathering
  - Resistance to a system process/forms/approval process
  - Limited in technology and technology integration
- Assumptions
  - Everyone is dissatisfied with the process.
  - Too many touches/highly manual.
  - Steering committee will approve and support team's recommendations.
  - Increase service levels and efficiencies without reducing full-time equivalents.
- Team Guidelines (see Code of Conduct)
- Resources (included in roles and SMEs not contemplated during the project planning phase)
- Preliminary Project Plan (10-step milestone level)
  - Steps 1–5 Training: Week 1
  - Steps 1–5 Fieldwork: Weeks 2–4
  - Steps 6–10 Training: Week 5
  - Steps 6–10 Fieldwork: Weeks 6–10
  - Celebration and Team Turnoff: Week 11 or 12

Step 3: What Are Three to Five Customer Requirements?

Voice of the Customer. The purpose of the customer survey, consistent with step 1, was to secure input from the customer segments to validate and in some cases refine key requirements, modify As-Is baselines, recalibrate To-Be performance targets, and provide valuable text responses. The team designed a VOC survey to be deployed early in fieldwork. The draft survey is presented next.

Step 4: What Are the Current Process (Map) and Issues?

The 10-step team was very efficient during its process mapping breakout session. It focused and rapidly developed five process maps for the HR requisition process for all four major medical centers and one for home health care. The visual review of the maps revealed and validated the issues and causes noted in earlier steps.

With limited time remaining in the breakout session, the 10-step team started to catalog the choke points for the first process map's first five steps. This brief analysis revealed these choke points:

- Process Map 1 Step 1
  - Budget limitations
  - Timeliness
  - Budget freeze
  - Inconsistencies between affiliates/department
- Process Map 1 Step 2
  - Multiple forms/multiple formats
  - Training
  - Locating form
  - Process flow of forms

- Which is your primary affiliate (locations listed)?
- Please best describe your role (hiring manager, HR, or other).
- How would you rate the following on a 1–5 scale:
  - Timeliness of the approval process
  - Number of required approvals
  - Overall satisfaction with the process
  - Training on how to use the forms correctly
  - Current prescreening process
  - Timeliness of the interview process
  - Training on how to use position manager

- Interview scheduling process
- Timeliness of background checks (HR only)
- Reference check process
- Making the offer process
- Ease in completing and submitting the form
- Access to the appropriate forms

- Process Map 1 Step 3
  - Multiple touches
  - Multiple tracking
  - Inconsistent/Multiple processes for benchmarking
  - Benchmarking not comprehensive
  - Back door approval
- Process Map 1 Step 4
  - Multiple touches

The team quickly realized that it would take a significant effort to fully understand the As-Is processes at all locations. This activity was placed on the first team meeting agenda for fieldwork in week 2.

Step 5: What Are the Prioritized Choke Points, Issues, and Root Causes?

The team further analyzed the content developed in step 4 to better understand the causes of issues. The team used the fishbone diagram described earlier in this chapter.

The 10-step team initially produced this problem statement for the head of the fish: "Our multiple requisition/application processes result in increased cycle time, generating rework and delayed hiring, increasing time to fill and costs."

The 8Ps and IT fishbone model was used. Categories of root causes or bones of the fish are described next.

- The product category root cause included multiple forms, multiple formats, and inconsistencies of manual and electronic versions.
- Process category root causes included lack of timeliness, lack of one unified process across the system, poor training, and multi-touch multi-tracking inconsistencies.

- People and skills category root causes included lack of training and inconsistencies in training.
- Pricing or costs category root cause included budget limitations and hiring freezes in some locations.
- Policy category root causes included inconsistent training and inconsistencies in policies system-wide.
- Procedure category root causes included timeliness inconsistencies, lack of systemwide procedures across affiliates and within affiliates, inconsistent use of benchmarking of process performance, and failure to follow procedures in limited cases.
- Place or location category root causes included lack of clarity about where to access forms, policies, approvals, and other aspects of the process.
- Technology category included two root causes of using different hiring software and pop-up blockers preventing use of applications.

At the conclusion of step 5, the team evaluated its performance across multiple attributes. The focus and intent of this exercise contributes to self-correcting teams that can weather challenges during their life cycle. The team voted using a 1–5 scale, with 5 being the highest grade, on five key factors of team performance. These included:

1. Established goals/agenda scored 4.
2. Used code of conduct and group roles scored 4.
3. Used tools/methods scored 3.
4. Freedom to participate (captured brain power) scored 4.
5. Overall meeting effectiveness scored 5.

Steps 1–5 Fieldwork

The fieldwork contained key findings that updated hypotheses developed during the two-day training and contained in the working papers. During fieldwork, the team deployed its internal customer (traveler) survey and gathered significant data that it analyzed.

Survey Results

- Which is your primary affiliate (locations listed)?
  - The team received replies from across the system with adequate representation from the affiliates with the highest number of requisitions.

- Please best describe your role (hiring manager, HR, or other).
  - 71% hiring managers, 14% HR, 15% other
- How would you rate the *timeliness* of the approval process (1–5 scale)?
  - Average rating score of 2.84
  - Rating score of 1 (lowest score): 11%; 2: 28%; 3: 26%; 4: 24%; 5 (highest score): 5%; not applicable: 6%
- What is the number of required *approvals*? (1–5)
  - Average rating score of 3.1 approvals per requisition
  - Rating score of 1: 8%; 2: 18%; 3: 30%; 4: 27%; 5: 8%; not applicable: 9%
- What is your *overall satisfaction* with the process (1–5 scale)?
  - Average rating score of 3.06
  - Rating score of 1 (lowest score): 8%; 2: 18%; 3: 35%: 4: 32%; 5 (highest score): 4%; not applicable: 3%
- How would you rate *training* on how to use the forms correctly (1–5)?
  - Average rating score of 3.20
  - Rating score of 1 (lowest score): 4%; 2: 22%; 3: 30%; 4: 25%; 5 (highest score): 12%; not applicable: 7%
- Current prescreening process: scored 3.22
- Timeliness of the interview process: 3.31
- Training on how to use position manager: 3.33
- Interview scheduling process: 3.36
- Timeliness of background checks (HR only): 3.37
- Reference check process: 3.39
- Making the offer process: 3.52
- Ease in completing and submitting the form: 3.54
- Access to the appropriate forms: 3.84

The 10-step team validated many of its earlier hypotheses on the timeliness, number of approvals, and overall satisfaction with the process. The team was surprised by much higher scores on the ease of completing and submitting forms and access to the appropriate forms.

Data Analyses The review of cycle times for internal and external hires against benchmarks revealed wide variations.

Internal Hires
- The industry benchmark average internal time to start in the top 25th percentile was 38 days; MidMichigan Health ranged from a low of 5 days to a high of 58 days.

- The five primary MidMichigan Health locations varied significantly:
  - Affiliate 1: average of 13.4 days
  - Affiliate 2: average of 17.4 days
  - Affiliate 3: average of 34.4 days
  - Affiliate 4: average of 43.4 days
  - Affiliate 5: average of 58.0 days

External Hires
- The industry benchmark average external hire time to start in the top 25th percentile was 48 days; MidMichigan Health ranged from a low of 1 day to a high of 135 days.
- The five primary MidMichigan Health locations varied significantly:
  - Affiliate 1: average of 37.1 days
  - Affiliate 2: average of 73.5 days
  - Affiliate 3: average of 50.7 days
  - Affiliate 4: average of 57.0 days
  - Affiliate 5: average of 49.6 days

Observations
Internal Hires
- The data by location provided the clearest evidence of variation in performance.
- Three of the five affiliates were performing at 25th-percentile levels.
- The data by location provided potential for best practice identification (from better performing locations) for To-Be designs during Days 3–4 training.

External Hires
- The data by location provided a clear indication of the wide variation in performance.
- One of the five affiliates was performing at 25th-percentile levels.
- The data by location provided limited potential for best practice identification (from the higher performing location) for To-Be designs during Days 3–4 training.

Steps 6–10 Training Days 3–4

During the two-day 10-step training, the team created solutions, a To-Be design, and implementation plans to realize value.

Step 6: What Are Future State or Desired Process Attributes?

The team engaged in a breakout session designed to leverage both creative and analytical thinking to develop a To-Be design for the core process.

The *creative* exercise resulted in these To-Be design elements:

- Collect data, measure current state
- Identify agree-on benchmark targets
- Planning future state and training for pilot
- Quick wins (requisitions)
- Pilot changes/integration/approval process/training
- Survey users and review benchmarks
- Plan for full roll-out
- Training staff
- Implement system-wide, culture change, ongoing benchmarks

The analytical, structured exercise reviewed the As-Is issues contained in the choke point tables and root cause diagrams. For each issue, the team developed To-Be solutions:

- Process, Policy, and Procedure
  - Standardize "system" process.
  - Streamline requirements of what requires approval beyond the department manager.
  - Minimize approval interactions among leadership.
  - Identify posting time frame by employee groups.
  - Interview process.
  - Start all new employees on Mondays.
- People and Skills
  - Training manager and HR approvers.
  - Accountability to follow process and meet benchmarks.
  - Reallocation of skills.
- Place and Location
  - Provide wireless, Wi-Fi infrastructure.
- Partner and Vendor
  - Position manager
  - HR systems vendor (Lawson)
  - Document imaging
  - Screening agency

- Technology
  - Standardized electronic requisition and status form and tracking capability
  - Integrated systems
  - Virtual meeting
  - Computers
  - Smart phones
  - iPads
  - Reference, background checks agency
  - Compensation service agreement and commitment

The 10-step team combined these two exercise outputs to define a comprehensive To-Be solution.

Step 7: What Improvement Level Is Expected—Final Goal Statement?

Based on the cumulative learning from the prior steps, the team revisited its initial goal statement and identified several new components to create significant value. The new targets also factor in benchmarks and best practices.

Preliminary Goal Statement   Reduce average cycle time in the requisition and hiring process by X days by developing a standardized system approach (process/forms/technology), resulting in increased end user satisfaction, decreased costs of $50,000, and increase service levels.

Revised Goal Statement   Reduce average cycle time in the requisition and hiring process from 45 to 38 days (25th-percentile benchmark) by developing a plan for an efficient, effective, and standardized system approach by week 12.

The process will result in decreased annual requisition processing and staff replacement cost savings for a total first-year net savings of $109,000 while increasing service levels to achieve MidMichigan Health's levels of operational excellence. Additional subsequent annual savings total $109,000 (five-year total savings $545,000).

Step 8: What Should the Future Process Be (New Map)?

The 10-step team incorporated the design elements from step 6 and the refined goal statement parameters from step 7 to design new processes. The new e-requisition process also reflected best practices for internal and external hires identified internally from high-performing affiliates.

Step 9: What Are the Barriers to Improvement? Countermeasures?

The 10-step team completed two analytics in step 9 to deal with change management issues: (1) force field analysis and (2) a stakeholder map and communications plan.

Force Field Analysis   The first exercise focused on preparation of a force field analysis. The purpose of this tool is for participants to think together about all the aspects of a desired solution. It is particularly useful for analyzing how to deploy change initiatives. A force field analysis is a structured approach to generating supports for and barriers to implementing a particular solution. The key steps in a force field analysis include:

1. Define the ideal state on the top right of the template.
2. Prioritize driving forces of those than can be strengthened.
3. Prioritize the restraining forces that can be removed or reduced.
4. Brainstorm force field actions to enhance driving forces and/or mitigate restraining forces.

The team followed the four steps, outputs included:

1. **Ideal State.** Top 25th-percentile e-requisition process (from external benchmarking service)
2. Driving forces that can be strengthened included:
   - One system request process
   - Shared services concept
   - Full utilization/maximization of technology we already have
   - System policies
   - Resources—strategies
   - Cost savings
3. Restraining forces that can be removed or reduced included:
   - Technology—integration of position manager module and Lawson system
   - Cost of integration
   - Manager buy-in to change in process step ownership
   - Approving organizations buy-in

- Accountability (lack of)
- Education and training (lack of or just in time)
- Existing contracts
- Resources, mostly time
- Hard and soft costs and validation

4. Brainstorm force field actions to enhance driving forces and/or mitigate restraining forces presented:
   - Education—process
   - Education—technology
   - Buy-in by users
   - Accountability—scorecard/job performance reviews (manager expectations)
   - System leadership buy-in
   - Policy redesign
   - Metrics and return on investment
   - Renegotiate contracts
   - Purchase integration for two IT systems (position manager and Lawson)

Stakeholder Map and Communications Plan Building on the force field analysis, the team built a stakeholder map that identified the anticipated roles people would play during solution deployment. The roles included:

- Change sponsors
- Change originators
- Change agents responsible for deploying or implementing the changes
- Change advocates
- Change blockers
- SME informants to provide information on the change

The stakeholder map provides insights into key constituencies. From the map, the team developed a summary communications plan that contained key actions that will enable the primary elements of the To-Be solution to gain traction in the organization. The team also developed specific messages for each stakeholder group.

- Hiring managers: Change in process and increase in accountability
- HR staff: Change in process, policies, and procedures; revisions and accountabilities
- Education: Training needs—new process

- System leaders: Support, buy in to change process
- CPM steering committee: Support and initial investment to secure savings
- Unions: Change in contract, posting process
- Other departments: Utilize technology and accountability

Step 10: What Do We Pilot? Results? What Is the Full Implementation Plan?

The team developed an action plan that contained over 25 action items or steps broken down into three categories:

1. Quick wins that could be deployed inside the team's 12-week life cycle
2. A pilot program to test changes and prepare for full implementation
3. To-Be changes that would be handed off to the process owner after the 12-week team cycle

Quick Wins   Quick wins approved by the 10-step Steering Committee during the 12 weeks enabled the team to demonstrate value prior to pilot or full implementation of the To-Be Solutions. The quick wins included:

- E-requisition form completion
- Funding for technology and education
- New hire to change processes and identify departmental needs
- HR approved the new E-requisition form
- Deployed universal reference checks and education verification on all hard-to-recruit and some nursing positions
- Leveraged ranking system for high-level positions (for all positions)

The 10-step team rated itself after each team meeting. Doing so enabled the team to identify and celebrate successes and to highlight those aspects of teamwork that could be improved. The team self-scored 5 out of 5 (the highest score) during its final meeting for each of these elements:

1. Established goals/agenda
2. Used code of conduct group roles
3. Used tools/methods
4. Freedom to participate
5. Meeting effectiveness

Improve Performance

The team identified financial first-year savings of $109,000; additional subsequent annual savings total $153,235 (five-year total savings $722,940). The nonfinancial opportunities are:

- Reduce average cycle time in the requisition and hiring process from 45 to 38 days (25th-percentile benchmark).
- Increased service levels.

I always thought that record would stand until it was broken.

—Yogi Berra

SUPPLY CHAIN MANAGEMENT: NEW PRODUCT REQUISITION 10-STEP CASE STUDY, *MANAGE INNOVATION*

Upon reviewing the process for requesting a new product for use in the OR [operating room], there was an average of nearly 12 months from time of request to a decision to stock. Our current system was broken to the point that the physicians either gave up or found other ways of getting products into the OR, sidestepping the process. Shortening the decision process and providing some guidance for the clinical supervisors for product review has resulted in under a 6-week turnaround time. A more robust review is now completed, answers back to physicians are now timely, and therefore less product is getting into the OR prior to a formal review. This has resulted in significant savings to the organization.

—Joan Herbert, Strategic Business Unit Director
(team leader)

Strategic Context

The new products team aligned with MidMichigan Health system Strategic Objective E: Operational excellence. The existing processes varied greatly by affiliate (entity), contained many manual steps, and caused long delays and missed opportunities to deploy new technologies and to optimize the cost benefit of new products.

This case study consists of these sections:

- **Steps 1–5 Training** encompasses working papers and content developed during the first two-day training team breakout sessions.
- **Steps 1–5 Fieldwork** shares key findings primarily from voice-of-customer surveys, data review, and analytics.

- **Steps 6–10 Training** consists of working papers and content developed during the second two-day training breakout sessions.
- **Improve performance** shares the financial and nonfinancial team findings to improve performance.

Steps 1–5 Training Days 1–2

Step 1: Have We Identified the Right Areas of Focus?

Since teams (by design) consisted of representatives from different functions that possessed varied understanding of the current process, step 1 focused the team to establish a baseline or common understanding of the current situation.

Customer Segments and Requirements   The team brainstormed the customer's requirements, prioritized them through voting, and drafted the Five Ups charts for each customer group.

The first customer group, *physicians*, had five primary requirements:

1. Reduce wait time from request of new product to approval.
2. Reduce variability of access to new products.
3. Reduce frustration with replacements (using old inventory).
4. Reduce dissatisfaction with process enforcement.
5. Reduce the lack of communication.

The team estimated As-Is and To-Be targets for each of the requirements. The team discussed the importance of a balanced set of targets that concurrently solved for multiple requirements of this process listed above.

The second customer group, *hospital staff*, also had five primary requirements:

1. Reduce the lack of communication.
2. Reduce the processing time of new requests.
3. Reduce the lack of input/knowledge into decisions.
4. Reduce inventory obsolescence.
5. Reduce the lack of product standardization.

The team estimated As-Is and To-Be targets for each of the requirements. The team discussed the importance of a balanced set of targets that concurrently solved for multiple requirements of this process listed above.

The third customer group, *patients*, had three primary requirements:

1. Reduce dissatisfaction with products.
2. Reduce patients' outmigration (leaving the system).
3. Reduce perception as an average provider.

The team estimated As-Is and To-Be targets for each of the requirements. The team discussed the importance of a balanced set of targets that concurrently solved for multiple requirements of this process listed above.

Causes of Issues   The team brainstormed a list of causes of customer problems. The team voted using a weighted voting method; the weighted voting totals are shown in parentheses:

- Approval process: too many touches, form design/understanding Pre-Anesthesia, Pre-Procedure Form (PAPPF) (38)
- Lack of standardization between affiliates and within affiliates, including physician offices (32)
- Vendor rep influence: pressure on physicians then blindsides purchasing (28)
- Rapid change in technology (19)
- Lack of communication (17)
- Reimbursement (13)
- Cost (13)
- Lack of standardization between hospital and physician offices (10)
- Forecast of needed products: how, when are items ordered, stored (9)
- Knowledge deficit of what we have versus what we don't have (5)
- Midland medical staff (OR) approval: don't meet frequently enough (2)
- Frustration between purchasing and clinical staff (2)
- Duplication (1)
- Differences in training: physicians and staff (1)
- Lack of single rep for each vendor for all affiliates (0)
- Value analysis team meeting frequency (0)
- Lack of compromise (0)
- Committed contracts (0)

Data Sets. The team identified key data sets to better understand the As-Is situation and avoid basing their discussions on anecdotes. The data sets would provide insights and facts to better analyze and validate and refine the goal statements. Data sets also provided the basis for refining or adjusting the scope of the project. The team determined that these data sets would be useful to gather to during the next four weeks of fieldwork:

- Invasive Imaging
  - Minimum total cycle time from request to approval
  - Maximum total cycle time request to approval
  - Range of total cycle time request to approval
  - Average total cycle time request to approval
- Operating Room
  - Minimum total cycle time request to approval
  - Maximum total cycle time request to approval
  - Range of total cycle time request to approval
  - Average total cycle time request to approval

Next the team defined the background, preliminary problem statement, and preliminary goal statement.

Background

- Physician and staff dissatisfaction
- Probably high-dollar implications
- Invasive imaging potential pilot—contained area versus OR
- Understanding of incremental cost of adding new items with small unit cost (patient and employee safety preventive issues)
- Extended timeline from request to response (prioritization of requests)
- Lack of communication plan
- Product evaluation process—how does it flow?
- What are the reimbursement implications?

Preliminary Problem Statement   There is dissatisfaction with the current process for new product review for both physicians and staff. We believe there is opportunity for some improvements and savings.

Based on the foregoing activities and analytics the team was positioned to establish a preliminary goal statement. As the team is only in step 1 of 10, the goal statement will be continuously refined and updated as more evidence and data become available.

Preliminary Goal Statement   Create a plan to reduce time (from X to Y) and improve satisfaction with the current new product request process by week 12 which provides standardization (resulting in improved quality/cost) and communication within all affiliates in a streamlined approach to benefit physicians, staff, and patients.

Step 2: What is the initial goal statement? Team charter?

Team Roles   Team member use of roles has supported improved team dynamics and performance. The 10-step team's sponsor and team leader roles were determined prior to the start of the project. However, remaining team members volunteered for the balance of the roles; brief descriptions are provided.

- Sponsor (oversees teams, reviews work, owns results): Diane Nold
- Team leader (sets guidelines, goals, weekly meetings): Joan Herbert
- Timekeeper (ensures deadlines are met): Dr. Watson
- Recorder (takes notes): Deb Mills
- Scribe (makes ideas visible in meetings): Lauree Hoag
- Monitor (adheres to methodology): Kathi Wilford
- Process observer (ensures participation): Ann Archuleta
- Spokesperson (reports to other groups): Melisa McLeod
- Team members: Michelle Brady, Bob Green, Vic Hosfeld, Ruth Kitzmiller, and Michael Thom

Code of Conduct   The team established a code of conduct to be observed during team meetings and phone calls in order to remain highly productive and meet its ambitious goals. The code of conduct incorporated cultural dimensions the team believed to be important to maintain good morale and working relationships. The code of conduct included these elements:

- No cell phones/PDAs, iPads, and so on.
- Set meeting agenda, allocate time and responsibilities at end of each meeting.
- SMEs are not team members.
- Ensure timeliness (calendar integrity—start / stop on time, be on time for meetings).
- Involve everyone (round robin).
- One idea at a time (no flops).
- No judgment of other's ideas (brainstorm).
- Obtain consensus.
- Prepare before meeting.
- Clearly define goals—get agreement.
- Adhere to roles.
- Be courteous . . . show respect.
- Commit to staying in meeting.

- No side discussions.
- Take turns talking.
- Foster honesty, openness, trust (no ridicule for throwing out idea).
- Two-knock rule.
- Have fun.
- Member check-out at meetings.

These exercises were consolidated with modifications into a more complete team charter that formed the team agreement.

Team Charter
- Issue/Problem
    - There is dissatisfaction with the current process for new product review for both physicians and staff. We believe there is opportunity for some improvements and savings.
- Goal Statement (preliminary)
    - Create a plan to reduce time (from X to Y) and improve satisfaction with the current new product request process by week 12, which provides standardization (resulting in improved quality/cost) and communication within all affiliates in a streamlined approach to benefit physicians, staff, and patients.
- Constraints
    - Reimbursement
    - Time—competing priorities, lack of communication
    - Existing contracts
    - Vendors
- Assumptions
    - Physician preferences (based on training, need communication)
    - Dissatisfaction exists with the process
    - Room for savings
    - Vendor control
    - Evaluate GPO (Group Purchasing Organization) options
- Team Guidelines
    - Teams roles are defined.
    - Core team meetings will meet once per week on Monday 12:00–1:30 (tentative).
    - Team leader will present to steering committee approximately every two weeks.
- Preliminary Project Plan (10-step milestone level)

- Steps 1–5 Training: Week 1
- Steps 1–5 Fieldwork: Weeks 2–4
- Steps 6–10 Training: Week 5
- Steps 6–10 Fieldwork: Weeks 6–11
- Celebration and Team Turnoff: Week 12

Step 3: What Are Three to Five Customer Requirements/Complaints?

Voice of the Customer. The purpose of the survey, consistent with step 1, was to secure input from the customer segments on their key requirements, As-Is and To-Be performance levels, and other provide valuable text responses. The team designed two VOC surveys to be deployed during fieldwork. The draft survey is presented next.

Survey 1: Survey for Surgeons, Cardiologists, Interventional Radiologists at All Affiliates

1. What is your specialty?
   - Open text
2. What affiliate do you practice at most often?
   - Affiliate locations A, B, C, or D
3. Do you know there is a process for new product requests?
   - Yes or No
4. Have you requested new products in the last year?
   - Yes or No
5. If yes, how many different products have you requested in the last year?
   - Enter 1–5
6. How many times has your new product request been denied?
   - Enter 1–5
7. What process did you use to place the request, i.e., with whom, in writing or verbally?
   - Various
8. Do you consider cost and reimbursement before making a request?
   - Yes or No
9. Where was the requested product to be used?
   - Hospital or physician office

10. How did you find out about the new product?
    - Course, colleague, vendor, patient request, journal
11. Do you feel knowledgeable about all the products available for your use within the health system?
    - Yes or No
12. Do you practice at other medical centers outside of MidMichigan Health?
    - Yes or No
13. If you practice at other facilities, please provide feedback on the ease of their new product request process.
    (1) Easier than MidMichigan's, (2) More difficult than MidMichigan's, (3) About the same as MidMichigan's, (4) N/A I have not requested a new product at that facility.
14. Rank your satisfaction with the product selection process at MidMichigan facilities.
    (1) Very Satisfied, (2) Moderately Satisfied, (3) Moderately Dissatisfied, (4) Very Satisfied
15. Suggestions for process improvement
    - Various

Survey 2: Survey for OR Value Analysis Team (VAT), Invasive Imaging VAT Team, and Clinical Department Managers

1. Do you belong to a VAT?
   - Yes (if so which one) or No
2. What affiliate do you primarily work at?
   - Location A, B, C, or D
3. Do you know that there is a new product request process?
   - Yes or No
4. What is your role in the new product request process?
   - Various
5. Do you feel like you have input for a new product?
   - Yes or No
6. Rank your satisfaction with the new product request process.
   (1) Very Satisfied, (2) Moderately Satisfied, (3) Moderately Dissatisfied, (4) Very Satisfied
7. What can we do to improve the process?
   - Various

Step 4: What Are the Current Process (Map) and Issues?

The 10-step team was very efficient during its process mapping breakout session. It focused and rapidly developed multiple process maps for new product request processes. The visual review of the maps revealed and validated the issues and causes noted in earlier steps.

With limited time remaining in the breakout session, the 10-step team started to catalog the choke points for the first process map's first five steps. This brief analysis revealed the next choke points:

Operating Room Process Choke Points
- Verbal product order.
- Requisition submitted by mail to purchasing. Just the requisition being completed and submitted, whether it was by mail, fax, or by hand was a choke point. This was because physicians did not fill them out correctly, and we continued to send them back to them if every blank was not filled in. Sometimes we were asking for information that the doctor did not have—such as catalog number and so on.
- Requisition submitted via fax to purchasing.
- Requisition submitted via hand to purchasing.
- Requisition is presented at department meeting. This was a choke point because often the physician didn't show up to the department meeting or the physicians would just all agree to bring in a product and not have cost/benefit info available.
- Purchasing coordinator talks with OR purchasing. This was replaced with the clinical supervisor for each section of the OR taking the lead to gather all information on a new product being requested—getting pricing from purchasing is just one of the steps now rather than the requisition being fully turned over to the purchasing coordinator.
- OR VAT team process. No physicians were on this committee, many people not familiar with what was being asked—physicians did not recognize this body as the ultimate authority for product approval.
- Coordinator gathers missing information.
- VAT reviews requisition. This was a vice presidential level VAT that hardly ever ends up meeting (as scheduled) and therefore reviews are delayed.
- Contact vendor for sourcing.

Invasive Imaging (II) New Product Process Choke Points
- Contact vendor. The II process was more streamlined due to the limited number of physicians and purchasing being integrated into the

department. In some ways the II process had some steps that were closer to a best practice.
■ Purchasing renegotiates pricing.
■ Requisition submitted to VAT.

The team quickly realized that it would take a significant effort during fieldwork to fully understand the As-Is processes at all medical center locations.

Step 5: What Are the Prioritized Choke Points, Issues, and Root Causes?

The team further analyzed the content developed in step 4 to better understand the causes of issues. The team used the fishbone diagram described earlier in this chapter. The 10-step team initially produced this problem statement for the head of the fish: "There is dissatisfaction with the current process for new product review for both physicians and staff. We believe there is opportunity for some improvements and savings." The team voted on the root causes with the vote totals shown in parentheses.

The 8Ps and IT fishbone model was used. Categories of root causes or bones of the fish are shown next.

■ Process (37 votes) category root causes included compliance enforcement, request is complicated, many redundancies, lack of standardization, too many steps and handoffs, and inconsistent communications.
■ People and skills (14) category root causes included different physicians by affiliate, multiple roles, lack of education, inconsistent communications, inconsistent prioritization, and different goals by person.
■ Policy category (10) root causes included quote formats by vendors, compliance and enforcement, lack of awareness of process, lack of standardization, and limited definition.
■ Product or vendor (9) category root causes included volume, multiple vendors for same product, vendor persistence, and vendor OR access.
■ The pricing or costs (8) category root cause included contract price negotiations, reimbursement rates, timing of vendor pricing, and quote formats vary by vendor.
■ Promotion category (0) root causes included patient requests based on vendor direct marketing and vendor solicitations.
■ Procedure (2) category root causes included prioritization in each step, sequence of steps, and workarounds.

- Place or location (0) category root causes included inconsistent prioritization, one affiliate slowing process resulting in others developing workarounds, different standards at each location, and multiple locations.

At the conclusion of step 5, the team evaluated its performance across multiple attributes. The focus and intent of this exercise contributes to self-correcting teams that can weather challenges during their life cycle. The team voted using a 1–5 scale, with 5 being the highest grade, on five key factors of team performance. These included:

1. Established goals/agenda scored 5.
2. Used code of conduct and group roles scored 5.
3. Used tools/methods scored 5.
4. Freedom to participate (captured brain power) scored 5.
5. Overall meeting effectiveness scored 5.

Steps 1–5 Fieldwork

The fieldwork contained key findings and updates to hypotheses developed during the two-day training and contained in the working papers. During fieldwork, the team deployed its internal customer surveys, gathered a significant amount of data for analyses, and performed two simulations of the process, one each for the OR and II.

Survey Results

Survey 1: Survey for Surgeons, Cardiologists, Interventional Radiologists at All Affiliates (12 respondents)

1. What is your specialty?
   - ENT = 2
   - Ophthalmology = 1

- OB/GYN =3
- GYN =2
- Ortho =1
- Interventional Radiology =1
- Surgery =1
- Skipped Question =1

2. What affiliate do you practice at most often?
   - Affiliate location A = 12
3. Do you know there is a process for new product requests?
   - Yes = 10, No = 2
4. Have you requested new products in the last year?
   - Yes = 8, No = 4
5. If yes, how many different products have you requested in the last year?
   - Enter 1–5 = 8
6. How many times has your new product request been denied?
   - Enter 1–5 = 6
7. What process did you use to place the request, i.e., with whom, in writing or verbally?
   - Written + Verbal = 1
   - Per Protocol = 1
   - With Inventory Coordinator = 1
   - OR Purchasing = 1
   - Filled out a Form = 1
   - Product Request Form or Verbal = 1
   - Verbally Requested to Trial a Device = 1
   - Skipped Question = 4
8. Do you consider cost and reimbursement before making a request?
   - Yes = 6, No = 3, and skipped question = 3
9. Where was the requested product to be used?
   - Hospital (or surgery center) = 7
   - Physician Office = 0
   - Skipped = 5

(Continued)

10. How did you find out about the new product?
    - Educational Conference = 5
    - Colleague = 4
    - Vendor = 5
    - Patient Request = 1
    - Journal (Literature) = 5
    - Skipped = 4
11. Do you feel knowledgeable about all the products available for your use within the health system?
    - Yes = 3, No = 5, Skipped = 4
12. Do you practice at other medical centers outside of MidMichigan Health?
    - Yes = 2, No = 10
13. If you practice at other facilities, please provide feedback on the ease of their new product request process.
    - Easier than MidMichigan's = 0
    - More difficult than MidMichigan's = 0
    - About the same as MidMichigan's = 0
    - N/A I have not requested a new product at that facility = 2
    - Skipped = 10
14. Rank your satisfaction with the product selection process at Mid-Michigan facilities.
    - Very Satisfied = 4
    - Moderately Satisfied = 3
    - Moderately Dissatisfied = 3
    - Very Dissatisfied = 1
    - Skipped = 1
15. Suggestions for process improvement.
    - Knowledgeable personnel making decisions in concert with the physician using the products in light of emerging/established literature supporting the change
    - More physician involvement
    - Need for better communication, awareness of available products and need for a quicker, simpler process

Survey 2: Survey for OR Value Analysis Team (VAT), Invasive Imaging VAT team and Clinical Department Managers (Results from 95 respondents appear)

1. Do you belong to a VAT?
   - Yes = 35 (37%), No = 60 (63%)
2. What affiliate do you primarily work at?
   - Affiliate A = 59 (63%)
   - Affiliate B = 3 (3%)
   - Affiliate C = 17 (18%)
   - Affiliate D = 9 (9%)
   - Skipped = 7 (7%)
3. Do you know that there is a new product request process?
   - Yes = 51 (54%)
   - No = 44 (46%)
4. What is your role in the new product request process?
   - Education
   - End user
   - VAT chair
   - Provide forms and assistance
   - Observer
   - Investigation and approval
   - Supervisor doing ordering
   - Supply contracts
   - Financial review
   - Ordering through Lawson
   - Request submitter
   - Evaluator
   - Recommender
   - Ensure consistency
   - Review of clinical products
5. Do you feel like you have input for a new product?
   - Yes = 61 (64%)
   - No = 27 (29%)
   - Skipped = 7 (7%)

(Continued)

6. Rank your satisfaction with the new product request process.
   - Very Satisfied = 6 (6%)
   - Moderately Satisfied = 38 (40%)
   - Moderately Dissatisfied = 24 (26%)
   - Very Satisfied = 9 (9%)
   - Skipped = 18 (19%)
7. What can we do to improve the process?
   - Utilize evidence based research and industry best practices
   - Better communication and education
   - Electronic list of all new products and impacted affiliates
   - Shorten the approval process time
   - Speed up the ordering of new products
   - Develop clear forms
   - Require physician participation
   - Differentiate between new technology and improved product
   - Get more input from end users at all affiliates
   - Automation involving all affiliates
   - More financial analysis
   - Be more patient focused
   - Prioritize requests
   - Define timelines

Data Analyses

- OR Process Time Study Simulation Approach
  - Spreadsheet was created to identify cycle times associated with each process.
  - Process flow was modified to accommodate suggestions associated with the cycle time data.
  - Data were linked with new process flow sheet to identify back-and-forth handoffs and choke points associated with cycle time variation.
  - All decisions were assumed to have 0 cycle time. If necessary, a new process was added to account for time assigned to decision in data spreadsheet.

- Maximum and minimum cycle times were used as surrogate for standard deviation for identifying variation.
- OR Process Time Study Simulation Results
  - Minimum total cycle time = 6 days
  - Maximum total cycle time = 209 days (+)
  - Range of total cycle time = 203 days
  - Average total cycle time = 107.5 days
- Invasive Imaging Time Study Simulation Approaches
  - Spreadsheet was created to identify cycle times associated with each process.
  - Process flow was modified to accommodate suggestions associated with the cycle time data.
  - Data were linked with new process flow sheet to identify back-and-forth handoffs and choke points associated with cycle time variation.
  - All decisions were assumed to have 0 cycle time. If necessary, a new process was added to account for time assigned to decision in data spreadsheet.
  - Max and min cycle times were used as surrogate for standard deviation for identifying variation.
- Invasive Imaging Time Study Simulation Results
  - Minimum total cycle time = 33 days
  - Maximum total cycle time = 293 days (+)
  - Range of total cycle time = 260 days
  - Average total cycle time = 163 days

Steps 6–10 Training Days 3–4

During the two-day 10-step training, the team created solutions, a To-Be design, and implementation plans to realize value.

Step 6: What Are Future State or Desired Process Attributes?

The team engaged in a breakout session designed to leverage both creative and analytical thinking to develop a To-Be design for the core process.

The *creative* exercise resulted in these To-Be design elements:

- Published list of current products and indications for use or other like products at all affiliates include ratings from providers
- Physician to submit electronic request—product, clinical outcomes

- Food and Drug Administration (FDA) approval, validation of clinical outcomes, pricing, best practices, reimbursement, standardization, other affiliates, current contract commitments
- Physician must have proper credentials to use products
- Vendor requirements—consistent and spelled out
- Product trial or demonstration
- Already covered above
- Covered above in trial/demonstration
- Covered under standardization
- Final recommendation presented to System Surgical Council where final decision is made
- Communication of outcome by System Surgical Council to requestor and newsletter to all physicians

The *analytical, structured* exercise resulted in these To-Be design elements:

- Process, Policy, and Procedure
  - Physician electronic request
  - Published list of current products
  - Checklist
- People and Skills
  - Physician electronic request
  - Published list of current products
  - Checklist
  - Physician credentials
- Place and Location
  - Published list of current products
  - Checklist
- Product
  - Physician electronic request
  - Published list of current products
  - Checklist
- Partner and Vendor
  - Checklist
- Technology
  - Physician electronic request
  - Published list of current products
  - Checklist

The 10-step team combined these two exercise outputs to define a comprehensive To-Be solution.

Step 7: What Improvement Level Is Expected (Final Goal Statement)?

Based on the cumulative learning from the prior steps, the team revisited its initial goal statement and identified several new components to create significant value. The new targets also factor in benchmarks and best practices.

Preliminary Goal Statement (steps 1–5)   Create a plan to reduce time (from X to Y) and improve satisfaction with the current new product request process by week 12, which provides standardization (resulting in improved quality/cost) and communication within all affiliates in a streamlined approach to benefit physicians, staff, and patients.

Revised Goal Statement   Create a plan to reduce time from current average of 163 days to an average of 31 days or less from time of request to decision and improve satisfaction with the operating room and invasive imaging new product noncapital request process by week 12. This streamlined approach will provide standardization (resulting in improved quality/cost and improved communication) within all affiliates to benefit physicians, staff, and patients, resulting in cost savings of at least $50,000.

Step 8: What Should the Future Process Be (New Map)?

The 10-step team incorporated the design elements from step 6 and the refined goal statement parameters from step 7 to design new processes. The new e-requisition process also reflected best practices for internal and external hires identified internally from high-performing affiliates.

Step 9: What Are the Barriers to Improvement? Countermeasures?

The 10-step team completed two analytics in step 9 to deal with change management issues: force field analysis and a stakeholder map and communications plan.

Force Field Analysis   The first exercise focused on preparation of a force field analysis. The purpose of this tool is for participants to think together about all the aspects of a desired solution. It is particularly useful for analyzing how to deploy change initiatives. A force field analysis is a structured approach to generating supports for and barriers to implementing a particular solution. The key steps in a force field analysis include:

1. Define the ideal state on the top right of the template.

2. Prioritize driving forces of those that can be strengthened.
3. Prioritize the restraining forces that can be removed or reduced.
4. Brainstorm force field actions to enhance driving forces and/or mitigate restraining forces.

The team followed the four steps, outputs included:

1. **Ideal State.** New product process
2. Driving forces that can be strengthened included:
   - Vendors
   - Physician satisfaction
   - Standardization
   - Cost savings
   - Increased volumes
   - Patients
   - Physician recruitment
   - Financial sensitivity/process improvement
   - Need for more education
3. Restraining forces that can be removed or reduced included:
   - Vendors
   - Physicians
   - Technology (new software needed)
   - Manpower needs to implement
   - EMR (electronic medical records) support capabilities
   - Current policies and culture (e.g., current VAT teams)
   - Physician recruitment
   - Cost of products/reimbursement
   - Uncertainty of education department structure
4. Brainstorm force field actions to enhance driving forces and/or mitigate restraining forces presented:
   - Pricing deadlines and policies to vendors
   - Develop catalog of available products with pricing
   - Implement technology to access catalog
   - Need for interfaces/databases expert
   - Educate physicians, recruiters, and staff to process
   - Redistribute hours and tasks
   - Consult with new chief information officer
   - Consult the Association of Healthcare Value Analysis Professionals for best practices
   - Clear and concise expectations to all
   - Empowerment

- Develop System Surgical Council (change of existing team with new charter)
- Checklist/Tracking tool development
- Communicate/educate current VAT teams on new process
- Modify policies to reflect new process and standardization

Stakeholder Map and Communications Plan   Building on the force field analysis, the team built a stakeholder map that identified the anticipated roles people would play during deployment of solutions. The roles included:

- Change sponsors
- Change originators
- Change agents responsible for deploying or implementing the changes
- Change advocates
- Change blockers
- SME informants to provide information on the change

The stakeholder map provides insights into key constituencies. From the map, the team developed a summary communications plan that contained key actions that will enable the primary elements of the To-Be solution to gain traction in the organization. The team also developed specific messages for each stakeholder group.

- Educators: Support with rollout implementation and newsletter
- Physicians: Notify educate on new process
- IT: Resources for database and resources (product catalog and database)
- Vendors: Distribute new policy
- Staff: Notify/educate on new process
- Purchasing: Notify/educate on new process
- Coordinators: Notify/educate on new process
- Specialty teams: Reach out to other affiliates for system Surgical Council membership
- VAT steering/administration: Notify/educate on new process
- Coders: Notify/educate on new process

Step 10: What Do We Pilot? Results? What Is the Full Implementation Plan?

The team developed an action plan that contained over 25 action items or steps broken down into three categories:

1. Quick wins that could be deployed inside the team's 12-week life cycle
2. A pilot program to test changes and prepare for full implementation
3. To-Be changes that would be handed off to the process owner after the 12-week team cycle.

Quick Wins Including Two Product Pilots

Quick wins approved by the 10-step steering committee during the 12 weeks enabled the team to demonstrate value prior to pilot or full implementation of the To-Be Solutions. The quick wins included developing a new product request form:

1. Request build of product catalog.
2. CEO and medical staff support for system-wide Surgical Council decision-making body.
3. Focus coordinator time on checklist (see To-Be process).
4. Physician new product request form.

The team ran two new product request pilots, one each for the OR and II. The results saved or avoided $84,600 ($423,000 over five years). The new product request form is presented next.

To-Be Physician New Product Request Form (elements to be included):

1. Request date
2. Requestor
3. Product name/description
4. Vendor name
5. Type of procedure
6. Reason for request
7. Is this a replacement for something you are already using? If so, what?
8. How often do you anticipate using this product?
9. Is a trial necessary?
10. How did you hear about the product?

New Product Request Checklist: Need Information Within 5 Business Days

1. FDA approval
   - Go to FDA.gov and search for item to determine if FDA-approved item. If not approved, end of checklist.

2. Contact affiliates
   - Is physician specialty group going to meet within the next 5 business days? If yes, bring info to group. If not, talk to specialists directly and contact coordinator at other affiliates to get initial input from each provider.
   - Is there another service within your organization utilizing a similar product?
   - Is product used or is something similar used?
   - If replacement, determine product, volume (on-hand inventory), cost.
3. Obtain system-wide department input:
   - Check with other providers doing same/similar procedures.
4. Check contracts
   - Check on J\pricing files.
5. Contact vendor/negotiate pricing
   - On consignment or not?
6. Contact coder
7. Estimated financial impact
   - # annual procedures × cost/savings
8. Best practice
   - Librarian to do best practice search

Improve Performance

The team identified these financial and operational improvements:

- Financial earnings improvement of $84,600 for two products ($423,000 over five years). Although MidMichigan Health reviews dozens of products annually, the team elected not to value all of them in the interest of conservatism.
- Reduce average cycle time in the new product process from 163 to 31 days.

  Every block of stone has a statue inside it and it is the task of the sculptor to discover it.

  —**Michelangelo**

NOTE

1. The case studies in this chapter are based on MidMichigan Health 10-Step Team Final Working Papers, April 14, 2012.

7

Support Units: 10-Step Team Best Practice Cases

Nothing is particularly hard if you divide it into small jobs.

—*Henry Ford*

THIS CHAPTER SHARES THE JOURNEY of two teams focused on MidMichigan Health system laboratory services and pharmacy services. Traditionally, these two vertically structured services operated within each of the four medical centers (hospitals) supporting core hospital operations, patients, and general and specialty medical practice areas. The 10-step teams changed this paradigm forever, reorienting and repositioning these service lines as "horizontal" strategic business units with clear and singular executive leadership to be operationally optimized and to serve all four medical centers.

LABORATORY SERVICES 10-STEP TEAM CASE STUDY, *OPTIMIZE THE SYSTEM*

The Laboratory System Integration team was charged with a very large scale task: In 12 weeks, identify and determine the optimal system laboratory services model and develop an implementation plan. Team member composition is crucial in building a team that possesses the knowledge, skills, and mind-set to be able to objectively evaluate all options."

> —Ann Dull, Director of Orthopedics and
> Rehabilitation Services (team leader)

The lab system team aligned with MidMichigan Health system Strategic Objective E: Operational excellence.[1] Lab structures, processes, policies, personnel, and other design factors varied greatly by affiliate (entity). A team was formed to explore opportunities for improvements along these design factors as well as improve response times and reduce costs and error rates.

This case study consists of the next sections:

- **Steps 1–5 Training** encompasses working papers and content developed during the first two-day training team breakout sessions.
- **Steps 1–5 Fieldwork** shares key findings primarily from voice-of-customer surveys, data review, and analytics.
- **Steps 6–10 Training** consists of working papers and content developed during the second two-day training breakout sessions.
- **Improve performance** shares the financial and nonfinancial team findings to improve performance.

Steps 1–5 Training Days 1–2

Step 1: Have We Identified the Right Areas of Focus?

Since teams (by design) consisted of representatives from different functions that possessed varied understanding of the current process, step 1 focused the team to establish a baseline or common understanding of the current situation.

Customer Segments and Requirements　The team brainstormed and initially defined five customer segments of lab services:

1. Patients
2. Physicians

3. Pathologists
4. MidMichigan Health System
5. MidMichigan Health physicians

For each customer segment, the team identified and prioritized customer requirements through voting, and drafted the Five Ups charts for each customer group.

The first customer group, *patients*, had a multitude of requirements, including:

* Painless blood draw
* Timeliness of results
* Right test
* Wait time in lab
* Safety patient identification
* Registration process
* Test menu
* Cleanliness
* Location, easy access
* Price (in network)
* Hours of operation
* Friendliness of staff
* Competent staff
* Patient choice of lab

The second customer group, *physicians*, had these requirements:

* Timeliness of results
* Timeliness of draw
* Accurate results
* Test menu one-stop shop
* Easy ordering process
* Cost for patients
* Difficulty finding results
* Lack of consultation services
* Lack of pathologist engagement
* Lack of connectivity.

The third customer group, *pathologists*, had these requirements:

* Lack of clinical lab management

- Lack of clinical competence
- Anatomic Pathology Laboratory Information system

The fourth customer group, *MidMichigan Health System*, had these requirements:

- Customer and physician satisfaction
- Lack of seamless lab operations
- Lack of standardization
- Total expenses
- Lack of operational efficiency

The fifth customer group *MidMichigan Health physicians*, had these requirements:

- Lack of operational efficiency
- Lack of standardization
- Customer and physician satisfaction
- Total expenses
- Lack of physician electronic options and connectivity

The 10-step team discussed the importance of a balanced set of targets that concurrently solved for multiple aspects of this process. For the listed customer groups, the team agreed to further prioritize the requirements and to establish As-Is and To-Be targets for all requirements.

Causes of Issues　The team brainstormed causes of customer problems and used the nominal group technique of grouping similar causes into six major themes for easier understanding. These groups included:

1. Two different pathology groups
   - Two different pathology groups—employed and independent —that have two different Anatomic Pathology Laboratory information systems and employed more likely to get second opinion
   - Lack of formal communication method between lab leadership
   - Lack of confidence in pathology results by some physicians
   - Lack of pathology involvement in patient care
   - Lack of referring physician's knowledge of pathologist practice
   - Lack of pathologist involvement; define expectations

2. Duplication of services, policies, procedures, and activities
   - Duplication of tests
   - Duplication of work
   - Duplication of policies and procedures (inconsistencies)
   - Duplication of services (i.e., customer service department)
   - Send-out services (duplication)
3. Different processes and standards
   - Charges different at all four hospitals
   - Different instrumentation
   - Different methods
   - Different normal ranges
   - Different organizational structure
   - Different purchasing processes
   - Supply distribution
   - Different document control system
   - Different quality management planning
   - Different decision making process
   - Different out-of-pocket charges
   - Different regulatory standards for inspections
4. Increased competition and lack of competitive edge
   - Paper test catalog not always up to date
   - No coordinated marketing efforts
   - Inability to interface in a timely fashion between physician offices or ourselves
   - Prices perceived to be high
   - Competition within medical centers (Each lab has its own bottom line. Each is responsible for resources that vary both in staffing levels and capital spending and overlapping geography.)
5. Lack of standardization with lab human resources
   - Phlebotomy turnover and training
   - Continuing education
   - No staff sharing
   - Job descriptions and competencies tested are different
   - Gladwin contract staff
   - Expected future turnover
   - Lack of succession planning
6. Physician office relations
   - Lack of client services to physicians and our offices

Data Sets. The team identified key data sets to better understand the As-Is situation. The data sets would provide insights and facts to better analyze and validate and refine the goal statement. Data sets also provided the basis to refine or adjust project scope. The team determined that the next data sets would be useful to gather during fieldwork:

- Benchmarking data from ABC Benchmarking,[2] an outside service
- Benchmarking data from XYZ Benchmarking, an outside service
- Internal benchmarking among locations
- Overall cost per test
- Organizational charts
- Test menus
- Existing business models
- Best practice business models

Next the team defined the background, preliminary problem statement, and preliminary goal statement.

Background   MidMichigan Health has four labs functioning at the four medical centers. Each lab functions independently. Labs A, B, and C are more similar in operations than D. A's physician services provides services for all A, B, and C. Lab D's physician services are provided by physicians employed by the medical center. Labs A and D have different laboratory information system platforms. D is moving to the same laboratory information system as the other three labs, anticipated completion after team close out. Market competition is increasing for lab services, and many providers are utilizing non-MidMichigan Health lab services due to perceptions of better customer service and communication, ease of order processing and result gathering due to computer connectivity, and better pathologist involvement in the patient care through consultation services and feedback. Increased pressure exists for MidMichigan labs to be part of bigger payer networks, which work to provide decreased costs to patients. Industry trend and standards suggest that a new more consolidated lab system may improve operational efficiency and service quality for MidMichigan Health.

Preliminary Problem Statement   Inefficiencies due to duplication and differences in lab policies, procedures, locations, and processes throughout the system are resulting in higher expenses and are affecting lab profitability.

Based on the preceding information, the team was positioned to establish a preliminary goal statement. As the team is just in step 1 of 10, the goal statement will be continuously refined and updated as more evidence and data become available.

Preliminary Goal Statement   Reduce total expense per test by 5% by reducing duplication of services and standardizing processes (by date to be determined) without reducing quality while maintaining customer satisfaction, resulting in savings of a minimum of $50,000.

Step 2: What Is the Initial Goal Statement? Team Charter?

Team Roles   Team member use of roles is proven to improve team dynamics and performance. The 10-step team's sponsor and team leader were selected prior to the start of the project. Remaining team members volunteered for the other the roles; brief descriptions are provided.

- Sponsor (oversees teams, reviews work, owns results): Diane Nold
- Team leader (sets guidelines, goals, weekly meetings, presents to steering committee): Ann Dull; Tricia Mangapora, assistant
- Timekeeper (ensures deadlines are met): Dean Cornell
- Recorder (takes notes): Cheryl Kotenko
- Scribe (makes ideas visible flipcharts/PC): Mark Kozak
- Monitor (adheres to methodology): Tracy Klapish
- Process observer (ensures participation): Cindy Fillmore, Sara Silvestro
- Spokesperson (reports to other groups): Kevin Russell
- Backups: Randy Wyse, Jason Williams

Code of Conduct   The team established a code of conduct to be observed during team meetings and phone calls in order to remain highly productive and meet its ambitious goals. The code of conduct incorporated cultural dimensions the team believed to be important to maintain good morale and working relationships. The code of conduct includes these elements:

- Thursdays 7:30 a.m.–9:00 a.m. in Midland
- No cell phones/PDAs, and so on. iPads okay for notes.
- Set meeting agenda at end of prior meeting with time allotments.
- Involve everyone—no idea is a bad idea. Feel free to talk!

- One idea at a time. Observer will keep track of other ideas.
- Obtain consensus.
- Prepare before meeting. Do homework.
- Define tool to meet objective.
- Be courteous . . . show respect.
- Commit to staying in meeting.
- No side discussions.
- Take turns talking.
- Foster honesty, openness, trust (no ridicule for throwing out idea).
- Two-knock rule.
- Have fun.

These exercises were consolidated with modifications into a more complete team charter, which formed a team agreement.

Team Charter

- Issue/Problem
  Inefficiencies due to duplication and differentiation in our policies, procedures, locations, and processes throughout the system resulting in higher expenses and affecting lab profitability.
- Goal Statement
  Initial: Reduce total expense per test by X% (to be determined) by reducing duplication of services and standardizing processes by date (to be determined) without reducing quality while maintaining customer satisfaction, resulting in savings of a minimum of $50,000.
- Constraints
  - Multiple processes, perceptions, procedures
  - Geographic requirements
  - Lab is a necessary service at each hospital
  - Information systems
  - Two pathology models
  - Magnitude and size of project
  - Fear of allocations
  - Fear of job loss
  - Resources such as courier services
- Assumptions
  - High costs per test
  - Inefficiencies exist

- Cost savings
- Team Guidelines (included in code of conduct)
- Resources (included in roles and additional subject matter experts [SMEs] not contemplated during the project planning phase)
- Preliminary Project Plan (10-step milestone level)
  - Steps 1–5 Training: Week 1
  - Steps 1–5 Fieldwork: Weeks 2–4
  - Steps 6–10 Training: Week 5
  - Steps 6–10 Fieldwork: Weeks 6–11
  - Celebration and Team Turnoff: Week 12

Step 3: What Are Three to Five Customer Requirements/Complaints?

Voice of the Customer. The purpose of the survey, consistent with step 1, was to secure input from the customer segments on their key requirements, As-Is and To-Be performance levels, and other valuable text responses. The team designed a voice-of-the-customer (VOC) survey to be deployed during fieldwork.

Step 4: What Are the Current Process (Map) and Issues?

The 10-step team focused initially on lab menus used across the system of the four medical centers. The 10-step team identified these choke points:

- Difficulty comparing costs per test between affiliates
- Analyzer/equipment differences between affiliates
- Data not available on a cost-per-test basis for all affiliates
- Labs have different norms for tests, and so on, due to being led by two pathology groups
- Lab information systems, not using to capacity/full capability
- Accrediting bodies/inspection process is different
- Relabeling, reordering, reprinting, re-registration causing significant inefficiencies
- Charge and reimbursement structures
- Supply distribution (ordering, receiving, etc.)
- Lack of tools/data to analyze profitability (reimbursement)

The organizational structures for all the labs were reviewed. Some observations are listed next.

- MidMichigan Health Laboratory Services currently operates in a partially centralized organization structure, with the Health System's corporate board of directors and separate board for each of its medical centers. This structure has permitted local control while offering corporate continuity and coordination.
- Laboratory services are provided within each of the four medical centers. The laboratories are geographically distant from one another (over 30 miles). Two laboratories have consolidated their midlevel and high-end esoteric testing at the location A medical center laboratory. Test consolidation between Lab A and Lab D has not yet occurred.
- Laboratory outreach services are provided to the four-county area by each medical center laboratory. The outreach programs do not share any infrastructure and are actually competing with one another for physician/clinic and long-term care laboratory business. These lab and off-site draw stations include:
  - Eight locations operated by Lab A.
  - Three locations operated by Lab C.
  - Seven locations operated by Lab D.

The team quickly realized that it would take a significant effort to fully understand all business model elements at all four locations.

Step 5: What Are the Prioritized Choke Points, Issues, and Root Causes?

In this step, the content developed in step 4 is further analyzed by the team to better understand the causes of issues. The primary tool in this step is the fishbone diagram. The 10-step team completed two fishbone analyses.

Fishbone 1   The 10-step team initially produced this problem statement for the head of the fish: "Inefficiencies due to duplication and differentiation in our policies, procedures, locations, processes throughout the system resulting in higher expenses and are affecting lab profitability."

The 8Ps and information technology (IT) model and its categories and root causes, or bones of the fish, are listed next.

- Product category root causes included different test menus; chemistry vendors differ, and service contracts.
- Process category root causes included different admitting processes, dedicated resources for certain functions in bigger labs, courier services. and Medicaid billing.

- People and skills category root causes included two pathology groups, pathologist concerns regarding systemization, staff concerns of systemization, and internal political issues.
- Pricing or costs category root causes included four different fee schedules, lack of standardized expenses, patient perception of price is different at all four sites, and different reimbursement rates.
- Policy and procedure category root causes included differing sets of norms and standards, and nonsystem policies.
- Place or location category root causes included logistics of transporting specimens, affiliate ownership of services, space issues for core lab.
- Technology category root causes included different analyzers and two different Laboratory Information System (LIS) platforms.
- The promotion category root cause included lack of branding.

Fishbone 2   The 10-step team initially produced this problem statement for the head of the fish: "Variations in administrative resources and responsibilities."

The 8Ps and IT model and its categories and root causes, or bones of the fish, are listed next.

- Product category root causes included blood supply: employees perceive differences in product.
- Process category root causes included four different customer ABC accounts, partial systemization, inconsistent quality management, inconsistent point of care, customer and client services resources, and four different customer ABC send-out processes.
- People and skills category root causes included age, competency of staff, job roles and responsibilities, pay structure, generalized versus departmentalized technicians, and customer and client services.
- The pricing or financial root cause included differences in financial resources.
- Policy and procedure category root causes included lack of document control, separate policies and procedures, two different intranet lab user guides, two different accreditation bodies, and lack of resources to prepare for surveys and peer reviews.
- Promotion category root causes included lack of use of marketing plan, lack of promotional plan, lack of lab identify, and lack of marketing resources.
- The place or location category root cause included lack of clinical input from pathologists.

- Technology category root causes included different two blood supply lab information systems (LIS), inconsistent human resources, and lack of connectivity with physician offices.

At the conclusion of step 5, the team evaluated its performance across multiple attributes. The focus and intent of this exercise contributes to self-correcting teams that can weather challenges during their life cycle. The team voted using a 1–5 scale, with 5 being the highest grade, on five key factors of team performance. These included:

1. Established goals/agenda scored 4.
2. Used code of conduct and group roles scored 4.
3. Used tools/methods scored 3.
4. Freedom to participate (captured brain power) scored 4.
5. Overall meeting effectiveness scored 4.

Steps 1–5 Fieldwork

The fieldwork contained key findings and updates to hypotheses developed during the two-day training and contained in the working papers. During fieldwork, the team deployed the internal customer surveys, gathered a significant amount of current and benchmarking data for analyses, and researched best practices.

Data Analyses

Current Status
- Summarized actual financial gross revenue, expense, and billable units by hospital for a six-month period. Pathologist-related revenues and expenses were excluded. Six-month data were doubled to reach annualized data.
- Contractual allowances were calculated at 71% for Medicare, 75% for Medicaid, and at three-year forecast rates for all other payors.
- Calculated labor, other expenses, and total costs per billable unit.
- Prepared three scenarios for the new state with the percentage of contractuals being the variable: optimistic, most likely, and pessimistic.

External Benchmarking Comparison
- Accumulated third-party benchmarking data for each hospital.
- Compared 25th- and 50th-percentile labor and other expense per billable unit data to actual results.

- Calculated opportunity for each category. If current results were better than benchmark, no opportunity impact was included.
- Annual opportunities identified are:
  - 50th-percentile benchmark comparison equated to $2,442,000 in potential earnings improvements.
  - 25th-percentile benchmark comparison equated to $3,588,000 in potential earnings improvements.

Internal Benchmarking Comparison

Compared internal results between hospitals and identified improvement opportunities: improve Lab D operations to Lab A levels; and improve Lab B operations to Lab C levels, which totaled $1,848,000:

- Labor variance totaled $960,000
- Other expenses $888,000.

Best Practice Research

In order to understand the industry trends for laboratory services, a literature search and review was completed. The most consistent component in all of the articles was the utilization of the work cell structure. In the traditional laboratory structure, the environment and the work processes are organized by grouping like instruments together. Technologists are specialists who manage one instrument utilizing a significant amount of batch processing, resulting in longer wait times while technologists wait for batches to build up. This batch processing causes bursts of work, swinging technologists between the extremes of overwork and idleness. When an instrument goes down, technologists stop to fix it, slowing everyone downstream.

In comparison, in the work cell structure, laboratory instruments are arranged in the order in which they are needed. Instead of having many operators shuttle back and forth across the lab, one cross-trained technologist can walk in a circle and operate all of the analyzers. In the work cell, single-piece first-in/first-out processing is utilized, and orders no longer sit waiting for the batch to build up. Technologists have a steady constant workflow. When an instrument malfunctions, the operator raises an alert flag, switches to a backup instrument, and continues working while a designated resource tech steps in to resolve the issue.

The major impacts of restructuring from the traditional to work cell laboratory structure are:

- Reduced overall turnaround time
- Reduced work in progress by eliminating batch processing
- Increased lab capacity
- Improved visual management with the ability to quickly assess the state of operations
- Reduced full-time equivalent (FTE) staffing requirements
- Optimized space requirements
- Reduced total operating costs

An example of the research into award-winning cases focused on Avera McKenna Hospital and University Health Center, Sioux Falls, South Dakota.[3]

Facts

- 490-bed magnet facility recognized for excellence in behavioral health, cancer care, and emergency medicine.
- In 2003 and 2004, recognized as a Distinguished Clinical Hospital by HealthGrades.
- In 2007, in Thomson Reuter 100 Top Hospitals.
- Lab employs 106 FTEs.
- 2.5 million tests per year.

Project Goal

- Root out wasteful processes before moving to a new facility.
- Reduce space requirements.
- Reduce headcount and turnaround time.

Process

- Team gathered data and videotaped the existing processes.
- Identified primary sources of waste and developed a series of corrective actions:

  - Consolidated tests that constituted 90% of the work volume into a single work cell.
  - Placed lab instruments in the order in which they are needed.

- Cross-trained staff permitting them to float according to demand.
- Identified standard procedures for each test.
- Switched from batch processing to single-piece, first-in/first-out processing.

Results
- Overall turnaround time dropped 46% from 68 to 37 minutes.
- Reduced FTE requirements by 12% from 120 to 106.
- Standing inventory was reduced by 30%.
- Increased lab capacity, allowing for the expansion of outreach programs to generate new revenue.
- Reduced space requirement by 17% from 6,000 to 5,000 square feet.
- Total savings estimated at $1,700,000.

Steps 6–10 Training Days 3–4

During the two-day 10-step training, the team created solutions, a To-Be design, and implementation plans to realize value.

Step 6: What Are Future State or Desired Process Attributes?

The team engaged in a breakout session designed to leverage both creative thinking and analytical thinking to develop a To-Be design for the core process.

The *creative* exercise resulted in these To-Be design elements:

- Map to integrated model.
- Pathology led focus groups.
- Determine physical logistics at each affiliate.
- Standardize equipment, supplies, and test processes.
- Determine timeline.
- Minimize costs per test.
- Determine test menu distribution.
- Communication to all stakeholders.
- Implement changes.
- Pulse check (check in with staff, focus groups, department meetings).
- Integration run time.
- Regulatory audits (expense per billable, stakeholder satisfaction, etc.).
- Monitor sustainability.

- Make any necessary modifications.
- Celebration of successful implementation.

The *analytical, structured* exercise to build the To-Be process included these design elements:

- Process/Procedures
  - Standardized admitting processes
  - Leverage availability of resources
  - Lab-focused courier services
  - Streamlined Medicaid billing
  - Systemize common departmental processes
- Policies
  - Implement lab document control system
  - Standardized lab user guide
  - Implement one accrediting body, with dedicated resource(s)
  - Implement one set of norms and standards
- Price/Promotion/Product
  - Establish lab brand and identity
  - Develop internal marketing/communication plan
  - Implement same prices
- Place
  - Additional space for core lab
  - Optimize lab space at all affiliates
  - Supply distribution and specimen transportation
- People/Skills
  - One pathology model
  - Leverage availability of resources
  - Integrated organizational structure
  - Implement succession planning
  - Standardized job descriptions and pay scales to allow for shared staffing
  - Dedicated resource for education/training
- Technology
  - Standardize instrumentation
  - One LIS platform
  - Physician connectivity

The 10-step team combined these two exercise outputs to define a comprehensive To-Be solution.

Step 7: What Improvement Level Is Expected–Final Goal Statement?

Based on the cumulative learning from the prior steps, the team revisited its initial goal statement and identified several new components to create significant value. The new targets also factor in benchmarks and best practices.

Initial Goal Statement Reduce total expense per test by X% by reducing duplication of services and standardizing processes by xxxx without reducing quality while maintaining customer satisfaction resulting in savings of a minimum of $50,000.

Revised Goal Statement One system lab using the shared services model will reduce duplication of services and activities. This will result in $1.70 million total expense savings annually (based on 50th-percentile performance from a benchmarking service) while maintaining customer satisfaction and quality.

Step 8: What Should the Future Process Be (New Map)?

The 10-step team incorporated the design elements from step 6 and the refined goal statement parameters from step 7 to design a new business model. The new lab system model reflected best practices from internal and external entities.

To-Be Lab System Model Design

- **Phase I.** This cross-functional and cross-affiliate corporate performance management team was formed to analyze integration of laboratory services for MidMichigan Health. Upon completion of the team's process, their outcomes were:
  - **Goal Statement.** To develop one system lab using a shared services model which will reduce duplication of services and activities. This will result in $1.7 million total expense savings annually while maintaining customer satisfaction and quality.
  - **Action Plan**
    - Develop an organizational structure for a shared services system lab model with a designated administrative lab leader and a system leadership team to optimize resources and reduce duplication of activities by four months in order to promote efficiency as measured in ABC benchmarking.

- Develop a pathologist model for a physician-led laboratory services system.
- Develop a phased implementation plan that synchronizes with the LIS implementation plan for a system lab model with a core lab and rapid response labs at the affiliates by eight months.
- **Phase II.** In early March, the MidMichigan Health Laboratory Services Integration Team was formed to complete the analysis and develop an implementation plan for centralization of laboratory services from all four medical centers. The analysis included:
  - A review of best practices for a multisite hospital system to provide laboratory services: integrated work cell model and fully automated work cell model.
  - From this review, identified that administrative responsibility, structure, and processes must be standardized and centralized prior to the implementation of a fully automated alternative.
  - Analyzed data by location under a core and rapid response lab structure, including:
    - Workloads
    - Capital equipment requirements
    - Space requirements
    - Supply expense impacts
    - Hours of operation
    - Staffing requirements
  - Prepared a gap analysis between the current structure and the desired future structure of capital equipment needs and staffing impacts.
  - Developed a plan for the implementation of an integrated work cell structure with Midland functioning as the core lab and rapid response labs at Gratiot, Clare, and Gladwin.
- **Phase III.** In one month, the pathology steering committee in conjunction with an expert consulting firm will develop a standardized pathology model for MidMichigan Health in order to implement a physician-led laboratory services system by nine months. This team will be led by Diane Nold and include Dr. Lydia Watson, Dr. Michael Stack, Mark Santamaria, Cindy Fillmore, and Deb Mills.
- **Phase IV.** In 10 months, after implementation of the integrated work cell structure and the pathology model, develop plans to improve laboratory operations to meet the ABC 50th-percentile benchmarking targets. Additional savings would be primarily realized through supplies, other nonlabor categories, pricing, and draw stations.

- **Phase V(a).** In 15 months, in conjunction with Phase V(b), evaluate the operational and financial implications to convert the work cells to a total automated laboratory line structure versus an unautomated line structure.
- **Phase V(b).** Starting in 15 months, this phase will focus on reaching the 25th-percentile targets, representing an additional annual opportunity of $1.1 million for laboratory services. MidMichigan Health has begun to differentiate clinical departments that must function at top quartile. Lab has been identified as one such department.

Step 9: What Are the Barriers to Improvement? Countermeasures?

The 10-step team completed two analytics in step 9 to deal with change management issues: force field analysis and a stakeholder map and communications plan.

Force Field Analysis   The first exercise focused on preparation of a force field analysis. This tool requires participants to think together about all the aspects of a desired solution and is especially useful for analyzing change initiatives. Force field analysis is a structured approach to generating supports and barriers toward implementing a particular solution. The key steps in a force field analysis are listed next.

1. Define the ideal state on the top right of the template.
2. Prioritize driving forces of those that can be strengthened.
3. Prioritize the restraining forces that can be removed or reduced.
4. Brainstorm force field actions to enhance driving forces and/or mitigate restraining forces.

   The output of these four steps includes:

1. **Ideal State.** Fully integrated system lab services
2. Driving forces that can be strengthened included:
   - Reduce cost
   - Standardization
   - Efficiency
   - Decrease duplication of services
   - Pathology involvement
3. Restraining forces that can be removed or reduced included:
   - Cost of implementation and rework

- Affiliate silos (financial)
- Resistance to change
- Staffing for 24-hour services
- Size and complexity of project
- Political ramifications
- Pathology involvement
- IT issues

4. Brainstorm force field actions to enhance driving forces and/or mitigate restraining forces presented in order of importance::
   - Phased approach to integration
   - LIS consolidation
   - Lab system designated administrative leader
   - System leadership team
   - Pathology model realignment

Stakeholder Map and Communications Plan   Building on the force field analysis, the team built a stakeholder map that identified the anticipated roles people would play during deployment of solutions. The roles included:

- Change sponsors
- Change originators
- Change agents responsible for deploying or implementing the changes
- Change advocates
- Change blockers
- SME informants to provide information on the change

The stakeholder map provides insights into key constituencies. From the map, the team developed a summary communications plan that contained key actions that will enable the primary elements of the To-Be solution to gain traction in the organization. The team also developed specific messages for each stakeholder group.

- MidMichigan Health & Affiliate Administration: Background and recommendations
- Lab staff: Background and recommendations
- Human resources and education: Staffing changes and implications
- Finance: Financial impact, shared services, allocations
- Pathologists: Background and recommendations
- Legal counsel: Shared services model
- Purchasing, couriers: Supplies ordering changes, delivery needs

- Patients: Any concerns about billing
- Outreach clients: Any changes in billing or services
- Medical staff: Any changes in services

Step 10: What Do We Pilot? Results? What Is the Full Implementation Plan?

The team developed an action plan that contained over 25 specific steps broken down into three categories:

1. Quick wins that could be deployed inside the team's 12-week life cycle
2. A pilot phase to test changes and prepare for full implementation
3. To-Be changes that would be handed off to the process owner after the 12-week team cycle

Quick Wins   Quick wins approved by the 10-step steering committee during the 12 weeks enabled the team to demonstrate the value of the To-Be solutions prior to pilot or full implementation.

After a complete review of the options, it is proposed to immediately implement an integrated model with work cell structure to incorporate these components:

- One system-wide administrative lead who has the authority and responsibility for laboratory services across MidMichigan Health.
- Adopt the work cell model for all laboratory sites to provide the next benefits:
  - Decrease overall turnaround time to perform at the 90th percentile for stat potassium, hemoglobin, and Troponin.
  - Reduce work in progress by eliminating batch processing so that samples do not sit in racks waiting for processing and analysis and test results do not wait for review and release.
  - Increase lab capacity to be identified.
  - Improve oversight of operations by being able to quickly assess the state of operations.
  - Reduce FTE staffing requirements and increasing cross-training.
  - Optimize space requirements, changes to be identified.
  - Reduce total operating costs by $1.7 million in Phase II.
- One core laboratory site located at Midland to include microbiology and anatomical pathology and utilize the work cell model for chemistry, urinalysis, coagulation, and hematology.

- ■ Three rapid response laboratory sites at Gratiot, Clare, and Gladwin to provide nonautomated services for blood bank and manual kits combined with utilizing a mini-work cell model for chemistry, urinalysis, coagulation, and hematology.
- ■ Standardize all instrumentation resulting in the replacement of chemistry instrumentation with Ortho Diagnostic chemistry instrumentation.
- ■ Support services to be consolidated to include functions of quality, accreditation, education, patient/client services, and customer service/processing.

After implementation is complete and current savings, quality, and efficiency targets are achieved, evaluate the operational and financial implications to convert the work cells to an automated laboratory line structure.

Improve Performance   The team identified these financial impacts totaling $1.7 million:

- ■ Phase I: Developed centralized model.
- ■ Phase II: Deploy centralized work cell structure: $1.7 million.

> Energy and persistence conquer all things.
>
> **—Benjamin Franklin**

PHARMACY SERVICES 10-STEP TEAM CASE STUDY, *SMARTER FORMULARIES*

Many technological advances within the health system had been made in the months preceding the initiation of our 10-step team that made this the perfect time for a standardized, system-wide approach. The inclusion of pharmacy and nonpharmacy team members was highly valuable and gave us a new perspective on potential solutions. We are very pleased with our team's results, which were particularly meaningful since we were able to find opportunities for significant cost savings while improving, not just maintaining, the quality of patient care.

> —Katie Sias, PharmD, Pharmacy Clinical
> Coordinator (team leader)

Strategic Context

The pharmacy 10-step team aligned with MidMichigan Health system Strategic Objective E: Operational excellence. The structure provided for one pharmacy at each of the four medical centers. The processes for ordering and filling prescriptions varied at each location. The overall system had not fully rationalized its formulary lists and was not fully realizing procurement discounts on prescription drugs.

This case study consists of the next sections:

- **Steps 1–5 Training** encompasses working papers and content developed during the first two-day training team breakout sessions.
- **Steps 1–5 Fieldwork** shares key findings primarily from voice-of-customer surveys, data review, and analytics.
- **Steps 6–10 Training** consists of working papers and content developed during the second two-day training breakout sessions.
- **Improve performance** shares the financial and nonfinancial team findings to improve performance.

Steps 1–5 Training Days 1–2

Step 1: Have We Identified the Right Areas of Focus?

Since teams (by design) consisted of representatives from different functions that possessed varied understanding of the current process, step 1 focused the team to establish a baseline or common understanding of the current situation.

Customer Segments and Requirements   The team brainstormed customer requirements, prioritized them through voting, and drafted the Five Ups charts for each customer group.

The first customer group, *physicians*, had five primary requirements:

1. Reducing cycle time for drug availability
2. Reducing the number of patients not being seen by pharmacists
3. Reducing the noncommunication of drug issues
4. Reducing inaccuracies of medical orders
5. Reducing inappropriate medication use

The team, based on its experience and estimation, established As-Is and To-Be targets for each of these customer requirements.

The second customer group, *nursing*, had five primary requirements:

1. Reducing cycle time for drug availability
2. Reducing the noncommunication of drug issues
3. Reducing the time spent on order clarification
4. Reducing nurse compounding
5. Reducing the waste or loss of bulk items

The team, based on its experience and estimation, established As-Is and To-Be targets for each of these customer requirements.

The third customer group, *patients*, had five primary requirements:

1. Reducing drug costs
2. Reducing length of stay
3. Reducing cycle time for drug availability
4. Reducing the waste or loss of bulk items
5. Reducing confusion over the home medication use process

The team, based on its experience and estimation, established As-Is and To-Be targets for each of these customer requirements.

The team recognized the importance of a balanced set of targets that concurrently solved for multiple aspects of this process.

Causes of Issues   The team brainstormed causes of customer problems. The team evaluated and voted on the list to prioritize the top five areas in which to focus its efforts:

1. Physician knowledge of medications and costs
2. Pharmacist knowledge and time
3. Drug shortages and brand/expensive medications
4. Medication waste/loss
5. Communication between disciplines

Data Sets. The team identified key data sets to better understand the As-Is situation. The data sets would provide insights and facts to better analyze, validate, and refine the goal statement. Data sets also provide the basis for refining or adjusting the scope of the project. The team determined that these data sets would be useful to gather during fieldwork:

▪ Cycle time for drug availability: Time to administration report versus time to verification report

- Patients not seen by clinical pharmacists (missed opportunities): Research best practices among other institutions
- Communication of drug issues: Administer survey
- Drug cost: Compile and review budgets
- Drug waste (home and bulk meds): Secure information from rounding and Electronic Medical Record (EMR) charge reporting.

Next, the team defined the background, preliminary problem statement, and preliminary goal statement.

Background   Medication costs make up the majority of the MidMichigan Health pharmacy budget (73%). With changes in inpatient reimbursement, it is critical that cost containment strategies are implemented. These strategies must never compromise the health system's ability to provide excellent care to patients. The pharmacy departments at MidMichigan currently lack a systematic approach to planning and prioritizing specific drug cost management strategies. Steps have been taken to systematize important pharmacy processes and policies (i.e., system-wide medication review by the Pharmacy and Therapeutics Committee). Also, advances in technology, such as the EMR, provide the departments with more detailed information about drug use and will significantly help with cost containment strategies. It is now essential to realize the full potential of these initiatives.

Preliminary Problem Statement   Inefficient pharmacy workflow is leading to longer cycle time to drug availability, increased cost, and lack of customer satisfaction.

Based on the preceding information, the team was positioned to establish a preliminary goal statement. As the team is just in step 1 of 10, the goal statement will be continuously refined and updated as more evidence and data become available.

Preliminary Goal Statement   Reduce cycle time and cost in formulary management by X, which provides improved formulary management to physicians, nurses, and patients resulting in a savings of at least $50,000.

Step 2: What Is the Initial Goal Statement? Team charter?

Team Roles   Team member use of roles is proven to improve team dynamics and performance. The 10-step team's sponsor and team leader were selected prior to the start of the project. Remaining team members volunteered for the other roles; brief descriptions are provided.

- Sponsor (oversees teams, reviews work, owns results): Robin Whitmore
- Team leader (sets guidelines, goals, weekly meetings): Katie Sias
- Timekeeper (ensures deadlines are met): Amy Behmlander
- Recorder (takes notes): Teresa Bailey, Ken Spencer
- Scribe (makes ideas visible in meetings): Tim Sassin, Bryan Cross
- Monitor (adheres to methodology): Tricia Sommer
- Process observer (ensures participation): Kristy Brown
- Spokesperson (reports to other groups): Teresa Bailey, Glenn King

Code of Conduct   The team established a code of conduct to be observed during team meetings and phone calls in order to remain highly productive and meet its ambitious goals. The code of conduct incorporated cultural dimensions the team believed to be important to maintain good morale and working relationships. The code of conduct includes these elements:

- No cell phones/PDAs, iPads, and so on (on vibrate).
- Set meeting agenda.
- Weekly meetings Tuesdays 3:00–4:30 p.m.
- SMEs are not team members.
- Ensure timeliness (calendar integrity, start/stop on time).
- Involve everyone (round robin).
- One idea at a time (two-knock rule).
- Be mindful of offsite members.
- No judgment of other's ideas (brainstorm).
- Obtain consensus (sponsor will break ties).
- Prepare before meeting.
- Clearly define goals; get agreement.
- Be courteous . . . show respect.
- Commit to staying in meeting.
- Have fun.

These exercises were consolidated with modifications into a more complete team charter that formed a team agreement.

Team Charter
- Issue/Problem
  Rising medication costs with no method to standardize containment.
- Goal Statement (revised)
  Reduce overall inpatient pharmaceutical expenditures through provision of more standardized formulary management and reduction of waste through improved medication delivery processes by X date while maintaining or improving patient quality and safety and physician satisfaction resulting in a savings of at least $50,000.
- Constraints
  - Physician and pharmacist participation
  - Pharmacist resources
  - Pharmacy and therapeutics committee approval
  - Consistency/standardization across system
  - Team member time
- Assumptions
  - Physician and pharmacist buy-in
  - Pharmacy and therapeutics committee approval
  - Data availability
  - Generics and drug classes to review
- Team Guidelines (see Code of Conduct)
- Resources (included in roles and additional SMEs not contemplated during the project planning phase)
- Preliminary Project Plan (10-step milestone level)
  - Steps 1–5 Training: Week 1
  - Steps 1–5 Fieldwork: Weeks 2–4
  - Steps 6–10 Training: Week 5
  - Steps 6–10 Fieldwork: Weeks 6–10
  - Celebration and Team Turnoff: Week 11 or 12

Step 3: What Are Three to Five Customer Requirements/Complaints?

Voice of the Customer. The purpose of the survey, consistent with step 1, was to secure input from the customer segments on their key requirements, As-Is and To-Be performance levels, and other valuable text responses. The team designed a VOC survey to be deployed during fieldwork. The draft survey is presented next.

1. Are you aware that the inpatient pharmacy offers the following services (yes, no)?
   - Antibiotic dosing
   - Anticoagulation dosing
   - Parental nutrition dosing
   - Admission medication reconciliation
2. How likely are you to use these inpatient pharmacy services including (1) not likely, (2) somewhat likely, (3) neutral, (4) likely, (5) very likely, (6) not applicable
   - Antibiotic dosing
   - Anticoagulation dosing
   - Parental nutrition dosing
   - Admission medication reconciliation
3. How likely would you be to use these inpatient pharmacy services if offered including (1) not likely, (2) somewhat likely, (3) neutral, (4) likely, (5) very likely, (6) not applicable?
   - Antimicrobial stewardship (the intent would be to optimize clinical outcomes while minimizing unintended consequences of antimicrobial use)
   - Emergency department pharmacist (the purpose would be to complete admission medication reconciliation, be available for drug information questions)
   - Intravenous to oral conversions (the purpose would be to ensure proper and timely conversion from parental to enteral administration with final approval by provider)
   - Intensivist team pharmacist (the purpose would be to ensure proper medication selection and use in critical care patients)
   - Pain management (the purpose would be to assist the provider in evaluating and monitoring a patient's acute and/ or chronic pain management)
   - Other (please specify)
4. How would you rate your knowledge on the cost of inpatient medications?
   - (1) no knowledge, (2) somewhat knowledgeable, (3) knowledgeable, or (4) very knowledgeable

5. How likely are inpatient medication costs to impact your prescribing patterns?
   ■ (1) not likely, (2) somewhat likely, (3) neutral, (4) likely, (5) very likely
6. What is your specialty?
7. At which affiliate do you see most of your patients?

Step 4: What Are the Current Process (Map) and Issues?

The 10-step team was very efficient during its process mapping breakout session. It focused and rapidly developed three process maps: (1) Pharmacy Verification/Consult Process, (2) Transport/Storage of Meds, and (3) Pharmacy and Therapeutics Committee Communication Process. The visual review of the maps revealed and validated the issues and causes noted in earlier steps.

The team breakout revealed these choke points:

1. Pharmacy Verification/Consult Process
   ■ Inappropriate consults
   ■ Consults currently required
   ■ Multiple verification resources
   ■ Knowledge deficit for current or potential pharmacy services
   ■ Physician communication
2. Transport/Storage of Meds
   ■ Technician to counter
   ■ Put in pocket
   ■ Set on counter inside med room
   ■ Set on top of med cart in hall
   ■ Misplaced
3. Pharmacy and Therapeutic Committee Communication Process
   ■ Breakdown in communication to appropriate groups
   ■ Minimal review when presented
   ■ Inefficient methods for distribution to physicians

The team quickly realized that it would take a significant effort to fully understand the As-Is processes at all locations.

Step 5: What Are the Prioritized Choke Points, Issues, and Root Causes?

The team further analyzed the content developed in step 4 to better understand the causes of issues. The primary tool in this step is the fishbone diagram.

The 10-step team initially produced this problem statement for the head of the fish: "Rising medication costs with no method to standardize containment."

The 8Ps and IT fishbone model's categories of root causes, or bones of the fish, are listed next.

■ Product category root causes included availability, appropriate use, and brand versus generic availability.
■ Process category root causes included appropriate use, intravenous to oral procedures, pharmacy and therapeutics committee, drug reorder levels, drug ordering, and price verifications and updates.
■ People and skills category root causes included pharmacy and therapeutics committee, physicians, nurses, and pharmacy staff.
■ Pricing or costs category root causes included drug shortages, drug waste, and coding.
■ Policy and procedures category root causes included brand versus generic availability, automatic substitution underutilization, and intravenous to oral policy.
■ The place or location category root cause included different practices among affiliates.
■ Technology category root causes included contract loading, intravenous to oral power plans, and pending discharge notifications.

Steps 1–5 Fieldwork

The fieldwork contained key findings and updates to hypotheses developed during the two-day training and contained in the working papers. During fieldwork, the team deployed the internal customer surveys and gathered a significant amount of data for analyses.

Survey Results

The 69 responses to the e-survey are shown next.

1. Are you aware that the inpatient pharmacy offers the following services?
   - Antibiotic dosing (68/69, 98.6%)
   - Anticoagulation dosing (68/69, 98.6%)
   - Parenteral nutrition dosing (66/69, 95.7%)
   - Admission medication reconciliation (28/69, 40.6%)
2. How likely are you to use these inpatient pharmacy services (1–6 scale)?
   - Antibiotic dosing: (1) not likely 10.1%, (2) somewhat likely 2.9%, (3) neutral 2.9%, (4) likely 14.5%, (5) very likely 65.2%, (6) not applicable 4.3%
   - Anticoagulation dosing: (1) not likely 11.6%, (2) somewhat likely 4.3%, (3) neutral 5.8%, (4) likely 7.2%, (5) very likely 65.2%, (6) not applicable 5.8%
   - Parenteral nutrition dosing: (1) not likely 21.7%, (2) somewhat likely 1.4%, (3) neutral 4.3%, (4) likely 5.8%, (5) very likely 58%, (6) not applicable 8.7%
   - Admission medication reconciliation: (1) not likely 18.8%, (2) somewhat likely 5.8%, (3) neutral 15.9%, (4) likely 20.3%, (5) very likely 30.4%, (6) not applicable 8.7%
3. How likely would you be to use these inpatient pharmacy services if offered?
   - Antimicrobial stewardship (the intent would be to optimize clinical outcomes while minimizing unintended consequences of antimicrobial use): (1) not likely 11.6%, (2) somewhat likely 4.3%, (3) neutral 11.6%, (4) likely 26.1%, (5) very likely 40.6%, (6) not applicable 5.8%
   - Emergency department pharmacist (the purpose would be to complete admission medication reconciliation, be available for drug information questions): (1) not likely 7.2%, (2) somewhat likely 7.2%, (3) neutral 10.1%, 4) likely 24.6%, (5) very likely 40.6%, (6) not applicable 10.1%
   - Intravenous to oral conversions (the purpose would be to ensure proper and timely conversion from parenteral to enteral administration with final approval by provider): (1)

(continued)

not likely 15.9%, (2) somewhat likely 4.3%, (3) neutral 15.9%, (4) likely 21.7%, (5) very likely 37.7%, (6) not applicable 4.3%
■ Intensivist team pharmacist (the purpose would be to ensure proper medication selection and use in critical care patients): (1) not likely 10.1%, (2) somewhat likely 7.2%, (3) neutral 15.9%, (4) likely 18.8%, (5) very likely 34.8%, (6) not applicable 13%
■ Pain management (the purpose would be to assist the provider in evaluating and monitoring a patient's acute and/ or chronic pain management): (1) not likely 13%, (2) somewhat likely 5.8%, (3) neutral 10.1%, (4) likely 21.7%, (5) very likely 44.9%, (6) not applicable 4.3%
■ Other (please specify): No free-text submissions
4. How would you rate your knowledge on the cost of inpatient medications?
■ (1) no knowledge 30.4%, (2) somewhat knowledgeable 52.2%, (3) knowledgeable 17.4%, or (4) very knowledgeable 0%
5. How likely are inpatient medication costs to impact your prescribing patterns?
■ (1) not likely 10.1%, (2) somewhat likely 20.3%, (3) neutral 24.6%, (4) likely 29.0%, (5) very likely 15.9%
6. What is your specialty?
■ 63 out of 69 providers responded to this question with varying free text responses.
7. At which affiliate do you see most of your patients?
■ Clare 4.3%, Gladwin 8.7%, Gratiot 20.3%, Midland 66.7%

Data Analyses

The review of data sets against benchmarks revealed wide variations for:

■ Cycle time for drug availability: Time to administration report versus time to verification report
■ Patients not seen by clinical pharmacists (missed opportunities): Research best practices among other institutions
■ Communication of drug issues: Administer survey
■ Drug cost: Compile and review budgets

■ Drug waste (home and bulk meds): Secure information from rounding and EMR charge reporting

At the conclusion of Step 5, the team evaluated its performance across multiple attributes. The focus and intent of this exercise contributes to self-correcting teams that can weather challenges during their life cycle. The team voted using a 1–5 scale, with 5 being the highest grade, on five key factors of team performance:

1. Established goals/agenda scored 5.
2. Used code of conduct and group roles scored 5.
3. Used tools/methods scored 5.
4. Freedom to participate (captured brain power) scored 5.
5. Overall meeting effectiveness scored 5.

Steps 6–10 Training Days 3–4

During the two-day 10-step training, the team created solutions, a To-Be design, and implementation plans to realize value.

Step 6: What Are Future State or Desired Process Attributes?

The team engaged in a breakout session designed to leverage both creative thinking and analytical thinking to develop a To-Be design for the core process. The *creative* exercise resulted in these To-Be design elements:

■ Set specific protocols and restrictions for certain medications.
■ Educate/train providers.
■ Maintain consistent pharmacy stance.
■ Open communication.
■ Maximize computerized physician order entry.
■ Hold providers accountable.
■ Educate/train pharmacists, define roles.
■ Give them an easy and good process.
■ Timely interventions and learn from mistakes.

The *analytical, structured* exercise to build the To-Be process revealed these design elements:

■ Process/Procedure

- Expanding clinical services to optimize medication use.
- Centralized verification
- Multiple intravenous medication batches
- Change large volume parenteral medications to on-demand dispensing
- Improve pharmacy and therapeutics committee as well as drug short-age communication
- Policy
  - Metric to hold providers accountable
  - Maximize automatic substitution policies
- Pricing
  - Eliminate unnecessary drug classes for inpatients
- Place/Location
  - Standardize processes across affiliates
- People/Skills
  - Adding FTEs to provide clinical services
  - Educating providers and pharmacists
- Technology
  - Discharge/transfer notification
  - Computerized physician order entry communication and optimization

The 10-step team combined these two exercise outputs to define a comprehensive To-Be solution.

Step 7: What Improvement Level Is Expected—Final Goal Statement?

Based on the cumulative learning from the prior steps, the team revised its initial goal statement twice and identified several new components to create significant value. The new targets also factor in benchmarks and best practices.

Revised Goal Statement #1   Reduce overall inpatient pharmaceutical expenditures through provision of more standardized formulary management and reduction of waste through improved medication delivery processes by X date while maintaining or improving patient quality and safety and physician satisfaction resulting in a savings of at least $X.

Revised Goal Statement #2   Reduce overall pharmaceutical budget by an annual total of $292,000.

- Reduce overall inpatient anti-infective pharmaceutical expenditures per adjusted discharge through provision of more standardized formulary management beginning in two months while maintaining or improving patient quality and safety and physician satisfaction, resulting in an annual savings of at least 10%.
- Reduce overall inpatient pharmaceutical expenditures through an expanded auto-substitution program beginning in two months while maintaining or improving patient quality and safety and physician satisfaction, resulting in an annual savings.
- Reduce IV drug waste through implementation of multiple IV medication batches, change in Gratiot IV waste protocols, and development of a pharmacy technician patient access list, resulting in an annual savings of $x.

Step 8: What Should the Future Process Be (New Map)?

The 10-step team incorporated the design elements from step 6 and the refined goal statement parameters from step 7 to design new processes. The new process also reflected best practices from high-performing affiliates.

Step 9: What Are the Barriers to Improvement? Countermeasures?

The 10-step team completed two analytics in step 9 to deal with change management issues: force field analysis and a stakeholder map and communications plan.

Force Field Analysis The first exercise focused on preparation of a force field analysis. This tool requires participants to think together about all the aspects of a desired solution and is especially useful for analyzing change initiatives. Force field analysis is a structured approach to generating supports and barriers toward implementing a particular solution. The key steps in a force field analysis are listed next.

1. Define the ideal state on the top right of the template.
2. Prioritize driving forces of those that can be strengthened.
3. Prioritize the restraining forces that can be removed or reduced.
4. Brainstorm force field actions to enhance driving forces and/or mitigate restraining forces

The team followed the four steps, outputs included:

1. **Ideal State.** Optimal drug therapy
2. Driving forces that can be strengthened included:
   - Financial implications
   - Improved patient care
   - Decreased length of stay
   - Delayed bacterial resistance
   - Improved cycle time
   - Increased affiliate pharmacist time
   - Improved communication
   - Improved job satisfaction
   - Physician satisfaction
3. Restraining forces that can be removed or reduced included:
   - Physician loss of control
   - Physician push back
   - Affiliate pharmacist push back
   - Available pharmacy time
   - Midland pharmacist push back
   - Current pharmacy and therapeutic committee process
   - Provider frustration from medication records
4. Brainstorm force field actions to enhance driving forces and/or mitigate restraining forces presented in priority order:
   - Provider awareness prior to implementation and ongoing
   - Pharmacist awareness prior to implementation and continuing education
   - Increase accountability of pharmacy and therapeutics recommendations through all levels of the health system
   - Change pharmacy roles to provide a more focused workflow
   - Show providers and pharmacists improvement from changes

Stakeholder Map and Communications Plan   Building on the force field analysis, the team built a stakeholder map that identified the anticipated roles people would play during solution deployment. The roles included:

- Change sponsors
- Change originators
- Change agents responsible for deploying or implementing the changes
- Change advocates

- Change blockers
- SME informants to provide information on the change

The stakeholder map provides insights into key constituencies. From the map, the team developed a summary communications plan that contained key actions that will enable the primary elements of the To-Be solution to gain traction in the organization. The team also developed specific messages for each stakeholder group.

- Providers: Communication process
- Pharmacists: Workflow, CPM results
- Infectious disease team: Communication
- Chiefs of staff: Communication

Step 10: What Do We Pilot? Results? What Is the Full Implementation Plan?

The team developed an action plan that contained over 25 action items or steps broken down into these categories:

- Quick wins that could be deployed inside the team's 12-week life cycle
- Pilot phase to test out changes and prepare for full implementation
- To-Be changes that would be handed off to the process owner after the 12-week cycle

Quick Wins　　Quick wins approved by the 10-step steering committee during the 12 weeks enabled the team to demonstrate value of their To-Be Solutions prior to pilot or full implementation. The quick wins included:

- A new process for more robust physician pharmacy and therapeutics committee involvement
- Reduced drug waste through change in intravenous medication labeling procedure at Gratiot pharmacy
- Expanded adjacent office space in Midland

Improve Performance　　The team identified these financial and operational improvements:

- Reduce overall pharmaceutical budget by an annual total of $290,000 (five-year total of $1,450,000).

- Reduce overall inpatient anti-infective pharmaceutical expenditures per adjusted discharge through provision of more standardized formulary management beginning week 12 while maintaining or improving patient quality and safety and physician satisfaction, resulting in an annual savings.
- Reduce overall inpatient pharmaceutical expenditures through an expanded automatic substitution program beginning week 12 while maintaining or improving patient quality and safety and physician satisfaction, resulting in an annual savings.
- Reduce IV drug waste through implementation of multiple IV medication batches, change in affiliate IV waste protocols, and development of a pharmacy technician patient access list, resulting in an annual savings.

I do not feel obliged to believe that the same God who has endowed us with sense, reason, and intellect has intended us to forgo their use.

—**Galileo Galilei**

 ## NOTES

1. The case studies in this chapter are based on MidMichigan Health 10-Step Team Final Working Papers, April 14, 2012.
2. Pseudonyms are used for all company names.
3. Thomas P. Joseph, "Design of Lean Work Cells: A Lean Lab Layout," *Medical Laboratory Observer* (August 2006).

CHAPTER EIGHT

Core and Specialty Businesses: 10-Step Best Practice Cases

Do your duty and a little more and the future will take care of itself.

—*Andrew Carnegie*

THIS CHAPTER FOCUSES ON CORE AND SPECIALTY SERVICES within the MidMichigan Health care system. Core or central to the medical centers, the Emergency Department (ED) is often the first point of contact for patients. Should ED diagnoses warrant further services, patients will experience the Care Coordination process through discharge. MidMichigan Health provides numerous specialty services. The orthopedics services team focuses largely on hip and joint replacements, and the women's health services team focuses on preventive mammographic screening. The cases include:

- Emergency Department: Improve throughput, customer scores, and revenue.
- Care Coordination: Improve medical outcomes.
- Orthopedic Services: Standardize and save.
- Women's Health Services: Grow the business.

EMERGENCY DEPARTMENT 10-STEP TEAM CASE STUDY, *IMPROVE THROUGHPUT, CUSTOMER SCORES, AND REVENUE*

Bob Paladino's 10-step team design was one of the most effective methods I have ever utilized for identifying, implementing, and evaluating the need and results of process improvement. We were grateful to have support from our administrative team as well as multiple representatives from areas that directly affected our length of stay in the ED. Our team included representatives from radiology, lab, registration/admitting, ED physicians, education, ED nurses, ED clerks, finance, and customer service.

—Stephanie Petras, RN, BSN, MA, MSA, CEN

Strategic Context

The ED team aligned with MidMichigan Health system Strategic Objective E: Operational excellence.[1] The ED wait times were having an impact on patient satisfaction scores, and a number of patients left before treatment (LBT), impacting revenue.

This case study consists of the next sections:

- **Steps 1–5 Training** encompasses working papers and content developed during the first two-day training team breakout sessions.
- **Steps 1–5 Fieldwork** shares key findings primarily from voice-of-customer surveys, data review, and analytics.
- **Steps 6–10 Training** consists of working papers and content developed during the second two-day training breakout sessions.
- **Improve performance** shares the financial and nonfinancial team findings to improve performance.

Steps 1–5 Training Days 1–2

Step 1: Have We Identified the Right Areas of Focus?

Since teams (by design) consisted of representatives from different functions that possessed varied understanding of the current process, step 1 focused the team to establish a baseline or common understanding of the current situation.

Customer Requirements   The team brainstormed patient customer's requirements, prioritized them through voting, and drafted the Five Ups charts. The patient customer group had eight prioritized requirements:

1. Cycle time triage to bed placement
2. Triage to physician
3. Triage to discharge
4. Triage to admittance
5. Registered nurse (RN) assess to physician evaluation
6. Triage to disposition
7. Pain control
8. Customer satisfaction scores

The team established As-Is and To-Be targets for each of the requirements. However, the team recognized that baseline data would have to be collected to validate the current situation. The team discussed the importance of a balanced set of targets that concurrently solved for multiple goals of this process.

Causes of Issues   The team brainstormed and prioritized causes of customer problems. The top four issues were:

1. No fast track or support staff, such as midlevel providers
2. Limited dedicated SC shift coordinators coverage
3. Delay in disposition to door
4. Slow response by consultants

Data Sets. The team identified key data sets to better understand the As-Is situation. The data sets would provide insights and facts to better analyze and validate and refine the goal statement. Data sets also provide the basis for refining or adjusting the scope of the project. The team determined that the next data sets would be useful to gather during fieldwork:

- Cycle time triage to bed placement
- Triage to physician
- Triage to discharge
- Triage to admittance
- RN assess to physician evaluation

- Triage to disposition
- Customer satisfaction scores

Next the team defined the background, preliminary problem statement, and preliminary goal statement.

Background

- Multiple requisition forms and processes
- Inefficiencies in productive time
- Lack of leveraging technology
- Lack of communication among all users
- Perceived low satisfaction among all users

Preliminary Problem Statement　Unsatisfactory patient quality of care scores for the ED when compared to the ED peer group. The key measure is the percentage of patients who rate the service excellent.

Based on the preceding information, the team was positioned to establish a preliminary goal statement. As the team is just in step 1 of 10, the goal statement will be continuously refined and updated as more evidence and data become available.

Preliminary Goal Statement　Our goal is that the Emergency Department will achieve this fiscal year, a two point increase in the percent of those who respond excellent when asked about their overall quality of care experience in the Emergency Department.

Step 2: What Is the Initial Goal Statement? Team Charter?

Team Roles　Team member use of roles is proven to improve team dynamics and performance. The 10-step team's sponsor and team leader were selected prior to the start of the project. Remaining team members volunteered for the other roles; brief descriptions are provided.

- Sponsor (oversees teams, reviews work, owns results): Mike Erickson
- Team leader (sets guidelines, goals, weekly meetings): Stephanie Petras
- Timekeeper (ensures deadlines are met): Missy Simmons
- Recorder (takes notes): Renae Foco and Brad Van Fulpen

- Scribe (makes ideas visible in meetings): Karma Beutel
- Monitor (adheres to methodology): Andrea Millard and Tricia Magnapora
- Process observer (ensures participation): Lyn Hintz and Andrea Millard
- Spokesperson (reports to other groups): Jan Penney

Code of Conduct

The team established a code of conduct to be observed during team meetings and phone calls in order to remain highly productive and meet its ambitious goals. The code of conduct incorporated the cultural dimensions the team believed to be important to maintain good morale and working relationships. The code of conduct includes these elements:

- Set meeting agenda, allocate time.
- Ensure timeliness (calendar integrity; start/stop on time).
- Involve everyone (round robin).
- One idea at a time (no flops).
- No judgment of other's ideas (brainstorm).
- Obtain consensus.
- Prepare before meeting.
- Clearly define goals—get agreement.
- Define roles.
- Define tool to meet objective.
- Be courteous . . . show respect.
- Commit to staying in meeting.
- No side discussions.
- Take turns talking.
- Foster honesty, openness, trust (no ridicule for throwing out idea).
- Supermajority.
- Have fun.

These exercises were consolidated with modifications into a more complete team charter, which formed a team agreement.

Team Charter

- Issue/Problem

Unsatisfactory patient quality-of-care scores for the ED when compared to the ED peer group. The key measure is the percentage of patients who rate the service excellent.

- Goal Statement

  Our goal is that the Emergency Department will achieve this fiscal year, a two point increase in the percent of those who respond excellent when asked about their overall quality of care experience in the Emergency Department.

- Constraints
  - Lack of dedicated fast-track staff
  - Wait time is too long
  - Pain control
- Team Guidelines (included in code of conduct)
- Resources (included in roles and additional subject matter experts [SMEs] not contemplated during the project planning phase)
- Preliminary Project Plan (10-step milestone level)
  - Steps 1–5 Training: Week 1
  - Steps 1–5 Fieldwork: Weeks 2–4
  - Steps 6–10 Training: Week 5
  - Steps 6–10 Fieldwork: Weeks 6–10
  - Celebration and Team Turnoff: Week 11 or 12

Step 3: What Are Three to Five Customer Requirements/Complaints?

Voice of the Customer. The purpose of the survey, consistent with step 1, is to secure input from the customer segments on their key requirements, As-Is and To-Be performance levels, and to review other valuable text responses. The team agreed to use the existing hospital ED telephone survey deployed daily to ensure consistency in measurement. The score measured the percent of responses in each of the five categories: Excellent, Very Good, Good, Fair, or Poor.

Step 4: What Are the Current Process (Map) and Issues?

The 10-step team developed a process map for patient in the ED for one medical center with the highest volume. The visual review of the maps revealed and validated the issues and causes noted in earlier steps.

The 10-step team started to catalog the choke points in the process map. The most impactful choke points included:

- Waiting room to treatment room
- RN evaluation to MD evaluation or standing orders
- Clerk receiving chart with orders
- Clerk ordering diagnostic studies
- Obtaining results
- MD reviewing results
- Consulting another physician
- Disposition time to leaving ED

Step 5: What Are the Prioritized Choke Points, Issues, and Root Causes?

In this step, the content developed in step 4 is further analyzed by the team to better understand the causes of issues. The primary tool in this step is the fishbone diagram. The 10-step team initially produced this problem statement for the head of the fish: "Patient Excellent scores are too low."

The 8Ps fishbone model's categories and attendant root causes or bones of the fish are listed next.

- Pricing or costs category root causes included copay rates and overall costs increases.
- Promotion category root causes included self-promotion, advertising in waiting room, lack of positive promotion, and unrealistic expectations set by other providers.
- People and skills category root causes included fishbowl setting, inconsistent scripting, inconsistent interactions, staffing levels, and resistance to change attitude.
- Process category root causes included diagnostic testing, decision to admit, lack of standing orders, inconsistent greeter, physician order for pain reduction, transport process inconsistent, clerk process inconsistent, and patient admission.
- Place or location category root causes included location—distance to ancillary services, room placement, bed availability, central nurses' station design, and no holding area.
- Policy category root causes included X-ray Department in ED, consulting difficulties, and standing orders.
- Procedure category root causes included patients' perceived lack of control.
- Product category root causes included lack of monitors, patients' perceived needs not met, lack of availability of selected services.

At the conclusion of step 5, the team evaluated its performance across multiple attributes. The focus and intent of this exercise contributes to self-correcting teams that can weather challenges during their life cycle. The team voted using a 1–5 scale, with 5 being the highest grade, on five key factors of team performance. These included:

1. Established goals/agenda scored 4.
2. Used code of conduct and group roles scored 5.
3. Used tools/methods scored 4.
4. Freedom to participate (captured brain power) scored 5.
5. Overall meeting effectiveness scored 4.

Steps 1–5 Fieldwork

The fieldwork contained key findings and updates to hypotheses developed during the two-day training and contained in the working papers. During fieldwork, the team deployed the internal customer surveys and gathered a significant amount of data for analyses.

Survey Results

The team reviewed the weekly results for Overall Quality of Care, which revealed these percentages rated Excellent:

- Week 1: 45.0% of 160 patients surveyed
- Week 2: 46.9% of 162 patients surveyed
- Week 3: 47.6% of 170 patients surveyed
- Week 4: 53.2% of 171 patients surveyed
- Week 5: 45.4% of 194 patients surveyed
- Week 6: 47.2% of 199 patients surveyed
- Week 7: 42.9% of 203 patients surveyed
- Week 8: 49.4% of 180 patients surveyed
- Week 9: 43.5% of 184 patients surveyed
- Week 10: 44.9% of 127 patients surveyed

The 75% percentile benchmark level is consistently in the 53% to 55% range weekly. So the As-Is baseline is regularly below the desired benchmark level.

The 10-step team validated the weekly Excellent scores and also identified the benchmark 75th-percentile weekly scores for peer group hospitals. These two data sets provided insight into the potential gap the team might undertake to close.

Data Analyses

The team determined these data sets would be useful to gather during fieldwork:

- ED Cycle Time Analysis: ED Triage to Physician
  - Cycle time triage to bed placement: 19 minutes
  - Cycle time bed to RN: 10 minutes
  - RN to physician: 51 minutes
  - Triage to physician: 74 minutes
- ED Cycle Time Analysis: ED Order to Physician Review
  - Order to clerk: 7 minutes
  - Clerk to result time: 54 minutes
  - Result to physician review: 39 minutes
  - Total order to physician review: 82 minutes
- ED Cycle Time Analysis: ED Disposition to Leave ED
  - Disposition to patient placement: 34 minutes
  - Patient to bed assign: 17 minutes
  - Bed assign to bed ready: 9 minutes
  - Bed ready to leave ED: 60 minutes
  - Disposition to leave ED: 43 minutes
- ED Cycle Time Analysis: ED Patient Door-to-Door Summary
  - Triage to physician: 74 minutes
  - Total order to physician review: 82 minutes
  - Disposition to leave ED: 43 minutes
  - Triage to leave ED: 204 minutes
- ED Cycle Time Analysis: ED Patient Door-to-Door Summary by Acuity level (1 is high and 5 is low)
  - Acuity level 5: 211 minutes
  - Acuity level 4: 198 minutes
  - Acuity level 3: 160 minutes
  - Acuity level 2: 120 minutes
  - Acuity level 1: 86 minutes
- Year-over-Year Comparison: Total Left Before Treatment Cases per Month
  - Month 1 last year 42, this year 60, an increase of 42.9%
  - Month 2 last year 30, this year 77, an increase of 156.7%
  - Month 3 last year 64, this year 82, an increase of 21.9%
- Comparison Three Months: Total Left Before Treatment Cases per Month
  - Month 1 60 increased in month 2 of 77, an increase of 28.3%
  - Month 2 77 increased in month 3 of 82, an increase of 6.5%

Steps 6–10 Training Days 3–4

During the two-day 10-step training, the team created solutions, a To-Be design, and implementation plans to realize value.

Step 6: What Are Future State or Desired Process Attributes?

The team engaged in a breakout session designed to leverage both creative thinking and analytical thinking to develop a To-Be design for the core process. The *creative* exercise resulted in these To-Be design elements:

- Offer discharge instructions—speedy, accurate, understandable
- Easy: No guesswork, patient well informed
- Free warm blanket, stitches out for free, warm atmosphere, friendly faces, free beverages
- Clean appearance
- Personal attention, handoff, communication to next patient care provider
- Attention to detail: Pain management, physician spending time, accurate charting, completed green form
- Amenities such as magnetic resonance imaging (MRI), computed tomography (CT), diagnostics, clean room, television, telephone, wireless, food when able, warm blanket, ticker mattress on stretcher
- Competent staff, timely available testing
- Promotion: ED signs, billboards, accurate and easy way-finding, additional signs around campus
- Speed: Decreased length of stay (LOS), turnaround time, limited waiting room time
- Cost effective: Transparency in billing, easily understandable, no unrequired tests, no copay, reduce our costs to provide service
- Location: Easy to identify, close to vital services
- Personal touch: Introductions are made, visible teamwork, exceeding patient expectations
- Reduced cycle time: Door to bed to door
- Quality: Accurate diagnosis and skilled treatment, quality ancillaries

The *analytical, structured* exercise to build the To-Be process included these design elements:

- Process, policy, and procedure
  - Discharge instructions: Speedy, accurate, understandable

- No guesswork, patient well informed
- Handoff: Communication to next care provider
- Pain management
- Physician spending time, accurate charting, completed green form
- More staffing, more rooms
- Philosophy (fast track): Staff buy-in fast track for low-acuity patients, assigned staff and time
- Utilization of techs (transport, etc.)
- Decreased LOS, turnaround time, limited waiting room time
- Transparency in billing, easily understandable, no unrequired tests, no copay, reduce our costs to provide service
- Door to bed to door
- Standing orders
- Dedicated shift coordinators
- Computerized physician order entry
- Admitting physician: See patient on floor
- People and Skills
  - No guesswork, patient well informed
  - Warm blanket, stitches out for free, warm atmosphere, friendly faces, free beverages
  - Handoff: Communication to next patient care provider
  - Competent staff, timely available testing
  - Introductions are made, visible teamwork, exceeding patient expectations
  - Door to bed to door
  - Accurate diagnosis and skilled treatment, quality ancillaries
- Place and Location
  - Clean appearance
  - ED signs, billboards, accurate and easy way-finding, additional signs around campus
  - Easy to identify, close to vital services
- Partner and Vendor
  - MRI, CT, diagnostics, clean room, TV, telephone, wireless, food when able, warm blanket, ticker mattress on stretcher
  - Transparency in billing, easily understandable, no unnecessary test, no copay, reduce our costs to provide service
  - Reinforce bylaws
- Technology
  - Accurate diagnosis and skilled treatment, quality ancillaries

- MRI, CT, diagnostics, clean room, TV, telephone, wireless, food when able, warm blanket, ticker mattress on stretcher
- Electronic medical records (EMR)

The 10-step team combined these two exercise outputs to define a comprehensive To-Be solution.

Step 7: What Improvement Level Is Expected—Final Goal Statement?

Based on the cumulative learning from the prior steps, the team revisited its initial goal statement and identified several new components to create significant value. The new targets also factor in benchmarks and best practices.

Preliminary Goal Statement
Our goal is that the Emergency Department will achieve this fiscal year, a 2-point increase in the percentage of those who respond excellent when asked about their overall quality of care experience in the Emergency Department.

Revised Goal Statement
The team determined a compound goal statement consisting of three related measures:

1. Our goal is that the Emergency Department will achieve this fiscal year, a two point increase in the percent of patients who respond excellent when asked about their overall quality of care experience in the Emergency Department
2. Our goal is to decrease the total cycle time spent in the ED by an average of 30 minutes over the next six- month trial period. This will be accomplished by implementing current standing orders, interdepartmental fast track, and dedicated shift coordinators in the ED.
3. We project that the reduced wait time will result in a 50% decrease in LBT patients, which represents net income opportunity of $158,000.

Step 8: What Should the Future Process Be (New Map)?

The 10-step team incorporated the design elements from step 6 and the refined goal statement parameters from step 7 to design new processes. The new ED process also reflected best practices from high-performing affiliates.

Step 9: What Are the Barriers to Improvement? Countermeasures?

The 10-step team completed two analytics in step 9 to deal with change management issues: force field analysis and a stakeholder map and communications plan.

Force Field Analysis

The first exercise focused on preparation of a force field analysis. This tool requires participants to think together about all the aspects of a desired solution and is especially useful for analyzing change initiatives. Force field analysis is a structured approach to generating supports and barriers toward implementing a particular solution. The key steps in a force field analysis are listed next.

1. Define the ideal state on the top right of template.
2. Prioritize driving forces of those that can be strengthened.
3. Prioritize the restraining forces that can be removed or reduced.
4. Brainstorm force field actions to enhance driving forces and/or mitigate restraining forces.

   The team output included:

1. **Ideal State.** Improved ED patient satisfaction and LBT earnings through a reduction in cycle time
2. Driving forces that can be strengthened included:
   - Medical Executive Review Committee (MERC): Reduce congestion in ED
   - Administration: Patient scores
   - Patients: Increased satisfaction
   - Staff morale: Improved flow
   - Fast track: Improved throughput
3. Restraining forces that can be removed or reduced included:
   - MERC: Resistance to change
   - Administration: Operations
   - Current process
   - Staff resistance to change
   - Physical layout
4. Brainstorm force field actions to enhance driving forces and/or mitigate restraining forces:
   - MERC: Business case vis-à-vis data; reduce physician on-call pay
   - Patient scores may impact compensation
   - Provide excellent care to drive patient volumes

- Consistent excellence of care
- Staff recognize additional time provided for direct patient care
- Staff education and transparent communication
- Positive approachable attitudes by department champions
- Expedited care for all patient acuity levels
- MERC data: Hourly census, best practices, decreased liability
- Increased comfort from consistent care plan

Stakeholder Map and Communications Plan   Building on the force field analysis, the team built a stakeholder map that identified the anticipated roles people would play during deployment of solutions. The roles included:

- Change sponsors
- Change originators
- Change agents responsible for deploying or implementing the changes
- Change advocates
- Change blockers
- SME informants to provide information on the change

The stakeholder map provides insights into key constituencies. From the map, the team developed a summary communications plan that contained key actions that will enable the primary elements of the To-Be solution to gain traction in the organization. The team also developed specific messages and expectations for each stakeholder group.

- MERC: Schedule fast-track physician and standing orders
- Nurses, clerks: Overview of planned process, ownership and participation in the plan
- Patients: Survey, data collection, telephone, scripting of care
- Administration: Support in changing the process
- Ancillary services: Communication and involvement in the plan
- Survey company: Increase by 2% during FY11
- Inpatient units: Decrease rework and increase throughput

Step 10: What Do We Pilot? Results? What Is the Full Implementation Plan?

The team developed an action plan that contained over 25 specific steps broken down into three categories:

1. Quick wins that could be deployed inside the team's 12-week life cycle
2. A pilot phase to test out changes and prepare for full implementation
3. To-Be changes that would be handed off to the process owner after the 12-week cycle.

Quick Wins   Quick wins approved by the 10-step steering committee during the 12 weeks enabled the team to demonstrate value prior to pilot or full implementation of their To-Be solutions. The quick wins included:

- Using standing orders
- Leveraging a fast-track system
- Approving two full-time equivalent positions for dedicated shift coordinators

The pilot of these quick wins had an immediate positive impact:

- Data showed decrease in overall length of stay in the ED by 30 minutes from implementation of partial plan.
- The To-Be pilot secured buy-in from the ED physicians, nurses, and clerks.

Improve Performance   The team identified these financial and operational improvements:

- Financial earnings improvement through reduced LBTs of $158,000; additional subsequent annual savings total $158,000 per year (five year total savings $790,000).
- Achieve a two-point increase in the percentage of those who respond excellent when asked about their overall quality of care experience in the ED.
- Decrease the total time spent in the ED by an average of 30 minutes over the next six-month trial period.

> By always thinking unto them. I keep the subject constantly before me and wait till the first dawning's open little by little into the full light.
>
> **—Isaac Newton (on how he made discoveries)**

 ## CARE COORDINATION 10-STEP TEAM CASE STUDY, *IMPROVE MEDICAL OUTCOMES*

The 10-step team provided the structure and framework for a cross-affiliate team to come together with a common goal to improve patient outcomes and at the same time gain important operational efficiencies that are crucial in the current economic state of health care today. The 10-step process facilitated teamwork, validated our current process and problems, and ultimately guided our problem-solving process to ensure the implementation of best practices.

—Tammy Terrell, RN, BSN, Director of Nursing,
MidMichigan Medical Center–Gratiot (team leader)

Strategic Context

The care coordination 10-step team aligned with MidMichigan Health system Strategic Objective E: Operational excellence. The existing care coordination processes varied by affiliate (entity), contained many manual steps, and caused delays and missed opportunities to classify patient entry status for appropriate designation. These processes and factors impact revenue, claim denials, patient LOS, and patient readmission rates.

MidMichigan Health currently has an inconsistent coordination of patient care process, which results in customer dissatisfaction, deficiency in quality metrics/initiatives, and lost revenue. We need to bridge any gaps to the upcoming EMR. Some of our challenges were:

- Multiple manual touch points (different between the affiliates)
- Inconsistent social work and utilization review (UR) processes
- Cumbersome quality data collection process (not timely)
- Retrospective versus concurrent review process
- Unnecessary or redundant testing
- Lack of staff involvement in care plan and interdisciplinary team
- Lack of consistent physician advisor process that holds physicians accountable
- Lack of structured discharge process
- Role confusion
- Hours of coverage do not meet demand
- Lack of standardized forms
- Need to bridge current paper process to the upcoming EMR

Our goal was to have consistent (system-wide) coordination of patient care services that results in customer satisfaction, improved care management, improved quality metrics/initiatives, and enhanced revenue capture.

This case study consists of the next sections:

- **Steps 1–5 Training** encompasses working papers and content developed during the first two-day training team breakout sessions.
- **Steps 1–5 Fieldwork** shares key findings primarily from voice-of-customer surveys, data review, and analytics.
- **Steps 6–10 Training** consists of working papers and content developed during the second two-day training breakout sessions.
- **Improve performance** shares the financial and nonfinancial team findings to improve performance.

Steps 1–5 Training Days 1–2

Step 1: Have We Identified the Right Areas of Focus?

Since teams (by design) consisted of representatives from different functions that possessed varied understanding of the current process, step 1 focused the team to establish a baseline or common understanding of the current situation.

Customer Segments and Requirements
The team brainstormed customer groups, identified and prioritized group requirements through voting, and drafted the Five Ups charts for each customer group.

The first customer group, *patients*, had five primary requirements:

1. Education
2. Communication
3. Coordinated timely care
4. Cost of care
5. Involvement in care

The second customer group, *family or patient representative*, was believed to be an extension of the patient and has the same five primary requirements:

1. Education and resources
2. Communication
3. Coordinated timely care
4. Cost of care
5. Involvement in care

The third customer group, *physician*, has five primary requirements:

1. Accurate information
2. Point person
3. SBAR (Situation, Background, Assessment, and Recommendation) and communication
4. Timeliness
5. Control or medical management

The fourth customer group, *interdisciplinary team (IDT)*, generally consisting of nurses, case workers, and administrators, has five primary requirements:

1. Reducing any miscommunications
2. Increasing involvement in care
3. Improving authority and empowerment
4. Increasing use of a point person
5. Increasing the accuracy of insurance information

The fifth customer group, *payors (insurers)*, has five primary requirements:

1. Increasing efficiency of care
2. Increasing accuracy of information
3. Improving costs
4. Increasing the timeliness of notification
5. Increasing the quality and safety data

The sixth customer group, *external partners*, has four primary requirements:

1. Increasing the timeliness of notification
2. Improving coordinated care
3. Increasing accurate patient handover communications
4. Increasing access to the plan of care

The team, based on its experience on prior 10-step teams, decided to baseline information during fieldwork to establish As-Is and To-Be targets for each of the requirements.

Causes of Issues   The team brainstormed causes of customer problems. The team captured causes for all customer segments in one exercise:

- Multiple facilities
- Different processes
- Multiple touch points
- Not everyone is on the same page working toward the same goal
- Silo mentality on the care team—no captain
- Inconsistent social work and UR processes
- Quality data collection processes (vary and not always timely)
- Retrospective instead of concurrent review
- Delays/wait times in care process
- Unnecessary testing/redundancy
- IT system workflows (unknown to this team)
- Lack of staff involvement in care plan and IDT
- Staff rework
- Lack of physician advisor process/not timely
- Lack of structured discharge process
- Payor initiatives and penalties
- Lack of seven-day-a-week coverage
- Role confusion
- Multiple forms/lack of standardized forms

Data Sets. The team identified key data sets to better understand the As-Is situation. The data sets would provide insights and facts to better analyze and validate and refine the goal statement. Data sets also provide the basis for refining or adjusting the scope of the project. The team determined that these data sets would be useful to gather during fieldwork:

- Revenue recognition (write-downs) for patients designated as inpatient later diagnosed as outpatient in total and by four hospital locations.
- Revenue recognition (missed revenue) for patients designated as outpatient who should have been diagnosed as inpatient in total and by four hospital locations.
- LOS in total for system and by four hospital locations
- LOS by specific diagnoses in total for system and by four hospital locations
- Readmission rates in total system and for selected diagnoses
- Readmission rates by four hospital locations for selected diagnoses
- Insurance denials volume in total and by four hospital locations
- Insurance denials dollars in total and by four hospitals

Next, the team defined the background, a preliminary problem statement, and a preliminary goal statement.

Background

- Multiple facilities, different processes, different payment methodologies
- Multiple touch points
- Not everyone on the same page working toward the same goal
- Silo mentality on the care team—no captain
- Inconsistent social work and UR processes
- Quality data collection processes (vary and not always timely)
- Retrospective instead of concurrent review
- Delays/wait times in care process
- Unnecessary testing/redundancy
- Merlin workflows (unknown to this team)
- Lack of staff involvement in care plan and IDT
- Staff rework
- Lack of physician advisor process/not timely
- Lack of structured discharge process
- Payor initiatives and penalties

Preliminary Problem Statement   Inconsistent coordination of patient care services results in customer dissatisfaction, deficiency in quality metrics/initiatives, and lost revenue.

Based on the preceding information, the team was positioned to establish a preliminary goal statement. As the team is just in step 1 of 10, the goal statement will be continuously refined and updated as more evidence and data become available.

Preliminary Goal Statement   To have consistent coordination of patient care services that results in customer satisfaction, improved quality metrics/initiatives, and enhanced revenue capture.

Step 2: What Is the Initial Goal Statement? Team Charter?

Team Roles   Team member use of roles is proven to improve team dynamics and performance. The 10-step team's sponsor and team leader were selected prior to the start of the project. Remaining team members volunteered for the other roles; brief descriptions are provided.

- Sponsor (oversees teams, reviews work, owns results): Shelli Wood
- Team leader (sets guidelines, goals, weekly meetings): Tammy Terrell
- Timekeeper (ensures deadlines are met): Pam Wieske

- Recorder (takes notes): Christie Mann
- Scribe (makes ideas visible in meetings): Cheryl Kotenko
- Monitor (adheres to methodology): Andrea Muladore
- Process observer (ensures participation): Rachel Peltier and Carolyn VanWert
- Spokesperson (reports to other groups): Rachel Peltier and Carolyn VanWert
- Team members: Chandra Morse, Sherry Taunt, Jan Penney, Kellie Warner, and Jerri Liphard

Code of Conduct

The team established a code of conduct to be observed during team meetings and phone calls in order to remain highly productive to meet its ambitious goals. The code of conduct incorporates the cultural dimensions the team believed to be important to maintain good morale and working relationships. The code of conduct includes these elements:

- No cell phones/PDAs, iPads, and so on.
- Set meeting agenda, allocate time.
- SMEs are not team members.
- Ensure timeliness (calendar integrity; start/stop on time).
- Involve everyone (round robin).
- One idea at a time (no flops).
- No judgment of other's ideas (brainstorm).
- Obtain consensus.
- Prepare before meeting.
- Clearly define goals—get agreement.
- Define roles.
- Define tool to meet objective.
- Be courteous . . . show respect.
- Commit to staying in meeting.
- No side discussions.
- Take turns talking.
- Foster honesty, openness, trust (no ridicule for throwing out idea).
- Two-knock rule.
- Have fun.
- No experts in the room.
- Take risks.
- What happens in the boardroom stays in the boardroom.

- Allow and work through conflict.
- Send notification (not files) when posting on J: drive.

These exercises were consolidated with modifications into a more complete team charter, which formed a team agreement.

Team Charter
- Issue/Problem
    Inconsistent coordination of patient care services results in customer dissatisfaction, deficiency in quality metrics/initiatives, and lost revenue
- Goal Statement (revised)
    Consistent coordination of patient care services results in customer satisfaction, improved quality metrics/initiatives, and enhanced revenue capture.
- Constraints
    - Individual schedules
    - Holidays
    - Competing priorities
- Assumptions
    - Enough time and manpower to complete task
    - Everyone will contribute
    - Avoid solutions that cannot be measured in the time frame
    - Core team will meet weekly
    - Decisions by consensus
- Team Guidelines (included in the code of conduct plus the next considerations due to the team consisting of representatives from multiple locations)
    - Utilize technology such as Live Meetings.
    - Every Wednesday 2 p.m.–4 p.m.
    - Location = Midland Conference Room (near Harlow).
    - No meeting the week between Christmas and New Year's.
    - If missed meeting, individual is responsible for finding out what was missed and prepares their assignments for the next meeting
- Resources (included in roles and additional SMEs not contemplated during the project-planning phase.
- Preliminary Project Plan (10-step milestone level)
    - Steps 1–5 Training: Week 1
    - Steps 1–5 Fieldwork: Weeks 2–4
    - Steps 6–10 Training: Week 5
    - Steps 6–10 Fieldwork: Weeks 6–10
    - Celebration and Team Turnoff: Week 12

Step 3: What Are Three to Five Customer Requirements/Complaints?

Voice of the Customer. The purpose of the survey, consistent with step 1, is to secure input from the customer segments on their key requirements, As-Is and To-Be performance levels, and other valuable text responses. The team designed a voice-of-the-customer (VOC) survey to be deployed during fieldwork. The draft survey is presented next.

Physician Questions
- When there are multiple physicians on a patient's case, I know who is coordinating the overall plan of care for the patient.
  - Yes
  - No
- Rank the ease of communication between yourself and the following members of the care team: (using a 1–5 scale with 1 = lowest, 5 = highest)
  - Nursing
  - Quality resource management
  - Social work and transition planning
  - Pharmacy
  - Rehab services (therapy)
  - Midlevel providers
  - Other physicians
  - Other _____
- Rank the accuracy of information you receive from these disciplines in order to optimize the patient's care: (using a 1–5 scale with 1 = lowest, 5 = highest)
  - Nursing
  - Quality resource management
  - Social work and transition planning
  - Pharmacy
  - Rehab services (therapy)
  - Midlevel providers
  - Other physicians
  - Other _____

(continued)

> - Rank your working knowledge of the following regulatory issues: (using a 1–5 scale with 1 = lowest, 5 = highest)
>   - Core measures
>   - Insurance requirements for reimbursement
>   - Nursing home/extended care facility placements
>   - Home care/hospice
>   - Medical necessity for inpatient care
>   - Observation status
>   - Bundled payments
>   - Medicare denials

Step 4: What Are the Current Process (Map) and Issues?

The 10-step team was very efficient during its process mapping breakout session. It focused and rapidly developed process maps for all four major medical centers. The visual review of the maps revealed and validated the issues and causes noted in earlier steps. With limited time remaining in the breakout session, the 10-step team started to catalog the key steps and choke points. The high-level process narrative follows:

- Patient in bed
- UR function reviews within 24 hours
  - Preauthorization/insurance validation
  - Core measure assessment
  - Daily continued stay reviews
  - Daily nurse conference/team conferences
  - Daily data gathering for quality review/quality assessments (differs at each site)
  - Meet with physician to determine the plan
  - Physician advisor review
  - Reissue important message from Medicare (within two days of admission)
- Discharge planning begins within 24 hours of high-risk admission or specific referral
  - Meet with patient and families to determine needs
  - Make appropriate referrals

- Coordinate transition to the next level of care (complex process)
- Attend care management/IDT meetings
- Medical social workers (done differently at each site)
  - Initial assessment within 24 hours
  - Counseling and education
  - Addressing complex problems

The team quickly realized that it would take a significant effort to fully understand the As-Is processes and choke points at all locations and agreed to conduct these exercises during the fieldwork phase.

Step 5: What Are the Prioritized Choke Points, Issues, and Root Causes?

The team further analyzed the content developed in step 4 to better understand the causes of issues. The primary tool in this step is the fishbone diagram.

The 10-step team initially produced this problem statement for the head of the fish: "Inconsistent coordination of patient care services results in customer dissatisfaction, deficiency in quality metrics/initiatives, and lost revenue."

The 8Ps and IT root cause model's categories and root causes, or bones of the fish, are listed next.

- Process, procedure, and policy category root causes included lack of policies governing physician reviews, lack of standard policies, multiple touch points, quality data collection process varies, retroactive instead of concurrent reviews, delays and wait times, unnecessary testing or redundant testing, lack of structured discharge process, duplication of work, fragmented care, different payor initiatives, and multiple different forms.
- People and skills category root causes included varied skill levels, confusion on role definitions, some confusion on authority, physicians, seven-day scheduling coverage, not everyone on the same page, not all have the same goals, departmental focus (silos), low staff involvement on IDTs, and family dynamics.
- Place or location category root causes included four different locations and inconsistent design of four locations.
- Technology category root causes included use of both automated versus paper medians, new technology workflows not fully understood by teams, multiple e-forms, lack of e-forms, and lack of electronic system.
- Pricing and product categories did not have root causes contributing to the problem statement.

Steps 1–5 Fieldwork

The fieldwork contained key findings and updates to hypotheses developed during the two-day training and contained in the foregoing working papers. During fieldwork, the team refined meeting agendas, continued process maps, evaluated choke points, deployed internal customer surveys, and gathered a significant amount of data for analyses.

Standard Agenda

During fieldwork, the care coordination team developed a standard agenda to start to address this complex issue across all four locations.

- Review agenda
- Review minutes
- Progress reports
- Data analysis overview
- Review timeline
- Recap assignments/timeline
- Debrief meeting
- Date next meeting

Process Flows and Choke Points

The team developed a standard process flow to enable comparisons among the four locations. The patient process flow by time phase illuminated these choke points:

- **Day of admission and first 24 hours.** Variation in review tools and software, variations in staff types and levels, variations in roles, and lack of a formal process for physician advisor review
- **Day 2 and dailies.** Variation in review tools and software, variations in staff types and levels, variations in roles, and lack of a formal process for physician advisor review
- **Outliers.** Lack of consistent process to address LOS issues continuum of care issues among physicians, families, and patients
- **Additional stay tasks.** No consistent process, variations in roles and responsibilities, and variations in staffing

Steps 6–10 Training Days 3–4

During the two-day 10-step training, the team created solutions, a To-Be design, and implementation plans to realize value.

Step 6: What Are Future State or Desired Process Attributes?

The team engaged in a breakout session designed to leverage both creative thinking and analytical thinking to develop a To-Be design for the core process.

The *analytical, structured,* and *creative exercises* to build the To-Be model included these design elements:

- Process, Policy, and Procedure
  - Consistent care management process
  - Concurrent review
  - Medical staff endorse process
  - Utilize real-time reports
  - Consistent communication plan of regulatory requirements
  - Create centralized repository of reference materials: J: drive/Web to ensure compliance
  - Consistent care management policies
- People and Skills
  - Newly defined care management process with one point person
  - Define skill mix and job descriptions
  - Define and add designated physician advisors
  - Seven-day/week coverage
  - Physician engagement
  - Care management infrastructure/organizational chart
  - Comprehensive education
  - Know and understand regulatory requirements
- Product/Equipment
  - Utilize bed board, patient list, and the like
  - Standardized reference manuals
- Place and Location
  - Patient in bed consistently at each affiliate
  - Determine location for designated physician advisors
- Partner and Vendor
  - Physician advisors/consultant
  - Cross-continuum collaboration

- Meeting regulatory initiatives
- Technology
    - Implementation of Merlin
    - Review orders
    - Perform patient assessment
    - Initiate order sets
    - Utilize IDT summary
    - Utilize departmental process
    - Automated InterQual (third party service provider) criteria/IT system form
    - Designate one central warehouse for quality data
    - Establish predetermined prompts

Step 7: What Improvement Level Is Expected—Final Goal Statement?

Based on the cumulative learning from the prior steps, the team revisited its initial goal statement and identified several new components to create significant value. The new targets also factor in benchmarks and best practices.

Initial Goal Statement   Consistent coordination of patient care services results in customer satisfaction, improved quality metrics/initiatives, and enhanced revenue capture.

Final Refined Goal Statement   Reduce the variability in care coordination utilizing evidence-based practice which results in decreased length of stay (by X), decreased readmissions (by X), improved process (core) measure outcomes (by X), and increase patient satisfaction (by X), which results in an improvement of X percent revenue capture; plan completed by week 12 and full implementation by week 28. The team was still gathering data to establish their goal targets during the fieldwork and Training Days 3–4.

Step 8: What Should the Future Process Be (New Map)?

The 10-step team incorporated the design elements from step 6 and the refined goal statement parameters from step 7 to design new processes. The team researched award-winning hospital systems, conducted phone interviews, and incorporated best practices into the new care coordination process.

1. Adopt a system view of patient flow, not a hospital-centered view.

2. Collaboration across multiple functions (quality, ED, operating room, inpatient units, discharge, residents, and physicians).
3. Incorporate three processes in scope: patient access management, patient throughput, and discharge planning.
4. Use ADT index consisting of admission workload, discharge workload, and transfer workload contributing factors to focus integrated case management teams.
5. Establish primary metrics across all four hospitals: ADT Index, LOS, ED diversion hours, occupancy rate and census disparity, delays in discharge, 30-day readmission rates.
6. Create a patient placement center (aka air traffic controller) with a focus on:
   ▪ Bed tracking based on algorithms for efficient placement and doctor rounds
   ▪ Nursing staffing levels
7. Form multidisciplinary care coordination teams charged with identifying ways to improve throughput.
   ▪ Establish one department having authority and accountability and consolidating all reporting for case management, discharge planning, and utilization review.
   ▪ Department contained triads based on acuity, volume, and location.
   ▪ Added finance counselor to triad.
   ▪ Approach internal doctors/hospitalists midsummer.
   ▪ Add complex care teams.
8. Establish a rapid admission unit.
   ▪ UMMC established a 20-bed rapid admission unit, staffed eight hours per day, to provide a place for patients who are waiting for inpatient beds.
   ▪ LOS among several different patient populations, including long-term care, critical care, and intensive care patients.
9. Leverage technology for tracking all metrics.
10. Daily bed briefings to reconcile house-wide bed availability and bed board accuracy.
11. Non-RNs delegated responsibility for entering discharge data.
12. Detroit Medical Center (DMC) has predetermined daily discharge times.
13. Establish director of patient logistics overseeing house-wide throughout and key functions:
    ▪ Transportation
    ▪ Bed placement
    ▪ ADT

14. Patient transfer tracing enabled by common patient pathways (to minimize transfers).
    - 80/20 review indicates a few diagnoses contributed disproportionally to transfers:
        - Heart attack, heart bypass surgery, pneumonia, and the like.
        - Medical necessity criteria for transfers.
15. Streamlined admissions documentation to shorten admission cycle time from 30-minute to 13-minute assessment time and reduce burden on staff through elimination of duplicate requirements and leverage EMR.
16. Discharge prewire; preadmission segregating population into outpatient, inpatient, and those inpatients requiring additional care.
17. Dedicated ADT nurse to expedite ADT activities by:
    - Identifying peak demand for ADT.
    - Redeploying experienced, adaptable staff.
    - Charging nurse hours directly to units served.
18. Demand-driven housekeeping schedule.
    - Perform root cause analysis for bed turnaround delays.
    - Housekeeping staff to support bed turnaround cycle time.
    - Replicate these steps across system.
19. Inpatient staging unit: Determine criteria to establish peak hours—virtual model.

Step 9: What Are the Barriers to Improvement? Countermeasures?

The 10-step team completed two analytics in step 9 to deal with change management issues: force field analysis and a stakeholder map and communications plan.

Force Field Analysis   The first exercise focused on preparation of a force field analysis. This tool requires participants to think together about all the aspects of a desired solution and is especially useful for analyzing change initiatives. Force field analysis is a structured approach to generating supports and barriers toward implementing a particular solution. The key steps in a force field analysis are listed next.

1. Define the ideal state on the top right of the template.
2. Prioritize driving forces of those that can be strengthened.
3. Prioritize the restraining forces that can be removed or reduced.
4. Brainstorm force field actions to enhance driving forces and/or mitigate restraining forces.

The team exercise resulted in the following outputs:

1. **Ideal State.** Consistent care coordination process
2. Driving forces that can be strengthened included:
   - EMR
   - Regulatory requirements
   - Best practices
   - Customer expectations
   - Improved quality of care
   - Finances
   - Physicians
   - Data transparency
   - Implement physician advisor
3. Restraining forces that can be removed or reduced included:
   - EMR
   - Physicians
   - Regulatory requirements
   - Change management
   - Staff buy-in
   - Finances/staffing
   - Physical locations of affiliates
   - Patient/family expectations
   - Outside vendors/outside agencies
4. Brainstorm force field actions to enhance driving forces.
   - Enhance driving forces.
     - Education
     - Work in conjunction with EMR
     - Build best practices in our care coordination process
     - Future infrastructure would support regulatory compliance
     - Implement physician advisor(s)
     - Daily collaborative rounds
     - Communication
   - Mitigate restraining forces.
     - Decentralized UR process
     - Daily collaborative rounds
     - Role definition
     - Communication
     - Research and partner with best sub-acute providers
     - Education

> ■ Financial analysis/validate value of refined care coordination process

Stakeholder Map and Communications Plan   Building on the force field analysis, the team built a stakeholder map that identified the anticipated roles people would play during solution deployment. The roles included:

- Change sponsors
- Change originators
- Change agents responsible for deploying or implementing the changes
- Change advocates
- Change blockers
- SME informants to provide information on the change

The stakeholder map provides insights into key constituencies. From the map, the team developed a summary communications plan that contained key actions that will enable the primary elements of the To-Be solution to gain traction in the organization. The team also developed specific messages for each stakeholder group.

- Physicians: Communication/education
- Patient and families: Collaborative rounds
- Quality Management Review (QMR), Utilization Review (UR), Master of Social Work (MSW) staff: Delineation of roles, training, reorganization of staffing
- Nursing staff: Communication/education
- EMR: Request capabilities/communicate change where necessary
- IDT: Delineation of roles, training, reorganization of staffing
- Vendors/external referral agencies: Communication/Education
- Administration/finance: Obtain buy-in and approval

Step 10: What Do We Pilot? Results? What Is the Full Implementation Plan?

The team developed an action plan that contained over 25 action items or steps broken down into these categories:

- Quick wins that could be deployed inside the team's 12-week life cycle
- Pilot phase to test out changes and prepare for full implementation

- To-Be changes that would be handed off to the process owner after the 12-week cycle

Quick Wins   Quick wins approved by the 10-step steering committee during the 12 weeks enabled the team to demonstrate value prior to pilot or full implementation of their To-Be Solutions. The quick wins included:

- Implement physician advisor.
- Use tools within EMR.
- Initiate supplemental paper forms.
- Pilot recommendations for best practice.
  - Daily IDT rounds (led by CM)
  - Complex care rounds
  - Social work screening for complex cases
  - Concurrent reviews
  - Screening in ED
- Hand-off of potential/parking lot items.
- Resource tool kit (from corporate performance management [CPM] team).

Improve Performance   The team identified these financial and operational improvements:

- The process increased annual earnings by $647,240 while increasing service levels to achieve MidMichigan Health's levels of operational excellence. Five-year total earnings improvements of $3,236,200.
- The LOS (in days) improved by location for specific diagnoses:
  - Hospital A Chronic Obstructive Pulmonary Disease (COPD) went from 4.15 to 3.79 LOS, a reduction of 8.7%.
  - Hospital B COPD went from 4.76 to 4.12 LOS, a reduction of 13.4%.
  - Hospital B Chronic Heart Failure (CHF) LOS went from 4.33 to 4.04, a reduction of 6.7%.
- The readmission rate percentage by location for specific diagnoses:
  - Hospital A COPD went from 8.13% to 4.96%, a 39% reduction.
  - Hospital A CHF went from 6.78% to 5.63%, a 17% reduction.
  - Hospital C COPD went from 6.37% to 5.04%, a 20.9% reduction.
  - Hospital C CHF went from 6.70% to 5.65%, a 15.7% reduction.
  - Hospital D CHF went from 7.73% to 5.58%, a 24.3% reduction.

Science knows no country, because knowledge belongs to humanity, and is the torch which illuminates the world. Science is the highest personification of the nation because that nation will remain the first which carries the furthest the works of thought and intelligence.

—**Louis Pasteur**

ORTHOPEDICS DEPARTMENT 10-STEP TEAM CASE STUDY, *GROW THE BUSINESS*

The CPM process allowed us to bring together key members through-out the system to focus efforts on a common initiative. This focus allowed us to achieve optimal results in a short time period that other-wise may have taken years to achieve. Barriers that may have existed otherwise between affiliates were instantly broken down as all team members were tasked with the same goal. It was awesome to see every-one come together and achieve such success.

—Ann Dull, Director of Orthopedics and
Rehabilitation Services (team leader)

Strategic Context

The orthopedics team aligns with MidMichigan Health system Strategic Objective E: Operational excellence. The existing process for requisitioning orthopedic supplies, such as implants for hip and knee joint replacement surgeries, was not optimizing cost management practices. The insurance reimbursement rate was not increasing to cover increased vendor costs; thus, the health system's earnings were being compressed. Multiple vendors and implant systems across the affiliates were resulting in difficulty managing the vendor contracts, supply inventory, and staff competence.

The case study consists of the next sections:

- **Steps 1–5 Training** encompasses working papers and content developed during the first two-day training team breakout sessions.
- **Steps 1–5 Fieldwork** shares key findings primarily from voice-of-customer surveys, data review, and analytics.
- **Steps 6–10 Training** consists of working papers and content developed during the second two-day training breakout sessions.

- **Improve performance** shares the financial and nonfinancial team findings to improve performance. .

Steps 1–5 Training Days 1–2

Step 1: Have We Identified the Right Areas of Focus?

Since teams (by design) consisted of representatives from different functions that possessed varied understanding of the current process, step 1 focused the team to establish a baseline or common understanding of the current situation.

Customer Segments and Requirements   The team identified three customer segments, brainstormed and prioritized their requirements, and drafted the Five Ups charts for each customer group.

The first customer group, *patients*, had five primary requirements:

1. Patient satisfaction—overall MidMichigan Health experience
2. LOS
3. Pain rating
4. Medical outcome
5. Cost

The team, based on its experience and estimation, established As-Is and To-Be targets for each of these requirements. It was understood that some of these requirements represented trade-offs, such as the LOS and pain rating; several were positively correlated. (It isn't necessarily accurate to say a shorter LOS may have a trade-off with a subsequent higher pain rating. For instance, the shorter LOS reduced overall costs and improved some aspects of the patient satisfaction.)

The second customer group, *physicians*, had six primary requirements:

1. Medical outcomes—reduced infections and dislocation
2. Improved availability and utilization of the operating room
3. Less physician surgical time, ease of implant use
4. Increased physician satisfaction with vendor representation
5. Increased operating room (OR) staff competency with total joint procedures
6. Total physician revenue

The team, based on its experience and estimation, established As-Is and To-Be targets for each of these requirements.

The third customer group, *OR staff*, had six primary requirements:

1. Reductions in infections and dislocation
2. Reduced physician surgical time
3. Vendor customer service in OR
4. Improved OR room turnover (patient flow)
5. Reduced number of hip and joint systems per vendor
6. OR financial margin

The team, based on its experience and estimation, established As-Is and To-Be targets for each of these requirements.

It became clear that the sheer scope of this effort would be significant, should the team choose to address all three customers and their collective 17 requirements (although some overlap). The team recognized that ensuing steps would be used to sharpen its focus and narrow its scope.

Causes of Issues   The second breakout exercise consisted of brainstorming causes of customer problems. The team felt at this stage that it would be important to capture all causes and prioritize those that mapped back to the greatest number of requirements. The prioritized list is shown next; reasons 1 to 6 (shown in italics) secured the most votes.

1. *Inadequate data (not timely, inaccurate and incomplete)*
2. *Patient requests for specific implants*
3. *Vendor relationships with doctors*
4. *A lot of implant systems for staff to know*
5. *Cost of implants*
6. *Rapidly changing implant technology*
7. Lack of demand matching for implants with patient needs
8. Inconsistent communication from physician office to OR
9. OR scheduling the physicians block time (for surgery)
10. Late physicians
11. Inaccurate requests from doctors
12. Lengthy time intensive process for new products
13. Lack of physician commitment to new equipment process; untimely requests from doctors for supplies needed for procedure
14. Decreased hospital reimbursement overall

15. Decreased physician reimbursement
16. Patient wait times
17. OR turnover
18. Staff competency
19. Nondedicated OR staff
20. Too many equipment trials at once

Data Sets. The team identified key data sets to better understand the As-Is situation. The data sets would provide insights and facts to better analyze, validate, and refine the goal statement. Data sets also provide the basis for refining or adjusting the scope of the project. The team determined these data sets would be useful to gather during fieldwork:

- Physician factors for selection of implant
- Implant utilization rates by vendor
- Implant cost by patient age
- Implant utilization rates (vendors, models, types), volumes, and costs by physician
- Implant utilization rates (vendors, models, types), volumes, and costs by affiliate hospital
- Reimbursement rates for types of implants
- Vendor contracts and key terms and conditions
- Reimbursement (revenue) and payor mix: commercial, Medicare, and Medicaid data
- National benchmarking trends for implant costs as a percentage of reimbursement

Since teams consist of representatives from different functions with a varied understanding of the current process, during step 1 the team sought to establish a baseline or common understanding of the current situation. The next two templates call for defining the background and a preliminary problem statement.

Background   Total hip and knee implant technology is changing at an ever-accelerating rate. Implant manufacturers are touting improved outcomes in terms of longevity, improved fit, and function without data confirming these claims. Medical centers are under constant pressure to reduce length of stay for patients and reduce the cost of the stay due to declining reimbursement. Thus, MidMichigan Health has been asking physicians to consider demand matching and implant cost when choosing a total hip or total knee implant. The utilization of higher-demand and thus higher-cost implant systems seems to be increasing. Physicians based at Hospital A have not been receptive to this pressure and feel that MidMichigan Health is asking them to sacrifice quality. The physicians in Midland do not feel that OR staff is knowledgeable regarding the different implant systems. The OR staff members are having difficulty with consistent skill level due to the accelerating rate of technology and systems being used in the OR. The medical center is struggling with storage space capacity, and purchasing is struggling with pricing and containing costs on systems due to multiple vendors and systems. The physicians also feel they need greater access to the OR for their patients. Thus, overall, the physicians may be growing dissatisfied with MidMichigan Health.

Preliminary Problem Statement   Current orthopedic utilization trends by MidMichigan Health orthopedic surgeons are resulting in increased implant costs per procedure for primary total hip and total knee replacements. Pressure on the physicians to decrease supply expenses has decreased physician satisfaction, especially in Hospital A.

Preliminary Goal Statement   Increase the orthopedic operating margin by $150,000 as a part of MidMichigan Health's goal of operational excellence in nine months.

Step 2: What Is the Initial Goal Statement? Team Charter?

Team Roles
Team member use of roles is proven to improve team dynamics and performance. The 10-step team's sponsor and team leader were selected prior to the start of the project. Remaining team members volunteered for the other roles; brief descriptions are provided.

- Sponsor (oversees teams, reviews work, owns results): Scott Currie
- Team leader (sets guidelines, goals, weekly meetings): Ann Dull
- Timekeeper (ensures deadlines are met): Krista Klein
- Recorder (takes notes): Ann Archuleta
- Scribe (makes ideas visible in meetings): Ann Archuleta
- Monitor (adheres to methodology): Kathi Wilford
- Process observer (ensures participation): Cindy Hough
- Spokesperson (reports to other groups): Ruth Kitzmiller

Code of Conduct   The team established a code of conduct to be observed during team meetings and phone calls in order to remain highly productive to meet its ambitious goals. The code of conduct incorporates the cultural dimensions the team believed to be important to maintain good morale and working relationships. The Code of Conduct includes the following elements:

- Team will meet Thursdays from 7:00 a.m. to 8:30 a.m. in Midland.
- Secure meeting will be set up for those who are unable to physically attend in Midland.
- We will respect everyone's time and come prepared to start the meeting on time and end on time.
- Everyone is encouraged to share ideas and thoughts. All members are responsible to monitor participation.
- We will pursue one idea at a time and not hold sidebar conversations during the primary conversation.
- We will respect everyone's ideas and opinions, remaining open and objective.
- We will seek to obtain consensus.
- We will define our goal and obtain agreement.
- We will define our roles and respect them.
- Be courteous . . . show respect.
- Commit to staying in meeting.
- We will foster honesty, openness, trust.

Next the team defined the background, preliminary problem statement, and preliminary goal statement.

Team Charter
- Issue/Problem
    Current Orthopedic utilization trends by MidMichigan orthopedic surgeons are resulting in increased implant costs per procedure for primary total hip and total knee replacements.
- Revised Goal Statement
    Reduce total hip and knee primary joint implant costs per procedure by 4% as part of MidMichigan Health's goal of operational excellence in nine months while maintaining high-quality patient outcomes and physician satisfaction
- Constraints
    - Data collection

- Working with three affiliates
- Skepticism of physicians and vendors
- Need to respect physician choice
- Timeline
- Regular job responsibilities
- Assumptions
  - None noted.
- Team Guidelines (see Code of Conduct)
- Resources (included in roles and additional SMEs to be identified)
- Preliminary Project Plan (10-step milestone level)
  - Steps 1–5 Training: Week 1
  - Steps 1–5 Fieldwork: Weeks 2–4
  - Steps 6–10 Training: Week 5
  - Steps 6–10 Fieldwork: Weeks 6–11
  - Celebration and Team Turnoff: Week 12

Step 3: What Are Three to Five Customer Requirements/Complaints?

Voice of the Customer. The purpose of the survey, consistent with step 1, is to secure input from the customer segments on their key requirements, As-Is and To-Be performance levels, and other valuable text responses. The team narrowed the scope to include VOC surveys for only physicians. The rationale was to align the primary decision maker who impacted the greatest number of customer requirements. Patients were already being surveyed on their patient experience separately, and these data could be secured without an additional survey.

Early draft physician survey questions are presented next.

- What metrics do you use to measure your patient's surgical outcome?
- Do you feel these outcomes are supported and achieved by the medical center staff?
- What are your three top issues or concerns in regard to the OR and medical center support for you in performing total joint procedures?
- What is your perception of MidMichigan Health's operating room turnover time?

- How satisfied overall are you with the competency and service provided by the surgical technicians in the OR? (1 being most satisfied, 5 least satisfied)
- Comments/explanation for ranking:
- Would you be willing to participate in a vendor standardization project for total joints? This may include exploring how many vendors we utilize as well as how many different components from each vendor.
- Please rank the following in importance to you in relation to total joint procedures (1 being most important, 8 least important):
  - _____ Ability to schedule OR time for my procedures
  - _____ Total joint implant ease of use
  - _____ OR staff competency
  - _____ Vendor representation for total joint implants
  - _____ Patient outcomes for total joint implants
  - _____ My revenue generated by total joint procedures
  - _____ Cost impact to the patient
  - _____ Financial impact to the health system for total joint procedures
  - _____ Other: _____
- Please add any additional comments or information you feel would help us.

Step 4: What Are the Current Process (Map) and Issues?

The 10-step team was very efficient during its process mapping breakout session. The team created a high-level map consisting of 15 steps and included swim lanes for physicians, patients, orthopedic vendors, OR staff, and related specialists (e.g., MRI). The visual review of the maps revealed and validated the issues and causes noted in earlier steps.

The 10-step team brainstormed and prioritized the choke points for the process map; these included:

1. Data collection (similar to the data sets identified in a prior step)
2. Lack of education on the array of implants (and ever-changing technologies)

3. Lack of standardization of implants
4. Varied levels of staff competency with the matrix of implant systems
5. Lack of physician knowledge of costs for implants and reimbursement for the medical center

The team recognized it would have to validate these during fieldwork.

Step 5: What Are the Prioritized Choke Points, Issues, and Root Causes?

The team further analyzed the content developed in step 4 to better understand the causes of issues. The primary tool in this step is the fishbone diagram.

The 10-step team initially produced this abbreviated problem statement for the head of the fish: "Increasing implant costs by procedure."

The 8Ps and IT fishbone model's categories of root causes, or bones of the fish, are listed next.

- Product category root causes included lack of physician stake in implant costs, increased vendor pricing, use of high-cost implants, new implant technologies, and rapid pace of change in technologies.
- Process, procedure, and policy category root causes included ineffective product identification and selection process, physicians and offices not following a standard process, and poor communications between physicians and the OR.
- People and skills category root causes included varied level of staff education, physician reliance on vendor for product knowledge, vendor influence on selection, and vendor relationship with physicians.
- Pricing or costs category root causes included payor reimbursement rates and payor mix.
- Place or location category root causes included OR turnover time, number of ORs, and block timing of surgeries.
- The technology category root cause focused on internal technologies, which included the number of various information systems.

Steps 1–5 Fieldwork

The fieldwork contained key findings and updates to hypotheses developed during the two-day training and contained in the working papers. During fieldwork, the team deployed the internal customer surveys and gathered a significant amount of data for analyses.

Survey Results

Survey results confirmed the physician's six requirements noted previously by the team, such as OR turnover, staff competence, and ability to utilize the implant of choice.

Data Analyses

The team determined that these data sets would be useful to gather during fieldwork:

- Physician factors for selection of implant
- Implant utilization rates by vendor
  - Vendor 1 accounted for 44% of total expenditures.
  - Vendor 2 accounted for 30% of total expenditures.
  - Vendor 3 accounted for 24% of total expenditures.
  - Vendor 4 accounted for 2% of total expenditures.
- Implant utilization rates (vendors, models, types), volumes, and costs by hospital
  - Vendor 1 accounted for 100% of implant costs at Hospital 1.
  - Vendor 3 accounted for over 80% of implant costs at Hospital 2.
- Implant cost by patient age
  - The extensive regression analyses of cost per hip implant to patient age ranging from 35 to 85 years did not reveal any discernible patterns and dispelled the myth that expensive replacements were going to older patients unnecessarily.
  - The extensive regression analyses of cost per knee implant to patient age ranging from 35 to 85 years did not reveal any discernible patterns and dispelled the myth that expensive replacements were going to older patients unnecessarily.
- Implant volumes by physician
  - Ten physicians completed 562 replacements with three providing 80% of the total.
    - Physician 1 completed 181 replacements, 32% of total.
    - Physician 2 completed 175 replacements, 31% of total.
    - Physician 3 completed 96 replacements, 17% of total.
    - Physicians 4 to 10 completed 126 replacements, 20% of total.
- Average cost by physician for hip replacements
  - Two physicians preferred implants that cost 20% and 30% more respectively than the system average.

- One physician preferred implants that cost 20% less than the system average.
- The balance of physicians preferred implants with average costs within 5% of the system average.
- Average cost by physician for knee replacements
  - Two physicians preferred implants that cost approximately 15% more respectively than the system average.
  - One physician preferred implants that cost 20% less than the system average.
  - The balance of physicians preferred implants with average costs within 5% of the system average.
- Reimbursement (revenue) and payor mix: commercial, Medicare, and Medicaid data
  - 63% of implants were reimbursed at Medicare and Medicaid rates, which had increased $500 per implant per year in the past two years.
  - 37% of implants were reimbursed at commercial and corporate rates.
  - Implant costs are 65% of total inpatient charges.
- Vendor contracts and key terms and conditions

  Two vendors' contracts were coming up for renewal in the next 12 months.

Observations
- Three physicians account for 80% of the implant procedures.
- Two hospital locations have preferences for their own single vendors.
- Two vendors account for 74% of total spending.
- Only two physicians prefer more expensive hips.
- Only two physicians prefer more expensive knees.

Further analyses revealed that changing behaviors of a few physicians' practices and preferences could have significant impacts on average and overall implant costs.

Steps 6–10 Training Days 3–4

During the two-day 10-step training, the team created solutions, a To-Be design, and implementation plans to realize value.

Step 6: What Are Future State or Desired Process Attributes?

The team engaged in a breakout session designed to leverage both creative thinking and analytical thinking to develop a To-Be design for the core process.

The *creative* exercise resulted in these To-Be design elements:

- Physician determines whether total joint surgical intervention is needed.
- Patients may do Internet searches or see ads on TV, magazine, newspaper, or rely on advice from surgeon.
- Physicians pick a system.
- Physicians review implant features and match patient need and activity level to the implant features.
- Physician research longevity of implant (data from vendor?).
- Best quality and expected outcome for patient.
- Consolidating purchases, accumulate data on purchase volume for non-implant products from same vendors
- Research how long is the implant expected to last. Potential revisions?
- Manage new technology releases.
- Ease of mobility for patient.
- Better understand vendor value proposition.

The results of the *analytical, structured* exercise to build the To-Be process included these design elements:

- Process, Policy, and Procedure
  - Physician determines that total joint surgical intervention is needed using evidence-based medicine and clear selection criteria.
  - Physician maintains best quality and expected outcomes for patient.
  - Standardized and controlled process request for new products.
  - Standardized and controlled process request for implant system requests (could be stock or not).
- Product
  - Manageable number of systems for inventory management, purchasing, and staff competency.
- People/Skills
  - Health system to educate and promote services for patients who may search the Internet or see ads on TV, magazine, newspaper, or rely on advice from surgeon.
  - Ease of mobility for patient.
  - High physician skill as viewed by the patient.
  - Highly skilled OR staff that is competent and confident in the systems used by the physicians.

- Place/Location
  - Convenient and safe locations
  - Excellent reputation for quality services and customer service
  - Convenient parking
  - Attractive appearance
  - Private rooms providing privacy and comfort
  - State-of-the-art technology to provide quality patient care
- Partner/Vendor
  - Standardized vendors
  - Physicians to have stake in implant selection and cost
  - Physicians to collaborate with health system to manage costs and patient outcomes
  - Cost transparency with physicians
- Technology (internal, not product technology)
  - Report utilization and cost data to physicians on a regular basis
  - Easy and efficient data collection
  - Functional interfaces between software

The 10-step team combined these two exercise outputs to define a comprehensive To-Be solution.

Step 7: What Improvement Level Is Expected—Final Goal Statement?

The team revisited its preliminary goal statement to incorporate new information discovered during fieldwork and step 6. The new targets also factor in benchmarks and best practices.

Preliminary Goal Statement   Increase the orthopedic operating margin by $397,000 as a part of MidMichigan Health's goal of operational excellence in nine months.

The team struggled to revise the goal statement and determined the next one would create a balance between cost savings and patient and physician value propositions.

Revised Goal Statement   Reduce total hip and knee primary joint implant costs per procedure by 4% as part of MidMichigan Health's goal of operational excellence in nine months while maintaining high-quality patient outcomes and physician satisfaction.

However, further analyses of the data and visits with the physician groups revealed that a more elegant solution based on more phased criteria would be warranted. The rationale for the goal considered these three phases and supporting design elements:

- Phase 1 Capitated Rate—reduced pricing initiative for implants
  - Institute capitation pricing.
  - Develop implant selection criteria.
  - Limit process to current vendors.
  - Work with new decision support system to identify tools for real time data collection.
  - Involve and engage physicians in every step.
- Phase 2 Limit Vendor Representative Access and Develop OR Staff Education Model
  - Work with staff and physicians to improve competency.
  - Explore staffing options to provide a form of dedicated teams or rotating experts and so on.
  - Limit vendor access and presence in OR.
  - Work with physician practices to limit vendor access and presence in orthopedic practice groups at each hospital.
- Phase 3 Competitive Bid—dual sourcing of implants
  - Long-term goal: Work with future physicians to coordinate implant usage with dual sourcing goal.

These phases and design changes identified time phased and incremental earnings improvements in a final goal statement shown next.

Final Goal Statement   Reduce total hip and knee primary joint implant costs per procedure through product standardization, utilization, physician engagement, physician collaboration, staff education, and vendor collaboration with negotiation, providing the best value implants meeting the patient's needs, as a part of MidMichigan Health's goals for operational excellence and physician collaboration.

1. **Capitated Rate.** Short-term goal: Reduce implant costs to 39.3% of Medicare national base rate reimbursement for diagnostic related group (DRG)-470 by six months for an annualized cost savings.
2. **Limit Representatives from OR and Educate Staff.** Midterm goal: Reduce implant costs further to 37% of Medicare national base rate

reimbursement for DRG-470 by 12 months, 2011 for an annualized cost savings.

3. **Competitive Bid.** Long-term goal: Reduce implant cost finally to 35% of Medicare national base rate reimbursement for DRG-470 by 24 months for an annualized cost savings.

The cumulative impact of all three phases will result in annual savings at maturity of $397,000.

Step 8: What Should the Future Process Be (New Map)?

The 10-step team incorporated the design elements from step 6 and the refined goal statement parameters from step 7 to design new processes. The new product requisition process also reflected best practices from external research.

Step 9: What Are the Barriers to Improvement? Countermeasures?

The 10-step team completed two analytics in step 9 to deal with change management issues: force field analysis and a stakeholder map and communications plan.

Force Field Analysis. The first exercise focused on preparation of a force field analysis. This tool requires participants to think together about all the aspects of a desired solution and is especially useful for analyzing change initiatives. Force field analysis is a structured approach to generating supports and barriers toward implementing a particular solution. The key steps in a force field analysis are listed next.

1. Define the ideal state on the top right of template.
2. Prioritize driving forces of those that can be strengthened.
3. Prioritize the restraining forces that can be removed or reduced.
4. Brainstorm force field actions to enhance driving forces and, or mitigate restraining forces.

The team outputs included:

1. **Ideal State.** Best-value implants meeting the patients' needs
2. Driving forces that can be strengthened included:
   - Correct implant on day of surgery
   - Demand matching with patient activity level and age

- Verify if implants are in current stock
- Verify if implants are on pricing lists
- Physician knowledge
- Utilize new technology
- Improved operating margin

3. Restraining forces that can be removed or reduced included:
   - Physician timing of implant system decision
   - Higher demand/cost implants
   - Space/storage/knowledge/inventory management
   - Discounts not applied to all items until further negotiated
   - Data collection, vendor influence
   - Price negotiations and staff knowledge
   - Increasing implant costs; utilization of high-demand/cost implants

4. Brainstorm force field actions to enhance driving forces and/or mitigate restraining forces:
   - Physician education
   - List of stock
   - List of cost in some fashion
   - Defined roles of MidMichigan Health team
   - Timing of surgery hospital preparation: Can physician office be more proactive?
   - When asked for something not in stock, discounts may not be "in place" compared to current stock items; need time to negotiate with vendor
   - System mind-set
   - Review physician office form for requesting implants
   - Communication with vendors
   - Develop selection criteria (physician and MidMichigan Health)
   - Share costs with physicians
   - Share data collection and reports
   - Improve data collection process
   - New products and technology controlled through value analysis team process
   - Change utilization habits
   - Develop standardization model
   - Enhance vendor relationship
   - Gain physician support
   - Include physician in negotiations and briefings
   - Staff education through/via:
     - Vendor classes

- Coordinator classes
- Education of roles in OR
- Sequence of events
- Physician training/teaching
- Recognition of physicians
  - Teaching in OR of new staff
  - Humor
  - Engagement or participation on initiatives

Stakeholder Map and Communications Plan Building on the force field analysis, the team built a stakeholder map that identified the anticipated roles people would play during solution deployment. The roles included:

- Change sponsors
- Change originators
- Change agents responsible for deploying or implementing the changes
- Change advocates
- Change blockers
- SME informants to provide information on the change

The stakeholder map provides insights into key constituencies. From the map, the team developed a summary communications plan that contained key actions that will enable the primary elements of the To-Be solution to gain traction in the organization. The team also developed specific messages for each stakeholder group.

- Patient: Patients will receive the highest-quality care at the best value
- Physician: Updates regarding plan
- Administration: Relay implementation plan
- Vendors: Contact vendors regarding negotiations
- OR Education: Team objectives and plan
- OR Purchasing: Updates regarding progress
- Main Purchasing: Update regarding progress

Step 10: What Do We Pilot? Results? What Is the Full Implementation Plan?

The team developed an action plan that contained over 25 action items or steps broken down into these categories:

- Quick wins that could be deployed inside the team's 12-week life cycle
- Pilot phase to test out changes and prepare for full implementation
- To-Be changes that would be handed off to the process owner after the 12-week cycle

Quick Wins   Quick wins approved by the 10-step steering committee during the 12 weeks enabled the team to demonstrate value prior to pilot or full implementation of To-Be solutions . The quick wins included:

- Survey pre-procedure process
- Conduct additional surveys with physicians and broaden support
- Continue data gathering and clean up data
- Gather data from remaining hospitals for validation
- Create the new data collection and reporting process
- Meet with physicians and finalize CPM team goals
- Celebrate the wins

Improve Performance   The team identified these financial and operational improvements:

1. **Capitated Rate.** Short-term goal: Reduce implant costs to 39.3% of Medicare national base rate reimbursement for DRG- 470 by six months for an annualized cost savings.
2. **Limit Representatives from OR and Educate Staff.** Midterm goal: Reduce implant costs to 37% of Medicare national base rate reimbursement for DRG-470 by 12 months for an annualized cost savings.
3. **Competitive Bid.** Long-term goal: Reduce implant cost to 35% of Medicare national base rate reimbursement for DRG-470 by 24 months for an annualized cost savings.

The cumulative impact of all three phases at maturity will result in annual savings of $397,000, or $1,985,000 over five years.

Efficiency is doing things right; effectiveness is doing the right things.

—**Peter Drucker**

WOMEN'S HEALTH SERVICES 10-STEP TEAM CASE STUDY, *GROW THE BUSINESS*

> The process allowed us to access a new perspective while providing the structure for our team to easily identify and effect the most beneficial changes.
>
> —Carole Calvert-Baxter, Director, Center for
> Women's Health (team leader)

Strategic Context

The Center for Women's Health (CWH) performed 8,484 mammograms—preventive screenings—on women in Midland County, Michigan; however, there are 14,000 to 18,000 women who meet the eligibility criteria for a mammogram. Nationally and locally mammography rates are suboptimal. The CWH team aligned with MidMichigan Health system Strategic Objective E: Operational excellence.

This case study consists of the next sections:

- **Steps 1–5 Training** encompasses developing working papers and content during the first two-day training team breakout sessions.
- **Steps 1–5 Fieldwork** shares key findings primarily from VOC surveys, data review, and analytics.
- **Steps 6–10 Training** consists of working papers and content developed during the second two-day training breakout sessions.
- **Improve performance** shares the financial and nonfinancial team findings to improve performance.

Steps 1–5 Training Days 1–2

Step 1: Have We Identified the Right Areas of Focus?

Since teams (by design) consisted of representatives from different functions that possessed varied understanding of the current process, step 1 focused the team to establish a baseline or common understanding of the current situation.

Customer Segments and Requirements The team brainstormed customer requirements, prioritized them through voting, and drafted the Five Ups charts for each customer group.

The first customer group, *patients*, had five primary requirements:

1. Overcoming radiation-based fear
2. Affordability
3. Complacency
4. Reducing uncertainty around recommended prevention
5. Diagnostic limitations

The team recognized that it would use fieldwork time to establish As-Is and To-Be targets for each of the requirements.

The second customer group, *physicians*, had five primary requirements:

1. Sensitivity and specificity
2. Reimbursement
3. Preauthorization
4. Radiation exposure
5. Lack of awareness, uncertainty around recommendations

The team recognized that it would use fieldwork time to establish As-Is and To-Be targets for each of the requirements.

Causes of Issues   The team brainstormed and prioritized causes of issues:

1. Equipment-based fears, claustrophobia, radiation exposure, pain with compression
2. Economy driving fears of affordability, cost/copays
3. U.S. Preventive Services Task Force guidelines recommendations published in November 2009
4. Uncertainty and confusion around recommendations
5. Complacency: no problems, why bother?
6. Physician practice (standard versus changing)
7. Fear of results—opt out of screening
8. Preauthorization issues for specialty services
9. Insurance coverage for newer technologies
10. Uninsured and underinsured patients
11. Media questioning need for exams for women 50 and under
12. Available funding from state, federal, local, Pardee Cancer Center-Midland
13. Lack of awareness of services available

14. Competitors aggressively promote breast services
15. Lack of awareness of quality accreditation measures achieved at CWH
16. Lack of knowledge of available funding (i.e., Breast and Cervical Cancer Control Program offered through the State of Michigan for eligible women, and restricted funds)
17. Limitations of current technology
18. Sensitivity and specificity
19. Other facilities may offer more "amenities"
20. Facility not a self-referring facility
21. Lack dedicated female surgeon
22. Patients seek services close to home

Data Sets. The team identified key data sets to better understand the As-Is situation. The data sets would provide insights and facts to better analyze, validate, and refine the goal statement. Data sets also provided the basis for refining or adjusting the scope of the project. The team determined that the next data sets would be useful to gather during fieldwork:

- Breast imaging volumes month by month
- Breast imaging volumes by day of the week
- Physician referral patterns including source physicians, volumes in total, volumes by week

Next, the team defined the background, preliminary problem statement, and preliminary goal statement.

Background

- Moved Breast Health Clinic and all breast-related services to a single facility on campus seven years earlier, with the exception of breast MRI and MRI-guided biopsies.
- Three years earlier digital mammography replaced film/screen analog system—went from five film/screen mammography units to two digital units.
- Limited capacity of only two units resulted in a two-month mammography backlog; some individuals sought services elsewhere.
- Added third unit this year, and patient flow improved significantly.
- Area facilities obtained digital mammography prior to CWH—percentage of patients left system seeking digital screening.
- Recent economic downturn may be impacting decreasing volumes.

- Uninsured and underinsured patients are concerned with affordability of exam.
- Perceived lack of awareness of existing restricted funds available to uninsured and underinsured.
- Recent studies and recommendations regarding screening for women 50 and under every year versus every two years may be impacting decreasing mammography volumes.
- General complacency of physicians and providers fueled by recent studies— may prevent women from being routinely screened.
- Increasing concern regarding radiation exposure—potential result of recent articles/media attention surrounding radiation exposure.
- Physician practice patterns (standard practice patterns versus changing practice patterns).
- Individuals requiring highly specialized equipment not available in system are receiving those services elsewhere.
- Physicians may be referring patients outside system.
- Women seeking the most amenities a facility can offer (i.e., aesthetic environment, massage, coffee, refreshments, etc.).

Preliminary Problem Statement

- Breast imaging volumes decreasing (primarily diagnostic mammography)
- Conflicting imaging standards and recommendations
- Physician practice patterns (previous and/or changing) as a result of conflicting guidelines
- Patients leaving system for highly specialized equipment (MRI breast biopsies [MBIs])

Based on the preceding information, the team was positioned to establish a preliminary goal statement. As the team is just in step 1 of 10, so the goal statement will be continuously refined and updated as more evidence and data become available.

Preliminary Goal Statement Increase outpatient volume by 4% or 600 procedures generating $75,000 in earnings by addressing the current national trend in decreasing utilization of breast imaging services, by removing real or perceived barriers to breast imaging, enhancing the patient experience for all breast-related imaging services, and by creating a public image that reflects the medical center's mission to provide the best in proven technology by a team that is dedicated to the needs of the community that it serves.

Step 2: What Is the Initial Goal Statement? Team Charter?

Team Roles   Team member use of roles is proven to improve team dynamics and performance. The 10-step team's sponsor and team leader were selected prior to the start of the project. Remaining team members volunteered for the other roles; brief descriptions are provided.

- Sponsor (oversees teams, reviews work, owns results): Lori Mault and Diane Nold
- Team leader (sets guidelines, goals, weekly meetings): Carole Calvert-Baxter
- Timekeeper (ensures deadlines are met): John Urban
- Recorder (takes notes): Kim Hartnagle
- Scribe (makes ideas visible in meetings): Lynne Carlson
- Monitor (adheres to methodology): Jody Greenacre and Kim Hartnagle
- Process observer (ensures participation): Warren Johnson and Bill Geyer
- Spokesperson (reports to other groups): Rod Zapolski
- SMEs: Mary Jahn and Gail Pelkey

Code of Conduct   The team established a code of conduct to be observed during team meetings and phone calls in order to remain highly productive to meet its ambitious goals. The code of conduct incorporates the cultural dimensions the team believed to be important to maintain good morale and working relationships. The code of conduct includes these elements:

- Agendas established for all meetings
- Clearly defined roles
- No side discussions
- Cell phone/pagers off during meeting
- Start and end on time
- Attendance: 100%
- Everyone must be prepared for all meetings
- Participation encouraged by all
- Respectful
- Agenda for next meeting set at the end of every meeting
- Voting by consensus/leader to validate

These exercises were consolidated with modifications into a more complete team charter, which formed a team agreement.

Team Charter

- Preliminary Problem Statement
    - Breast imaging volumes decreasing (primarily diagnostic mammography)
    - Conflicting imaging standards and recommendations
    - Physician practice patterns (previous and/or changing) as a result of conflicting guidelines
    - Patients leaving system for highly specialized equipment (MBI)
- Preliminary Goal Statement
    Increase outpatient volume by 4%, or 600 procedures, generating $172,200 in gross revenue by addressing the current national trend in decreasing utilization of breast imaging services, by removing real or perceived barriers to breast imaging, enhancing the patient experience for all breast-related imaging services, and by creating a public image that reflects the medical center's mission to provide the best in proven technology by a team that is dedicated to the needs of the community that it serves.
- Constraints: None noted
- Team Guidelines (see Code of Conduct)
- Resources (see Team Roles)
- Preliminary Project Plan (10-step milestone level)
    - Steps 1–5 Training: Week 1
    - Steps 1–5 Fieldwork: Weeks 2–4
    - Steps 6–10 Training: Week 5
    - Steps 6–10 Fieldwork: Weeks 6–10
    - Celebration and Team Turnoff: Week 12

Step 3: What Are Three to Five Customer Requirements/Complaints?

Voice of the Customer. The purpose of the survey, consistent with step 1, is to secure input from the customer segments on their key requirements, As-Is and To-Be performance levels, and other valuable text responses. The team designed two Voice of the Customer (VOC) surveys to be deployed during fieldwork.

Survey scores and scales were developed during fieldwork. The draft surveys are presented next.

Physician Survey

1. For healthy women with no history of concerns, what is your general recommendation for routine mammography screening?
2. To what degree do you find women confused about current national recommendations for screening mammography?
3. To what degree do you agree with the current "every year after 40" mammography recommendations (American College of Radiology [ACR], American Cancer Society) in light of recent studies and the differing position of the U.S. Preventive Services Task Force Guidelines?
4. Does your practice have a tickler system to remind women about scheduling routine physicals?
5. Do you use an internal tickler system to alert you that a woman is due for a routine screening mammogram?
6. Where do you typically refer patients who have suspicious breast findings?
7. What are the reasons you prefer the approach you take to the referral of patients with suspicious findings?
8. When you refer patients in need of breast-related services outside of MidMichigan Health, what factors generally drive that decision?
9. How much do quality accreditations influence your decision-making process when referring to a hospital-based breast health program? (National Accreditation Program for Breast Centers, [NAPBC] accreditation)

Patient Survey

1. How often do you have a routine exam with your physician?
2. How often do you get a mammogram?
3. What reason most fits you, if you do not get mammograms yearly?
4. How often does your physician discuss breast health and mammography during a routine exam?
5. What is your age range?
6. If the Center for Women's Health extended its hours for routine mammography, what times would be of most interest to you?

7. Did you use centralized scheduling to schedule your mammography appointment?
8. How many times did you have to call to schedule your appointment for this exam?
9. Approximately how long were you on hold to schedule your appointment?
10. Did you leave a voicemail to schedule your appointment? If yes, did someone return your call?
11. What could have been done to make it easier for you to schedule your appointment?

Step 4: What Are the Current Process (Map) and Issues?

The 10-step team developed a process map of the referral process that validated the issues and causes noted in earlier steps. The 10-step team identified these choke points (issues) for process map steps:

1a Routine mammogram not ordered
1b Lack of awareness of the importance of routine health screening visits
1c Patient lacks insurance for routine office visits
2a Normal practice pattern not to order routine mammogram
2b Lacks tickler system to alert for need of mammogram
2c Uncertainty and confusion around recommendations
3a Long wait to schedule procedure
3b Don't want to tie up office staff time scheduling mammogram for patient
4a Uncertain reason for outside referral – assumptions made
4b Lost revenue with potential for lost patient (may never return)
5a Conflicting standards causing uncertainty and confusion around recommendations
5b Providing information on pros/cons of annual screening
6a No access to health system
6b Not aware of current recommendations or need for routine screening
6c No insurance
6d Unaware of options for funding mammograms or access to mammograms without physician
6e Patient may not want personal physician
7a Unaware depth of services available at CWH

7b   Unaware of accreditation and what benefits it offers to patients

8a   Fear of pain

8b   Fear of results

8c   Equipment-based fears (radiation)

8d   Proximity—patient chooses facility closer to home

8e   Complacency

8f   Patient unaware they have choice to stay in system

9a   Radiologists do not write orders

9b   Patient must have physician to receive results

10a   Physicians lack capacity

10b   Physicians with capacity unwilling to accept insurance

10c   Physicians with capacity unwilling to accept patient

10d   Physicians with capacity unwilling to accept patient without insurance

11a   Unavailable films delay reading

11b   Delayed readings—frustrate referring physicians

11c   Delayed readings delay findings/treatment

12a   Patients bypassing CWH lose benefits of NAPBC accreditation

12b   Bypassing CWH fragments patient care services

12c   Potential for lost procedure resulting in lost revenue

13a   Seek program and services of dedicated female surgeon and program

13b   Not aware of BHP/BHC and NAPBC accreditation benefits to patients

13c   Seeking services not available within CWH or in system

The team recognized these potential causes would warrant further investigation during fieldwork.

Step 5: What Are the Prioritized Choke Points, Issues, and Root Causes?

In this step, the content developed in step 4 is further analyzed by the team to better understand the causes of issues. The primary tool in this step is the fishbone diagram. The 10-step team initially produced this problem statement for the head of the fish: "Decreasing Breast Related Volumes."

The 8Ps and IT fishbone model's categories and root causes. or bones of the fish, are listed next.

■ Product/Service category root causes included women select facilities with dedicated female breast surgeons, CWH breast accreditations not well known.

- Process and procedure category root causes included insurance coverage, not being a self-referring facility, and preauthorization for specialty services is cumbersome.
- People and skills category root causes included pain of mammogram, fear of results, complacency, and lack of awareness of available funding.
- Promotion category root causes included competitors heavily promote breast services and CWH accreditations not be well known.
- Place category root causes included patients may not be willing to travel to CWH and physicians refer patients to facilities closer to their homes.
- Policy category root causes included U.S. Preventive Services Task Force guidelines unclear, conflicting guidelines for uninsured and underinsured, decreasing funding from outside sources, and economy driving fears of affordability.
- The technology category root cause included referrals made outside system since it does not have the latest MRI technology.

At the conclusion of step 5, the team evaluated its performance across multiple attributes. The focus and intent of this exercise contributes to self-correcting teams that can weather challenges during their life cycle. The team voted using a 1–5 scale, with 5 being the highest grade, on five key factors of team performance. These included:

1. Established goals/agenda scored 4.
2. Used code of conduct and group roles scored 4.
3. Used tools/methods scored 4.
4. Freedom to participate (captured brain power) scored 5.
5. Overall meeting effectiveness scored 4.

Steps 1–5 Fieldwork

The fieldwork contained key findings and updates to hypotheses developed during the two-day training and contained in the working papers. During fieldwork, the team deployed the internal customer surveys and gathered a significant amount of data for analyses.

Physician Survey Results

The 10-step team surveyed physicians and summarized these findings:

- Only 37% of the respondents recommend yearly mammography screening.

- Physicians find 70% of their patients confused about the current national recommendations for screening mammography.
- Only 35% of the physicians agree with the current "every year after 40" mammography recommendations (ACR) in light of the recent studies and the differing position of the U.S. Preventive Services Task Force Guidelines.
- Only 35% of the physicians have a system in place to remind women about scheduling routine physicals.
- Only 5% have an internal tickler system to alert them that a woman is due for her mammogram.
- Greater than 90% of the physicians refer patients with suspicious findings to the CWH Breast Health Program for services.
- Reasons physicians refer patients in need of breast-related services outside MidMichigan Health are patient request, geographic considerations, and request for a female surgeon.

Patient Survey Results

- Ease of scheduling an appointment (103 respondents)
  - 89% of the participants used centralized scheduling to schedule their appointment.
  - When asked how many times they had to call to schedule their appointment, 92 reported one time, 9 reported two attempts, 2 reported three or more times.
  - When asked how long they remained on hold, 53 reported less than a minute, 29 reported 1 to 3 minutes, 7 responded 4 to 6 minutes, 4 reported 7 to 9 minutes, 2 reported 10 or more minutes.
  - Seven reported having to leave a voicemail; 4 reported that someone returned their call; 3 reported they did not receive a return call.
- What are the top three factors you consider when selecting a facility for your breast health needs? The responses are ranked from highest to lowest number of responses:
  a. Friendliness (44 respondents)
     1. Courtesy of staff
     2. Gentle compassion
  b. Expertise (39 respondents)
     1. Competent physicians and staff
     2. Confidence in physician and staff
     3. Competent professionals

   c. Location (32 respondents)
     1. Close to my home
     2. Location
     3. Nonhospital setting
     4. Availability
   d. Cleanliness (12 respondents)
     1. Cleanliness
     2. Warm environment
     3. Welcoming environment
     4. Facility
   e. Physician referral (11 respondents)
     1. Doctor's decision—highly respect opinion
     2. Doctor's order—I wasn't given options
   f. Equipment (9 respondents)
   g. Affordability (8 respondents)
     1. Cost
     2. Insurance coverage
     3. Insurance payment

The survey questions also focused on identifying root causes to resolve the problem discussed in steps 1 to 5. The questions and most frequent responses are:

- What prevents women from getting a routine mammogram?
  1. Conflicting guidelines
  2. Uninsured/underinsured
  3. Decreasing Breast and Cervical Cancer Control Program (BCCCP) funding
  4. Lack of awareness of restricted accounts for available funding
  5. Physicians didn't recommend
  6. Pain of the procedure
  7. Fear of the results
  8. Lack of transportation
  9. Hours of operation
- Why don't women choose CWH for breast-related services?
  1. Insurance acceptance (perceived versus real)
  2. Location
  3. Local options with similar technology
  4. Lack of awareness of equipment capability
  5. Lack of amenities (chocolate, coffee, massage)

6. Seeking female dedicated breast surgeons
7. Lack of competitive advertising ("Covenant Offers the Best Breast Health Care in the Region")
- Why don't physicians order routine mammograms?
  1. Recent conflicting guidelines
  2. Previous practice patterns—some physicians don't recommend annual mammograms
  3. Lack of reminder or tickler systems to alert physicians that annual mammograms are due
  4. Refer patient to a competitor
- Why aren't diagnostic procedures (MRI) performed at the center or in the medical center?
  1. Insurance-related issues
  2. Surgeons perform in office setting (ultrasound and biopsies)
  3. Women choose diagnostic workup where there are female dedicated breast surgeons
  4. Location
  5. Lack of awareness of equipment capability/services
  6. Lack of competitive awareness
- Why don't physicians refer to the breast health program?
  1. Lack of awareness of its existence and the services provided
  2. Lack of awareness of the program's benefits for their patients
  3. Lack of awareness of the NAPBC accreditation and what that means with regard to quality of care/services

Data Analyses

CWH's overall mammography screening volume for the past three years had increased modestly at 3.5% per year; however, the volumes by age bracket and by year showed significant variation.

- Overall number of mammography screenings: year 1: 9,813; year 2: 10,154; year 3: 10,512

  - Ages 30–39 years old
    - Year 1: 122; year 2: 131; year 3: 180
  - Ages 40–49 years old
    - Year 1: 2,242; year 2: 2,263; year 3: 2,594

- Ages 50–59 years old
  - Year 1: 3,345; year 2: 3,332; year 3: 3,389
- Ages 60–69 years old
  - Year 1: 2,268; year 2: 2,668; year 3: 2,658
- Ages 70–79 years old
  - Year 1: 1,836; year 2: 1,760; year 3: 1,691

Steps 6–10 Training Days 3–4

During the two-day 10-step training, the team created solutions, a To-Be design, and implementation plans to realize value.

Step 6: What Are Future State or Desired Process Attributes?

The team engaged in a breakout session designed to leverage both creative thinking and analytical thinking to develop a To-Be design for the core process.

The *creative* exercise resulted in these To-Be design elements:

- Find or market to customers
- Customer(s) survey to create awareness
- Communicate and education physicians and providers
- Acquire technology to advance services
- Recommunication with customers to create continuous dialogue
- Convenience have appointments available and timeliness of information to providers
- Improvement existing technology
- Continuous improvement and measure with scorecards
- Monitor revenue, expenses and budgets, evaluate end users to understand who is using service
- Volume analytics, understand referral patterns, quality or medical results, and provider statistics
- Volume growth for all tests
- Reevaluation of clinical treatments and services
- Export To-Be process or solutions to other strategic business units and affiliates

The *analytical, structured* exercise to build the To-Be process included these design elements:

- Process, Policy, and Procedure

- Find customer
- Custom survey
- Communicate/recommunicate to physicians and public customers and to physician sponsor (could be same or different as breast surgeon)
- Appointments, availability, and information to providers
- Performance Improvement (PI)-follow progress (scorecard)
- Monitor revenue/expenses
- Volume monitoring
- Referral patterns
- Quality results
- Patient/provider satisfaction
- Physician offices fax orders to facility
- Self-referring facility

- People/Skills
  - Speed of service
  - Technologists maintain job requirements
  - Customer service skills at all staff levels
- Product/Equipment
  - Implement existing equipment
  - Obtain/maintain stereotactic accreditation
  - Minimize downtime
- Place/Facilities
  - Coffee, chocolate
  - Location(s)
  - Access, "open when women work"
  - Lunch hour/extended hours
  - Quick for individuals to be seen/results
  - Decorated tastefully (artwork, cleanliness, special amenities)
  - One-stop shop
- Partner and Vendor
  - Identify technology vendor
  - Identify practice, referring patterns with providers
  - Real-time reads
  - Physician/radiologist patient interaction
- Technology
  - Acquire technology
  - Implement technology
  - Evaluate "newest" (MBI, etc.)

The 10-step team combined these two exercise outputs to define a comprehensive To-Be solution.

Step 7: What Improvement Level Is Expected—Final Goal Statement?

Based on the cumulative learning from the prior steps, the team revisited its preliminary goal statement to incorporate new information discovered during fieldwork and step 6. The new targets also factor in benchmarks and best practices.

Preliminary Goal Statement   Increase outpatient volume by 4% or 600 procedures generating $172,200 in gross revenue by addressing the current national trend in decreasing utilization of breast imaging services, by removing real or perceived barriers to breast imaging, enhancing the patient experience for all breast-related imaging services, and by creating a public image that reflects the medical center's mission to providing the best in proven technology by a team that is dedicated to the needs of the community that it serves.

Revised Goal Statement   Increase outpatient volume by 4% or 600 "screening" mammography procedures generating $75,000 in earnings by year-end at the Center for Women's Health. We will accomplish this by evaluating customer limitations, removing real or perceived barriers, and leveraging breast imaging services that maintain volumes and provide early detection to women.

Step 8: What Should the Future Process Be (New Map)?

The 10-step team incorporated the design elements from step 6 and the refined goal statement parameters from step 7 to design new processes.

Step 9: What Are the Barriers to Improvement? Countermeasures?

The 10-step team completed two analytics in step 9 to deal with change management issues: force field analysis and a stakeholder map and communications plan.

Force Field Analysis   The first exercise focused on preparation of a force field analysis. This tool requires participants to think together about all the aspects of a desired solution and is especially useful for analyzing change initiatives. Force field analysis is a structured approach to generating supports and barriers toward implementing a particular solution. The key steps in a force field analysis are listed next.

1. Define the ideal state on the top right of template.
2. Prioritize driving forces of those that can be strengthened.
3. Prioritize the restraining forces that can be removed or reduced.
4. Brainstorm force field actions to enhance driving forces and/or mitigate restraining forces.

The team followed the four steps, outputs included:

1. **Ideal State.** Increase mammographic volumes
2. Driving forces that can be strengthened included:
   ▪ Through negotiation, gain physician consensus on screening guidelines
   ▪ Become a self-referring facility
   ▪ Revenue enhancement
   ▪ Adopting new technology
   ▪ Early detection
   ▪ Consistently maintain Professional Research Consultants, Inc. results in top quartile
   ▪ Capturing patients through scheduling
   ▪ Improve turnaround time
   ▪ Increase access through expanded hours of services
3. Restraining forces that can be removed or reduced included:
   ▪ Confusion regarding current mammography guidelines
   ▪ Lack of physician champion/physician push-back
   ▪ Economy, declining reimbursement
   ▪ Cost/physician buy-in/sensitivity/specificity
   ▪ Radiation exposure concerns
   ▪ Physician support/patient and physician complacency
   ▪ Staff push-back to changes; physical plant; amenities
   ▪ Access/timing/central scheduling process/no ability to self-schedule
   ▪ Outside films
   ▪ Current hours Thursday, 7:30 a.m.–5:00 p.m. and Friday, 7:30 a.m.–4:00 p.m.; no lunch hour/evenings/weekends/require process changes/staff push-back
4. Brainstorm force field actions to enhance driving forces and/or mitigate restraining forces:
   ▪ Have surgeons/radiologists write a letter endorsing recommendations for women after 40 (seek select provider endorsement prior to sending letter)

- Follow letter up with physician office visits focusing on physicians who have significant variance in referral patterns (surgeon/radiologist/Cheri Hitchcock to escort/arrange)
- Identify a physician champion who will write and accept patient results
- Promoting services to include existing funds available programs and financial resources
- Expand hours of operation
- Implement process to decrease cycle time—by working with physicians to copy orders to CWH—ultimately centralized scheduling for follow-up (colored envelope—place with courier file)
- Promote this process—as benefit/risk reduction
- Grow revenue through adoption of new technologies
- Bring corporate analysis review to pre-radiation meeting on a semiannual basis
- Physicians create a communication system with patients regarding the importance of annual screening
- Ongoing staff education, consistent review of results
- Communication to staff that their involvement in providing excellent customer services is key to their incentive reward
- Well-appointed facility (chocolates, coffee, etc.)
- Identify a system to access outside films prior to the patient arriving at system
- Explore ability to accept digitized images (new Chief Information Officer [CIO])
- Ensure internal system is being monitored daily
- Work with radiologists to create a system follow-up on addition views (radiology wide)

Stakeholder Map and Communications Plan   Building on the force field analysis, the team built a stakeholder map that identified the anticipated roles people would play during deployment of solutions. The roles included:

- Change sponsors
- Change originators
- Change agents responsible for deploying or implementing the changes
- Change advocates
- Change blockers
- SME informants to provide information on the change

The stakeholder map provides insights into key constituencies. From the map, the team developed a summary communications plan that contained key actions that will enable the primary elements of the To-Be solution to gain traction in the organization. The team also developed specific messages for each stakeholder group.

- Radiologist, surgeons: Partnering
- Referring physicians: Onboarding
- CWH staff: Buy-in support
- Centralized scheduling: Partnering
- Customer: Communication
- Courier: Partnering and buy-in
- Administration: Buy-in
- Physician to accept self-referred patient: Partnering

Step 10: What Do We Pilot? Results? What Is the Full Implementation Plan?

The team developed an action plan that contained over 25 action items or steps broken down into the three categories:

1. Quick wins that could be deployed inside the team's 12-week life cycle
2. A pilot phase to test out changes and prepare for full implementation
3. To-Be changes that would be handed off to the process owner after the 12-week cycle

The team worked with marketing to conduct a mass mailing to former CWH patients who have not had a mammogram performed at the CWH for 18 months or more. The database consisted of over 8,000 patients. The team proceeded with a mailing that successfully generated additional screenings.

A pilot program was created at two offices to evaluate the potential for physicians' offices to batch and send mammograms orders to CWH. CWH contacted patients and has been successful in generating additional appointments. It has been positively received by patients and participating physicians. Based on the success of the pilot program, the program was expanded to two more physician offices to further increase referrals and use CWH staff to schedule. Additional practices have been brought online so volumes should continue to grow.

During the implementation phase, Finance has traced and calculated downstream procedures and developed predictable ratios for breast ultrasound, breast MRI, breast biopsies, radiation, surgical, and other ancillary services. Consequently, the team's initial value creation is considered conservative.

Improve Performance
The team identified these financial and operational improvements:

- Financial earnings annual improvement of $75,000 (five-year total savings $375,000)
- Number of mammograms of 600 procedures per year (five-year total of 3,000).

A wise man should consider that health is the greatest of human blessings, and learn how by his own thought to derive benefit from his illnesses.

—**Hippocrates**

 NOTE

1. The case studies in this chapter are based on MidMichigan Health 10-Step Team Final Working Papers, April 14, 2012.

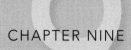

CHAPTER NINE

Improve Performance Self-Scoring Diagnostic and Roadmap

Give a man a fish, feed him for a day. Teach a man
to fish, feed him for a lifetime.

—*Proverb*

T THIS STAGE, HOW DOES A COMPANY get started accelerating
its performance improvement program? What are your current state
or baseline capabilities? Where are you on the corporate performance
management (CPM) maturity model with your improvement programs? How
well are you executing on five core Principle 4 Improve Performance best practices and the 35 new best practices to apply to teams every 12 weeks to realize
$450,000 annual growth or earnings improvement per team?

The next sections outline a systematic approach for completing self-scoring
diagnostics to baseline your As-Is capabilities and to chart your course toward
providing best-in-class and world-class customer, financial, process, and people

results. The sections provide three blueprints and link three bodies of knowledge to enable you to chart your journey to excellence.

1. Maturity Model Criteria
2. Five Key Principles of CPM Best Practice Blueprint
3. CPM 10-Step Improve Performance 35 Best Practices Blueprint

 ## MATURITY MODEL CRITERIA

MidMichigan Health realized over $450,000 in earnings improvement per team from the 10-step process—over eight times the targeted value—resulting in millions in earnings improvements while at the same time improving customer satisfaction scores, modernizing dozens of processes, and attaining better employee or people results.

MidMichigan Health leveraged the first five rounds of CPM teams to advance and mature its capabilities through CMU's level 1 (basic) through level 5 (optimized) model. This maturation then enabled MidMichigan Health to apply its level 5 optimized capabilities to an entire hospital in round 6 and system-wide teams in rounds 7 and beyond.

My hope is that by chronicling the maturation of your program, regardless of where you are on your journey, you will gain insights to help accelerate your program maturity and realize similar broad-based results.

- **Level 1 Initial.** Processes at this level (typically) are undocumented and in a state of dynamic change, tending to be driven in an ad hoc, uncontrolled, and reactive manner by users or events. The processes at this level are in a chaotic or unstable environment.
- **Level 2 Repeatable.** Some processes at this level are repeatable, possibly with consistent results. Process discipline is unlikely to be rigorous, but where it exists, it may help to ensure that existing processes are maintained during times of stress.
- **Level 3 Defined.** At this level, sets of defined and documented standard processes are established and subject to some degree of improvement over time. These standard processes are in place (i.e., the As-Is processes) and are used to establish consistency of process performance across the organization.

- **Level 4 Managed.** At this level, using process metrics, management can effectively control the As-Is process. In particular, management can identify ways to adjust and adapt the process to without measurable losses of quality or deviations from specifications. Process capability is established from this level.
- **Level 5 Optimized.** At this level, the focus is on continually improving process performance through both incremental and innovative technological changes/improvements.

Performance-minded leaders apply the five-level maturity model.

FIVE KEY PRINCIPLES OF CPM BEST PRACTICE BLUEPRINT

Companies, nonprofits, and government enterprises are regularly charting their CPM journeys to excellence using the self-scoring diagnostic shown in Exhibit 9.1. It incorporates a holistic view of the Five Key Principles of CPM; some call this blueprint as the Five Key Principles *Pentagon*. The Five Key Principles of CPM consist of 30+ best practices and include:

Principle 1. Establish CPM office and CPM officer
Principle 2. Refresh and communicate strategy.
Principle 3. Cascade and manage strategy.
Principle 4. Improve performance.
Principle 5. Manage and leverage knowledge.

The Five Key Principles core best practices enable performance-minded leaders to evaluate their CPM performance and the interrelationships among the five principles of their CPM programs. For instance, if your organization is spending too much time fighting fires trying to improve the business in Principle 4, it may be a symptom of poorly conceived strategies in Principle 2 or lack of adequate measurement in Principle 3. Or this scenario may present an opportunity for accelerating maturation of your Principle 4: Improve performance program. Informed practitioners translate their baseline scores on the core 30+ CPM best practices into a project plan as shown in the CPM best practices blueprint in Exhibit 9.2.

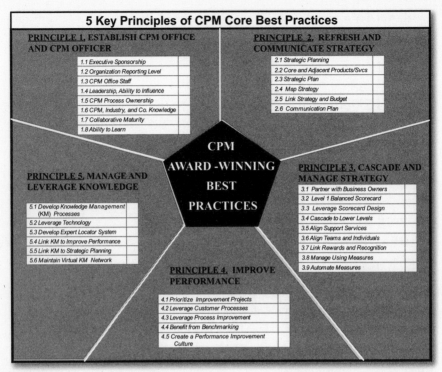

EXHIBIT 9.1 Five Key Principles Pentagon—Best Practices Scoring Diagnostic

---

EXHIBIT 9.2 Five Key Principles of CPM Maturity Model Blueprint

CPM Principles 1–5 Roadmap and Maturity	Year 1				Year 2				Year 3	
Key Supporting Processes	Q1	Q2	Q3	Q4	Q1	Q2	Q3	Q4	Q1	Q2
Principle 1: Establish CPM Office and CPM Officer										
1.1 Executive Sponsorship										
1.2 Organizational Level, Reporting Level										
1.3 CPM Office Staff										
1.4 Leadership, Ability to Influence										
1.5 CPM Process Ownership										
1.6 CPM, Industry, Company Knowledge										
1.7 Collaborative Maturity										

CPM Principles 1–5 Roadmap and Maturity	Year 1				Year 2				Year 3	
Key Supporting Processes	Q1	Q2	Q3	Q4	Q1	Q2	Q3	Q4	Q1	Q2
1.8 Ability to Learn										
Principle 2: Refresh and Communicate Strategy										
2.1 Strategic Planning										
2.2 Core, Adjacent Products										
2.3 Strategic Plan										
2.4 Map Strategy										
2.5 Link Strategy to Budgeting										
2.6 Communication Plan										
Principle 3: Cascade and Manage Strategy										
3.1 Partner with Business Owners										
3.2 Level 1 Balanced Scorecard (BSC)										
3.3 Leverage BSC Design										
3.4 Cascade BSC to Lower Levels										
3.5 Align Support Services										
3.6 Align Teams, Individuals										
3.7 Link Compensation										
3.8 Manage Using Measures										
3.9 Automate Measures										
Principle 4: Improve Performance										
4.1 Prioritize Improvement Projects										
4.2 Leverage Customer Processes										
4.3 Leverage Process Improvement										
4.4 Benefit from Benchmarking										
4.5 Create Performance Improvement (PI) Culture										
Principle 5: Manage and Leverage Knowledge										
5.1 Develop Knowledge Management (KM) Processes										
5.2 Leverage Technology										
5.3 Develop Expert Locator System										
5.4 Link KM to Improve Performance										
5.5 Link KM to Strategic Planning										
5.6 Maintain Virtual KM Network										

The Five Key Principles of CPM maturity model blueprint becomes a transparent planning tool to share with executive and management teams and employees at large. The blueprint serves as your North Star and helps you to manage organizational expectations on CPM services and their positive impact to the organization. If, for example, your baseline 4.3 Leverage Process Improvement is level 2 maturity, you may collaborate with the management team to work toward improving its maturity level one level per quarter. In Q2, you may aspire to attain level 3 maturity; in Q3, you target level 4 maturity; and finally, in Q4, you arrive at level 5 maturity. In a similar manner, you systematically chart your path or journey to excellence with all CPM best practices.

Since this book has more fully explored Principle 4: Improve performance through the journey at MidMichigan Health, I turn your attention to the second important tool for you to launch and manage your improvement program, the CPM 10-Step Improve Performance 35 New Best Practices Blueprint.

CPM 10-STEP IMPROVE PERFORMANCE 35 NEW BEST PRACTICES BLUEPRINT

As leader of your improvement program, you are probably a bit excited and nervous at the same time. I can attest to feeling both emotions leading Crown Castle International's CPM programs. This section provides you with a diagnostic scoring tool to chart your course deploying and maturing the 35 new Improve Performance best practices. The new best practices appear in Exhibit 9.3 and enable you to target the desired maturity level for each.

Imagine it is your first leadership or management team meeting, and you are sharing your improve performance plan. Experience shows that you will be negotiating and securing buy-in from your colleagues while simultaneously onboarding members of your CPM team to follow the project plan. When launching this process at Crown Castle International, I honestly appraised our 10-step problem-solving capabilities at level 1 maturity. This modest baseline provoked candid and engaging discussions with my colleagues (internal customers) to better understand which best practices they valued the most and at what rate they sought maturity. Their feedback for year 1 indicated a desire to rapidly accelerate a dozen best practices to level 5 maturity, develop a second dozen best practices to level 3 maturity, and make improvements to level 2 maturity for the balance of the best practices.

EXHIBIT 9.3 CPM 10-Step Improve Performance 35 Best Practices Blueprint

10-Step Improve Performance	Year 1				Year 2				Year3	
Best Practices	Q1	Q2	Q3	Q4	Q1	Q2	Q3	Q4	Q1	Q2
1. Portfolio of Projects										
2. Sponsorship										
3. Myth Busting										
4. Steering Committee—Composition										
5. Steering Committee—Meetings										
6. Steering Committee—Presentations										
7. Steering Committee—Governance										
8. Team Roster—Behavioral Composition										
9. Team Roster—CPM Experience										
10. Team Roster—High-Potential Team Members										
11. Team Roster—Configuration										
12. Team Roster—Pre Reading										
13. Team Roster—Planning										
14. Team Leader—Independence										
15. Team Leader—Experience										
16. Team Behavioral Life Cycle										
17. Team Member Participation										
18. Goal Statement—Compound Elements										
19. Goal Statement—Balanced										
20. Leadership Team Collaboration										
21. Training—Adult Learning										
22. Team Member CPE Credits										
23. CPM Certificate of Recognition										
24. Team Technology and Tools										
25. Team Technology Weekly Team Meetings										
26. CPM Leadership—Function										
27. CPM Leadership—Experts										
28. Benchmarking and Best Practices										

(continued)

EXHIBIT 9.3 (*Continued*)

10-Step Improve Performance	Year 1				Year 2				Year3	
Best Practices	Q1	Q2	Q3	Q4	Q1	Q2	Q3	Q4	Q1	Q2
29. CPM Team Leader—Turnover										
30. Implementation—Pilots										
31. Implementation—System										
32. Team Celebration										
33. Benefits Realization—Biweekly Reviews										
34. Benefits Realization—The Handoff										
35. Change Management—Communications										

Regardless of where you baseline your maturity for all 35 best practices, at this stage, it is advisable to secure input from your colleagues on the level of maturity they would like to attain for each best practice over the next six to eight calendar quarters. CPM is a team sport. It is vital that you engage and secure your colleagues' input. At MidMichigan Health, the leadership team supported all 35 best practices during its journey. The leadership team was practical and pragmatic, and recognized it was on a two- to three-year journey to excellence. Once MidMichigan Health attained level 5 maturity, it did not rest; rather, it applied these expert teams to ever-larger issues, including an entire medical center (see Chapter 4) and entire horizontal strategic business units (e.g., laboratory in Chapter 7).

 SUMMARY

MidMichigan Health CPM practitioners and contributors deserve special admiration and recognition for retaining their composure, professionalism, and collegial culture to realize outstanding results across customer, patient, financial, process, and people perspectives in the face of many market forces and adversity. The administrative and clinical executives and managers at MidMichigan Health are truly the type of leaders we need more of.

> Disciplining yourself to do what you know is right and important, although difficult, is the highroad to pride, self-esteem, and personal satisfaction.
>
> **—Margaret Thatcher**

About the Author

BOB PALADINO, founder of Bob Paladino & Associates, LLC (www .paladinoassociates.com), is a former executive and longtime thought leader and implementation practitioner in the CPM field. His firm advises boards of directors, executives, and governments, and offers a full suite of CPM services for rapidly implementing and integrating proven best practices to drive breakthrough results.

He contributes to leading research projects at several institutes and has established dozens of CPM offices and core processes for leading companies. He is a highly-sought-after speaker for industry and trade events and executive roundtables with experience in over 60 cities globally.

He donates royalties from all books to the United Flight 93 Tower of Voices national memorial as well as to Salute America's Heroes, an organization dedicated to providing aid to wounded and disabled military veterans and their families. He can be reached at bobpaladino@paladinoassociates.com.

Index